CW01665002

DIANA TOWNSEND

How It All Ended

Me, My Family and the Poltergeist volume 3

USSONS

First published by Ussons 2020

First edition

This book was professionally typeset on Reedsy.
Find out more at reedsy.com

Contents

Introduction

As children, my brother and I helped my father build a model circus.

At the time, it seemed a normal thing to do. I had no idea that the model would shape my entire life.

By the time I left school, my whole family were passionate model makers, and we decided to sell our home, buy a derelict school and convert it into a tourist attraction.

There were plenty of obstacles along the way, but eventually, we turned our dreams into reality.

But, as our business grew, we face a dilemma. Should we develop slowly, reinvesting the profits we made each year, or should we gamble everything by taking out a huge bank loan and renovate the old building in one go?

You can read the first part of our story in my two earlier books, ME, MY FAMILY AND THE POLTERGEIST and SUMMER DAYS.

And in case dealing with thousands of holidaymakers, temperamental crafts people, manic neighbours and unpredictable entertainers was not enough to keep us busy, we also shared the house with a ghost called Fred.

Chapter 1

Every year since opening Silverlands, we had taken a short holiday as soon as the summer season was over, but this year was different. This year was nineteen ninety, and we had a massive building programme ahead of us.

On the first day of October, the family gathered in the tearooms. Claire and Michael were at school, but Lucy was sitting beside me in a high chair sucking a rusk and watching everyone with serious eyes.

The tearooms felt empty without Abbie clearing tables, Martha bustling behind the counter or a display of cakes waiting for customers.

As Mum poured tea, my brother, David, produced a large paper bag from behind his back.

"If we're not allowed a holiday, I thought we could at least mark the occasion with an Eccles cake," he said.

"What occasion?" asked his wife, Phil.

"The first day of the new build, of course," David said as he tore the bag open with a dramatic flourish. "At last, we get to do all the things we've been planning."

"Not everything," Dad reminded him. "We're not touching the old swimming pool."

David lay the open bag on the table.

"Who cares about the pool? It can wait. This is a huge moment. We should celebrate."

"You're right." I nodded and took an Eccles cake.

"I know, I am," David went on happily. "When we first saw this place, no one with any sense would have believed we could make a success of it, but look at us now. Five years on and everything's going brilliantly."

"Yes. It's good to remember how far we've come," Mum agreed as she handed mugs around. "It's easy to concentrate on the problems and forget about the good things."

Bob, my husband, grinned as he took a mug.

"This time next year we'll be drinking tea in a proper restaurant and function suite," he said.

"Sooner than that," Mum corrected him. "It has to be ready by Easter."

"And it will be ready," Bob reassured her. "It's going to be amazing. By next spring our regulars won't recognise the place."

"Don't say that," Mum tutted. "It's not as if we're going to knock everything down and start again. It's still going to be Silverlands."

David sipped his tea.

"That's true, but don't underestimate what we're doing. These changes are massive. By the time everything's finished, we'll have opened up a whole new building for the model circus and live entertainment. The main house will have a superb restaurant for functions, like Bob said, and a huge indoor picnic area for bad weather. We'll even have the last two craft units up and running. I think that's pretty impressive."

"And don't forget the shop," Phil said. "It's going to be so much better with all the new display units."

"And there's the crazy golf and the outdoor games equipment," Bob threw in.

"And no one's mentioned the new terraces for the car park and widening the road leading up to them." I added.

"Remind me, how long do we have to finish all this?" Dad asked.

"Months and months," I laughed. "We've got the whole winter. There's going to be no rush at all."

Dino had been laying quietly beside Bob, but now he leapt to his feet and barked at a distant noise.

David frowned.

"Was that the doorbell?"

"It's probably the postman," Phil said. "Where's Ossie?"

"I thought he was with you?"

They looked at each other in dismay.

"Oh, no. Not again!" I groaned.

David hurried out of the tearooms and I raced after him along the corridor.

"You're supposed to be keeping Ossie inside," I scolded him.

"I thought he was with Phil. We can't keep him locked up all the time."

"But I warned you about the postman. He said if Ossie does it again, he's going to stop delivering."

David threw open the front door, and we were confronted by an indignant young man in a dark uniform and peaked cap.

"I'm so sorry…" David began, but the postman cut across him.

"He was waiting for me! Hiding in the bushes! There was no sign of him when I drove up, but the moment I got out… well, look at him."

The post office van was parked a few feet away, its engine still running. Through the windscreen I could see Ossie's black head and shoulders. He was sitting in the driver's seat, panting, and his huge white fangs gleamed in the morning light.

"I think he likes you. He just wants to be friends," I said, but the young man glowered at me.

"He won't get out. And he's got very big teeth. I can't waste time like this every morning."

David clapped his hands and pointed firmly to the ground beside him.

"Ossie! Come here!"

I waited hopefully, but the dog merely cocked his head to one side.

"Come here! Now!" David shouted.

Ossie pricked his ears and stared intently at us.

With a sigh of exasperation, David crossed to the van, grabbed Ossie by the collar and hauled him out of the driver's seat.

"I'm sorry about this," I said. "Ossie looks fierce, but he's a big softie, really. You can see that, can't you?"

The postman wasn't convinced.

"No. All I can see is that he's very big and very intimidating."

He stepped back as David dragged Ossie past, then climbed into the van, slammed it into reverse and shot off down the drive.

David let go of Ossie's collar and the dog watched the van disappear out of the gate before flicking his silky tail and trotting back inside the house.

"Do you think Ossie was really waiting for him?" I asked.

"Probably," David sighed. "He's a sneaky little bastard when he wants to be."

*****

Before work could start on the new restaurant, we needed to clear everything from the area and that meant moving the circus.

I knew it had to be done, but I was dreading it.

Normally, I consider myself to be a fairly laid-back person, but whenever we had to move the circus, I grew anxious. The model was the highlight of our exhibition and it would be a disaster if anything went wrong with it.

Although the circus contained over a hundred animated figures, they were all operated by one gigantic mechanism that was powered by a single motor. If any individual part was damaged the entire system was affected. This meant that even a small mishap could result in months of work and the circus would not be usable until everything was finished. Just thinking about it made me feel sick.

Dad had spent years travelling around Australia with his own full-size circus and the idea of packing everything into boxes and travelling each day seemed normal to him, but to me it was a nightmare.

The model had been designed to come to pieces, and each section had its own travelling case, but nothing was uniform. Each box had been individually built to fit a particular section and trying to put a section into the wrong case could easily result in it becoming stuck or being damaged.

I knew how easy it was to break the figures. When I was a child, Dad had carved the first of the acrobats that were to perform in the big top. I had begged to be allowed to hold it, and finally Dad had given in.

The tiny girl had her foot through a loop attached to a rope and her arms spread out gracefully on either side of her. As I twisted the rope she spun around and I was entranced.

I still don't know how she slipped from my fingers. One moment she was in my hands, the next she was lying on the kitchen floor in pieces.

Dad didn't tell me off. I'm sure he knew how upset I was, but it took weeks of work before the acrobat could fly again.

On another occasion, when the circus was on exhibition in Torquay, a local television crew arrived to interview us. They wanted to show the circus in the background, but the reflections from the glass panels distorted the view and we agreed to remove them.

The interviewer promised she would stay well away from the model, but as soon as she started asking questions, she stepped backwards and her elbow caught the golden carriage as it came around the parade track.

The interviewer was mortified, but the damage was done. The horses pulling the carriage were wrecked, and each one had to be rebuilt from scratch.

I couldn't bear the thought of anything going wrong now.

It was easy to explain to people that the carved figures and the tents were delicate and needed to be handled carefully, but it was more difficult to explain that the platform supporting the circus needed just as much care.

The platform consisted of six sections that bolted together to form one massive table. In total, it was three meters wide and seven meters long. The big top, menagerie tent and all the wagons and caravans were set into the table and a miniature road ran around the edge.

A parade of tiny vehicles moved constantly around the road, including a stagecoach and a golden carriage which were both pulled by teams of animated wooden horses. The mechanisms that drove the horses passed through tunnels below the table, and they would only work properly if all the sections were exactly aligned. A variation of even a few millimetres would be enough to cause problems.

To stop the table distorting, it had been reinforced with steel frames and this made it ridiculously heavy. Each section needed four people to carry it and I knew that if a section was dropped, or even bumped enough to spring it out of shape, we would not be able to reassemble the platform without stripping out the frames and re-aligning them.

Fortunately, we had a group of friends who had watched the model grow from its first beginning on our dining room table. They had helped us transport it to its first display in Torquay and had later moved it to Silverlands.

Now they turned out again.

I was grateful that our friends had volunteered to come and help us once again, but I couldn't help wishing we could manage on our own.

Mum understood. As the team of volunteers arrived, she whispered to me.

"Remember, dear, everyone's here because they care about the circus and want to help us. That's wonderful, isn't it?"

"Yes, of course it is," I mumbled guiltily.

A few minutes later, I spotted an unfamiliar face among the crowd.

"Who's that?"

David looked across the room.

"That's Mark. He lives in Chudleigh. He heard about the circus and asked if he could help."

"But you were only supposed to ask friends," I objected.

David stared at me in disbelief.

"He's a really nice guy, and he offered to help. What was I supposed to say?"

"No, would have been good," I sulked.

"You're impossible! Do you know that?" David's voice rose accusingly.

I did know I was being impossible, but I didn't want to admit it, so I looked offended instead.

"I just don't want any accidents," I sniffed.

David must have recognised my apprehension because he took a deep breath and changed his tone.

"Calm down and stop worrying. Why don't you help Dad with the belts?"

I nodded. Taking out the belts meant being under the table and away from everyone. It sounded like a good idea.

To my surprise, David gave me a quick hug.

"Honestly, everything's going to be fine."

Dad joined me under the table and we worked steadily stripping out the leather belts that connected the various mechanisms to the main drive. It was familiar work, and the aroma of dust and engine oil was oddly comforting. Slowly, I started to relax.

In the distance, I could hear the voices of the others as they unloaded travelling boxes from a storeroom.

"That's the last one," Dad said as he drew a belt from a pulley. "You go outside and I'll pass the shafting out to you."

I nodded, crawled to the end of the platform and slid out through the small door. Dad followed behind me and handed out the lengths of shafting one by one while I fitted them into the first travelling box. By the time we had finished David was busy removing windows from around the platform and Bob was packing dressing items such as tiny buckets, brooms, wheelbarrows and even miniscule children's toys into another box.

I paused and kissed Bob on the cheek as I passed.

"Are you OK?" he asked.

"Yes, of course. I'm fine."

As he reached out to pick up a pile of miniature sacks, a screwdriver that was lying near him rolled across the table and fell to the floor.

"Stop it!" I snapped.

Bob looked at me in surprise.

"What's the matter? It didn't do any harm. I must have caught it with my arm."

"I wasn't talking to you."

There was no one near us, and Bob's eyebrows rose in surprise.

I hadn't meant to speak out loud, but I knew that if I tried to explain it would only make matters worse, so I just smiled and walked away.

*****

Before we moved to Silverlands, I didn't believe in the paranormal, but over the years I had experienced enough strange things to be convinced the old property was haunted by a ghost called Fred.

I had tried to share my experiences with Bob, but he resolutely refused to believe the footsteps, bumps and missing items were caused by anything more than my over-active imagination.

I didn't want to argue with him, so I chose the path of least resistance and simply avoided the subject.

It wasn't usually too difficult. Creaking stairs and distant noises were harmless enough, and it didn't really matter if an occasional saucer fell out of a cupboard and cracked.

However, a few months ago, I had been shocked to discover that all the gas taps in the kitchen had been turned on full.

It was so unexpected and such an escalation from what had happened before that I found myself shouting at an empty, gas-filled room.

At the time, I had been afraid, but later, when I calmed down, I felt differently. There was no logical explanation for what had happened. It did not make any sense. And yet I couldn't bring myself to believe Fred meant us any harm.

Silverlands was an enormous building with endless winding corridors. The electrical wiring was ancient and illogical and many of the passages only had switches at one end so, in the evenings, switching the lights on and off as you moved from one wing to another was complicated. As a result, I found it easier simply to walk in the gloom.

At night, I sometimes carried a small torch, but more often than not, I didn't bother. I knew every twist and turn of the corridors. I loved the old house and felt safe there.

I didn't discuss the subject because I would have felt stupid talking about things that were not based on any form of logic, but I simply didn't believe there was anything evil lurking in the shadows.

I knew Fred was real, but I had no idea who or what he was or why he did the things he did. I wondered if he was trying to attract attention, and I began to think of him as a child who liked to show off. As if he was saying, 'Look at me! I've worked out how to do this!'

In my head, my ideas made sense, but I didn't want to have to justify them to anyone else.

David, on the other hand, could barely conceal his excitement about what had happened.

"We can't just ignore it," he had protested when I told him about the gas taps. "Who knows what's going to happen next?"

"Nothing," I had replied. "I told Fred not to do it again."

"Don't be ridiculous! You can't tell a ghost what to do. It's not a pet. You can't treat it like a stray dog!"

"Why not? If we're going to share this place, we have to learn to live together."

"Live together? That's hardly the right word, is it?"

"You know what I mean."

"No, I don't. We've no idea what's happening here. There's obviously some sort of force causing these things. We should try to find out what it is. Investigate it."

"You're right," I agreed grudgingly, "but we can't think about it now. There's too much else to concentrate on."

David hesitated.

"I suppose so," he said at last, "but I can't help thinking we're missing an opportunity."

In the days that followed, David's words echoed in my head.

Living with a ghost was an opportunity. But an opportunity for what?

It was something few people ever experience, and I felt I should record it in some way, and yet there was so little that was definite.

I wrote down a list of the things I had experienced and the approximate dates they had happened. Then I read them back and laughed. I imagined the look Bob would give me if I told him my jottings proved Fred was real. I knew the incidents were genuine because I had lived through them. I had experienced the sounds, the sights, even the smells that were associated with Fred but none of these things could be tagged and brought out in court as evidence.

The rest of the family had been as baffled as I had been by what happened in the kitchen. Bob asked whether a sudden change in gas pressure could have caused the taps to turn on by themselves, but when the rest of us dismissed the idea, he simply shrugged and went back to work.

Dad insisted we got an engineer in to check the gas supply, but he found nothing wrong.

For days, my mind kept searching for an explanation. Had Fred really been trying to attract attention? If so, he had certainly succeeded. But why? What did he want?

I thought back over the random things that had happened since we bought Silverlands, but I couldn't make sense of any of them.

In horror films, ghosts always have a reason for contacting the living. They have unfinished business of some sort. They want to pass on a message or give a warning. Did Fred want to tell us something? Or was he a bored teenager who enjoyed playing tricks?

"Did you do it because you thought it was funny?" I asked one night when I was alone in the kitchen, but there was no reply.

Now, as we lifted out the precious pieces of the circus and packed them away, I realised why I was feeling so apprehensive.

Leaving Dad disconnecting the harness on the stagecoach horses, I walked through into the kitchen. It was quiet and as I leaned against a worktop, I felt like an elastic band that had been stretched to breaking point.

Closing my eyes, I lowered my voice so that no one in the next room would hear me.

"Fred, you may be a ghost already, but if you ever touch the circus, I will kill you. Do you understand? Some things are not allowed."

I stood with my eyes closed for several minutes until, gradually I felt calmer.

"Please, Fred," I whispered, "don't do anything stupid."

*****

By the time Phil collected Claire and Michael from school, the circus had been stripped down into sections and was ready to be moved into its temporary home in the Enchanted Forest.

Lucy, my younger daughter, watched from her playpen as the two older children arrived like bouncing puppies eager to be included in the excitement. They helped carry metal struts and fetched tools and packed light bulbs into cartons until they were both exhausted.

Finally, everything was safely stored away, and we thanked our friends for their efforts with one of Bob's home-made curries. While the others chatted and laughed, Phil and I took the children up to bed.

Claire's eyes drooped as I read her a story and she soon drifted to sleep, but Lucy remained wide awake. She was now fourteen months old and could already walk unaided and form a few recognisable words. While Claire had always been a peaceful, contented baby, Lucy was the opposite. She was fiercely independent and had yet to sleep more than a few hours at a time.

Bob and I loved her dearly, but the continuing broken nights were a struggle.

"Claire was lucky she was born first," Bob muttered one night as he was woken, yet again, by Lucy's cries.

"Why?" I asked without opening my eyes.

"Because if Lucy had been first, she would have been an only child."

*****

Now that the circus and the dividing partitions had been removed, it was possible to see the whole area that was going to be our restaurant. It was enormous.

When Stokelake House was first built, it consisted of the main building and an impressive coach house and stable block that was laid out around an open courtyard.

Later, when the property was converted to a school, the front of the courtyard had been filled in with a two-storied classroom block that left only a small area at the back open to the sky.

Now, we intended to combine the ground floor of the classroom block with one wing of the stables to form the restaurant.

I had known it would be big, but now, as I stood in the middle and looked around, I felt excited and apprehensive in equal measures.

Mum was beside me, and I guessed she was feeling the same.

"Remind me, how many people is this for?" she asked as she looked at the dusty floor and sagging ceiling tiles.

"We're going to have tables and chairs for one hundred and sixty people, but the license will cover up to three hundred for functions."

Mum didn't answer. At that moment, if I had said we could fit a thousand people into the space, I think she would have believed me.

"And what has to be done first?"

"The windows." I nodded to the front of the building. "The metal frames have warped so much they won't open. They have to be replaced. The electricians will start on the wiring at the same time and once that's done, the new suspended ceiling will go up."

"Good. That's going to make a big difference," Mum said approvingly. "It looks odd with high ceilings at the far end and this horrible peeling concrete at this end."

"Yes, it's going to be amazing," I agreed, then broke off as a van drove past outside.

"That's Steve. Great. Now we can get started."

It was wonderful having the team of builders back. Within minutes of them arriving, the house was full of noise and bustle. We had arranged a detailed schedule with Steve, the foreman, and I knew every item in the budget by heart. We had allowed a ten percent contingency fund in case there was anything we had overlooked, but I was convinced we wouldn't need to use it.

During our first winter we had been bombarded by unexpected expenses but now, with more experience, I had checked every detail of our plans with the planning department, fire prevention officers, even the highways department and had double-checked with our solicitors to make sure there was nothing we had missed. This time I was confident we were fully prepared.

I checked with Steve that he had everything he needed and left him to organise his team.

It was a couple of hours later that David rushed into the shop where Phil and I were doing a stock take.

"Quick! The front of the building! It's collapsed!"

His face was white, and without a word, I scooped Lucy from her playpen and raced after him.

Steve was standing outside the restaurant picking lumps of render from his hair. Behind him, one of the window frames lay on the ground amid a pile of broken glass and concrete blocks.

"What happened?" I demanded. "Are you OK?"

Steve nodded.

"Don't worry, I'm fine. Paddy's gashed his hand but he'll live."

"Where is he?" Phil asked.

"In the kitchen washing the dirt off."

"I'll fetch the first aid kit," Phil said and hurried off.

"But what happened?" I persisted. "You were only supposed to be replacing the window frames."

"True. But no-one told us the place was booby-trapped."

"What do you mean?"

Lucy fidgeted, and I transferred her to my other hip.

"Normally, in a building like this, the walls are put up first, then the window frames are fitted into holes afterwards."

"Yes..."

"Well, this has been done differently. For some reason that I don't understand, the window frames were fitted as the walls were put up."

"Does it make any difference?" I asked.

Steve snorted at my ignorance.

"Look, I'll show you."

He led me to one of the remaining windows.

"You see? The metal part of the window frame is between the rows of concrete blocks. That means there's no way to replace it without cutting out the blocks."

"Is that what you were doing? Cutting out the blocks?"

"Not exactly. I was only trying to take out one piece. I wanted to see how much extra work it was going to be."

He pulled a screwdriver from his pocket and rammed it into the mortar between two blocks.

"But I didn't know about this. You see? This is the real problem."

He twisted the screwdriver from side to side, and the mortar crumbled to dust.

"The moment I put any pressure on the block, the whole section of wall under the window collapsed."

"And there's another problem," Steve went on. "There aren't any lintels."

"What do you mean?"

"Lintels. Big beams of wood or concrete. There should be one over every window to preserve the integrity of the wall. After the trouble we had with the flat roofs, I was expecting some problems, but I never dreamed we'd find anything like this."

He shook his head, and my heart began to pound.

"I'm afraid this whole wall is unsafe," he told me.

I looked and saw an ominous crack spreading up the front of the building.

"Oh, my God. How serious is it?"

"I don't know yet. You'll have to get the surveyor back."

Lucy pulled my hair, and I rocked her automatically. We were only halfway through the first day of the build and we were already in trouble.

"Right. I'll phone the surveyor straight away," I said. "Is there anything else you can get on with?"

"Plenty. We'll put some sheets of plywood over this and get started on the last two craft units."

"Good. Let's hope things go better over there."

*****

The surveyor couldn't come until the end of the week.

"We've barely started and we're behind schedule already," I complained to Bob when we were alone. "I was so sure things were going to go smoothly."

"Really? After what happened last time? Isn't that what they call the triumph of optimism over experience?"

"But we've done everything properly this time. We're much better prepared. It's not fair," I pouted.

Bob laughed and gave me a quick kiss.

"Stop panicking. It will all work out somehow. In the meantime, Penny's calling in to see us this afternoon. That should take your mind off things for a while."

Penny was the youngest of Bob's daughters from his first marriage and had inherited her father's wide smile and easy way with people. She worked as a deputy manageress in a shop in Exeter and Bob had told me that, one day, she wanted to open a shop of her own.

When she arrived, we took her on a tour of the buildings. Penny asked lots of questions and Bob explained the work we had planned.

When we reached the craft workshops Penny was particularly interested in the last two units. The flat roofs had been replaced earlier in the year, and now the walls were dry enough for the builders to re-plaster them.

"Do you have any craftspeople lined up?" she asked.

"Not yet, but we won't have any problems letting them," Bob told her.

"Before you do, I was hoping I could have one."

I looked at her in surprise.

"But what would you do with it?" Bob asked.

For a moment, I thought it was an impulsive suggestion, but as Penny explained her plans I realised she had given this some thought.

"I know you have a gift shop in the main house," she began, "but I think there's potential here for a craft shop that only sells locally made products. The craftspeople in the units are awesome but there are lots of other things that wouldn't conflict with them."

I nodded.

"I had thought about having more locally made products in the gift shop, but we just don't have room," I said. "I'm sure they'd be very popular."

"Yes, there's huge interest in craft work these days," Penny went on. "And I'm sure some of the craftspeople must find it difficult keeping their units open seven days a week during the summer. I could have a small display from each of them in the shop and then visitors could still buy their products even when they have to go out to get materials or pick the kids up from school."

"That does make sense," Bob agreed.

"I could even do talks each day about Devon traditions and how the different crafts evolved."

"That sounds brilliant, but be careful or your Dad will have you down on the entertainments schedule."

Penny laughed.

"Don't worry, I know what he's like. But I wouldn't mind. In fact, I could act as a manager for the whole craft block if you wanted me to," she offered. "It would be one less thing for you to worry about."

"You have no idea what you are suggesting!" I warned her. "Our craftspeople are not nearly as sweet and lovely as they would have you think."

I explained the running battle we had endured between Dougal the Woodcarver and Tom the Potter but Penny was not deterred.

"Okay." Bob grinned. "If you're serious, I think it's a great idea, but if the crafties drive you insane, don't say we didn't warn you!"

*****

When the surveyor arrived, I allowed him some time to assess the damage, then bombarded him with questions. I was desperate to know how big a setback we were facing.

"Is the building safe?" I asked him. "How much is it going to cost to repair?"

To my relief, he didn't seem unduly concerned.

"The good news is that the outside wall is not weight-bearing. The upper story is entirely supported by steel girders. Structurally, you will have to add lintels above the windows, and replace some grouting, but provided it's done straight away you shouldn't have any other problems."

I breathed a sigh of relief.

"Unfortunately, because of the poor standard of the original build, you will have to cut around the other window frames to remove them, but I'm sure your builder can handle that."

"Yes, he's already explained that problem."

"Good. Then I'll be on my way and send you a written report in due course."

When he had gone, I walked back and looked at the damaged wall. A skip was standing on the roadway waiting to be filled with waste from the building works and the window Steve had removed was propped against it. For the first time, I noticed how small it was.

"Steve, is there any reason why we have to replace the windows with identical ones?" I asked.

"Not really. It's not a listed building."

"That's what I was thinking. And if we have to put lintels in any way, would it be much more work to put in longer ones?"

Steve hesitated.

"I think you'd better tell me exactly what you have in mind," he said.

*****

"It will be a bit more money, but if we replace the little windows that are there now with wider French windows it will open up a fantastic view of the grounds," I said. "At the moment, the restaurant will be good, but this could make it spectacular."

The others were eating sandwiches and listening with doubtful expressions.

"But I thought we'd decided on everything. It's a bit late to change the plans now, isn't it?" Bob objected.

"Don't think of it as changing the plans. Think of it as seizing an opportunity," I suggested.

"We have to rebuild the wall anyway. It will only cost a small amount more to make the windows much bigger."

"It would make the room much lighter," Dad agreed.

"And I've had another idea," I went on. "We haven't really thought about the courtyard at the back of the restaurant. I think we should landscape it as a little garden. It gets quite a bit of sun in the middle of the day, and if we get big enough containers, we could have real trees in there. With the view of the grounds on one side and a secret garden on the other, it would have an incredible atmosphere."

"Have you costed any of this out?" Mum asked.

"I've done an estimate," I replied and handed around my notebook.

"How would we pay for it?" David asked.

"It would still be within the ten percent contingency figure," I explained.

"But that's for contingencies," Bob protested. "Emergencies, unforeseen disasters. How do we know we won't have any other things to deal with?"

"If you look at the figures, you'll see that rebuilding the wall with the same windows will cost eight percent. The new plans will be just over nine percent. We'll just have to make sure we don't have any more emergencies."

I had meant it as a joke, but no one laughed.

"In the circumstances, I think we ought to go for the bigger windows," Dad said at last.

There was a murmur of agreement from Mum and David, but Bob only shook his head.

"Does anyone object?" Dad asked. He waited for a moment, but no one spoke.

"In that case, it's decided," he said.

*****

It took nearly a month for Steve's team to rebuild the front wall of the restaurant and put in the missing lintels. Fortunately, the weather held, and the work went smoothly.

During that time, progress was being made in other parts of the property too. Dad and David had taken on the task of refurbishing the building that was going to become the new home for the model circus. It was structurally sound, but the walls were in poor condition and the views out of the windows revealed the last derelict buildings at the back of the school.

We had decided to repeat the circus tent theme that we had used before, and Dad was busy blocking in windows while David put up frames to support the striped material that would form the tent.

The building was approached by a long, windowless staircase from the main house. It was dark and gloomy and rather like climbing through a tunnel. We wanted to transform it into an exciting feature in itself, so we covered the walls and ceiling with the striped tent material and added hoops of bright lights and a sound system to play happy circus music.

Although Silverlands was closed to the public, Phil still had to look after the animals. Each morning she was occupied by feeding and cleaning, but in the afternoons, she stripped out the stock from the shop and took down the existing shelves to make space for the new units.

On busy days, visitors often blocked the entrance to the shop, and we hoped that a clearer route from one section to another would avoid so much congestion.

While the builders were occupied with the outside wall of the restaurant, I took the opportunity to convert the interior courtyard into a garden.

I wanted to create the impression that the garden had been established for a long time and was full of lush foliage, so I decided to raise the flowerbeds to lift the plants nearer to eye level for people sitting in the restaurant.

After retrieving a pile of second-hand concrete blocks from the skip, I helped myself to a bag of cement and began laying out the shapes of the flowerbeds.

The floor of the courtyard was concrete and there was a drain at one end, so I was careful to leave a path for drainage. When it rained, the water from the surrounding roofs was channelled into the yard and I didn't want puddles to form that could seep through the walls of the restaurant.

It only took me a few days to build three knee-high walls, cover them with a layer of cement, and fill them with soil. The flower beds were several meters long and had smooth curving outlines. They overlapped so the plants would give the impression of one continuous expanse of greenery, but I had left enough space to squeeze between them when I needed to do some weeding.

The largest bed was big enough to hold a water feature. Our local garden center sold pre-formed pond liners, and I found one that was the perfect size. Once it had settled into the soil, I asked two of the builders to help me carry a few large rocks into the courtyard and place them around the pond.

I was happy with the way my design was evolving, but I still felt it needed more height. The woodland that ran from the main lawn down to the road contained a wealth of self-seeded trees, and I was sure I could find something suitable.

Near to the boundary of our land, I spotted a grove of silver birches. The saplings were growing close together, and I contented myself they needed to be thinned if the remaining trees were to grow to maturity. I returned with a shovel and wheelbarrow and, in no time, I had a magnificent silver birch planted in one of the flower beds and three smaller saplings in another.

The flower beds were soon filled with ferns, and I planted decorative ivy to trail down and hide the walls. I intended to add bedding plants in the spring, but for now, I was pleased with the results.

Noticing David passing through the restaurant, I called him over to see what I had done.

"That's great." He smiled. "The visitors will love it."

"I'm glad you like it. Everything's going well, isn't it?"

"Yes, but I still can't get over how big it seems in here."

He looked around thoughtfully.

"I suppose it will feel better when it has tables and chairs in it."

"What do you mean?"

"Well, at the moment, it feels a bit like the motorway services, doesn't it?"

I was outraged.

"How can you say that? It isn't finished yet. It's going to have a serving counter right across there and new radiators there and there and a suspended ceiling..."

"But none of that's exciting, is it? It's all functional, but it's no different to what you get everywhere."

"It's a bit late to say so now," I exploded. "You should have said something earlier if you didn't like what we're doing."

"I did like it. It all looked fine on paper. But now we're standing here looking at this great big space... it just feels a bit bland."

A few minutes ago, I had felt on top of the world, but now my happy mood was shattered.

"I'm sorry you don't like it," I snapped, "but if you think it's dull, you'd better come up with something better, hadn't you? Anything you like. As long as we can do it ourselves, in addition to everything we're doing already. And it can't cost any money because we're already out of budget."

"Right. If that's how you feel, I will," David snapped back at me.

When he had gone, I looked around and realised he was right.

*****

The following morning David found me sitting in the office.

"Are you busy?" he asked coldly.

"No. Why?"

"You're probably going to say it's a stupid idea, but I want to know what you think of this."

He handed me a sheet of paper. A pencil drawing showed the walls at the far end of the restaurant, transformed into a row of arches.

"Wow. How would you do that?"

"It's not difficult. There're still some sheets of plasterboard in the storeroom at the back. They were left over from the first year when we changed our minds about plastering the walls in the Enchanted Forest."

"Can we go and look in the restaurant?"

"Sure."

As soon as I stepped into the shell of the restaurant, my mind visualised the row of arches around the end wall. I looked at the drawing again.

"It would look wonderful. I'm sorry I snapped at you yesterday."

"Don't worry. I'm used to working with a stroppy little sister."

"Don't push your luck," I frowned. "You were being pretty annoying yourself. How much timber would it take to frame it?"

"Don't worry. I'm sure I can exchange something."

I couldn't help but smile. David had collected militaria since he was a teenager, and sometimes he used it as his own form of currency. I wondered how many medals he would have to barter for a pile of timber.

"And the lights?" I asked.

"We've budgeted for them anyway. The question is, do you like it?"

"Yes. It's perfect. It would change everything. I think we should show this to the others."

Everyone loved David's design, and there were no objections to taking on the extra work.

"I'm glad you're all happy," I said, "because I've had an idea myself."

Bob groaned.

"It was David that started me thinking," I went on. "He was muttering about the restaurant looking like a motorway services because it's so big and open..."

"He said what?" Mum interrupted me.

"It's all right. He didn't mean it," I said quickly, "but it would be much more appealing if it was broken up into sections."

"You can't do that. If we have a big group coming in for a function, it needs to be one big space," Bob protested.

"Don't worry. I'm not talking about anything permanent."

"Then what are you talking about?"

"Dad, do you have any wheels?"

"What sort of wheels?" Dad asked.

"Little ones. Like you get under pianos."

My father was also a compulsive collector and had huge stores of almost everything.

"I might have. How many do you need?"

"About twenty."

"I'll have a look, but what do you have in mind?"

It was my turn to produce a drawing.

"Something like that," I said.

The rest of the family grouped around and looked at what I had drawn.

"And what is it, exactly?" Mum asked.

"I suppose you'd call it a mobile partition. We would need at least five of them. This part at the bottom is a big trough with concealed wheels underneath, and the top is a trellis made of wood. It could be any shape, but I've drawn it as a fan."

"It looks a bit like a sunrise," Phil said.

"How tall would it be?" David asked doubtfully.

"About 6 foot, but it won't take up much space because it will be narrow at the bottom."

Dad frowned.

"Won't it fall over?"

"Not if it's weighed down," I said quickly. "My plan is to fill the trough with plant pots and grow ferns up the trellis."

"That would be lovely," Mum admitted.

"And they'd be on wheels?" Phil asked.

"That's the plan. We could wheel them into the downstairs corridor when we need to use all the space in the restaurant, but normally, they would divide it into different sections."

"They would look very attractive," Mum said, and Dad nodded his approval.

"And they would match the garden theme in the courtyard," Phil added.

"But where would you get the timber?" David asked.

"I'm not sure yet," I said hopefully, "but I was wondering if you could arrange any more exchanges?"

Chapter 2

While the rest of us concentrated on the building plans, Bob spent most of his time contacting potential customers for our new function suite or coach companies who might be interested in arranging group visits.

We had never yet heard the terms World Wide Web or Internet, so his research involved innumerable phone calls, writing letters and visiting our local library.

The biggest problem was finding contact details for coach companies. In our first year, Bob had found it so difficult to get any information that he had spent hours sitting beside a roundabout on the outskirts of Torquay with a notebook and pen, scribbling down the names on the sides of coaches as they drove past.

Fortunately, once we became members of the Devon Association of Tourist Attractions, he persuaded the owner of another attraction to lend him a copy of a directory listing coach companies. It was several years out of date and only contained a phone number for each entry, but to us it was gold dust.

Every morning, Bob disappeared into the office and worked his way through the list, contacting each company in turn to find out if they operated in our area and offering to send them details about Silverlands.

It was slow work.

We knew the other attractions were doing the same thing. Many of them photocopied piles of standard letters and typed the name of each company onto the top line before posting them. Unfortunately, as photocopying always looked slightly fuzzy, the sharpness of the typed names made it obvious the letter was part of a group mailing.

Bob wanted our letters to stand out, so he always asked for the name of a person rather than a company and insisted we typed each letter individually.

His methods worked because we got a good response, but it meant typing hundreds of letters. Between us, we had three typewriters. Bob did the bulk of the typing, but Phil, Mum and I helped as much as we could.

At the beginning of November, Bob went to a DATA meeting. He always enjoyed catching up with the other members and usually came back in a cheerful mood, but this time he seemed subdued.

"How was everyone?" I asked.

"They were all right... but it wasn't a great atmosphere."

"Why not?"

"It seems everyone else was down this year."

"Down? What do you mean?"

"Their takings were down. I wasn't expecting it. We had a healthy increase, as you know, but we were the only ones. In fact, it was a bit embarrassing. Some places were a lot down and they were worried."

"That doesn't sound good. Did they have any idea what caused it?"

"The recession, of course. You really haven't been paying attention, have you?"

"Yes. The recession...."

I tried to look as though I knew what that meant, but Bob changed the subject.

"There was one piece of exciting news. Some of the others have started using a new system for their advertising. It's called a database."

"And what's that?"

"To be honest, I'm not sure, but it saves a lot of time. The guys from the Shire Horse Centre have got one and now they can print letters themselves instead of typing them."

"Really?"

"Yes. You have to put all your addresses into the database and then you can print out a pile of letters with each one addressed to a different person."

"That sounds incredible."

"Doesn't it just? But if we want to try it, we'll have to get a computer."

"And how much do they cost?"

"I've no idea, but I'm going to find out."

*****

The news that other attractions' visitor numbers had gone down worried me.

Our figures had increased steadily each year since we opened, and I had assumed everyone else's had too. I tried to think of an explanation, but nothing I came up with made any sense. Perhaps the figures were just a blip, or perhaps we were an exception. Or had we been enjoying the benefits of being a novelty? If so, how long could it last?

I found Mum and shared my concerns.

"Should we be worried, do you think?"

"No. It doesn't do any good," she replied briskly. "All that matters is that we focus on doing everything that's within our control. There's no point in worrying about the things that aren't."

I knew she was right, but I didn't know how to stop worrying. Perhaps if I had lived through the blitz in London as she had done, I would have understood.

I concentrated on getting as much done as possible each day. I kept lists of all the work on our schedule and ticked off jobs as they were finished. And, for the first time in my life, I made a point of watching the news every evening.

It was depressing.

Margaret Thatcher had been Prime Minister for more than ten years, but it was clear her long reign was coming to an end. Every night there were reports of rebellions in the Tory party and demands for change.

I had been a teenager when Mrs Thatcher came to power, and it was hard to imagine what would happen when she left. Despite the expectation, it came as a shock when she finally agreed to resign. Many people celebrated, but there was also a great deal of uncertainty about the future.

I had been too busy running the tearooms to notice at the time, but Saddam Hussein had annexed Kuwait in August, and now the UN Security Council issued a resolution calling for "all necessary means" to be used to force Iraq to withdraw.

No one seemed to know what that meant, but there was a general feeling we were on the brink of war.

"You don't really think there's going to be another war, do you?" I asked Bob, but he merely shrugged.

"I hope not, but I can't see Saddam Hussein backing down, can you?"

*****

Steve called me into the restaurant the day the new doors were fitted.

"There, what do you think?" he asked.

Until now, the empty holes had been blocked with plywood, and I was delighted with the transformation. Sunlight flooded across the dusty floor, and the room felt light and airy.

"I love them," I said honestly.

"Good. We've still got some plastering to do on the inside walls, but we should be able to move over to the craft units by the end of the week."

"That's great. So, it's ready for the plumbers to fit the radiators?"

"Yes, we'll be out of their way tomorrow."

I had arranged for the plumbers to be on standby, and now I contacted them to say we were ready to go ahead. I felt happy as I made the call, but I was not happy by the time I put down the receiver.

"What is it this time?" Bob asked as I burst into the office.

"I can't believe it! They've increased the price!"

"Calm down. Who's increased what?"

"The radiators, the piping, everything. It's all gone up."

"But the plumbers gave us quotes, didn't they?"

"Yes, but now they're saying they only guaranteed the labour costs. It's in the small print, apparently. If the cost of materials goes up, they're entitled to pass it on to us."

"How much is it?"

"A lot! About twenty percent of the total cost."

"That's a bit annoying."

I wanted to scream. It was more than a bit annoying. It was a disaster.

"What are we going to do?" I demanded.

"Is there anything left in the contingency fund?"

"Not enough."

"Then we'll have to cut back on something else."

For once, I wanted Bob to scream and shout, but he went on making phone calls.

I went to find David. He was helping Dad in his workshop and was as upset as I had been when he heard about the increase.

"That's ridiculous!" he protested. "If they gave us a quote, they should stick to it."

"To be fair, the quote did say it was only valid for thirty days," I admitted.

"But they accepted the order. They can't just ask for more money now," David persisted.

Dad was bending wire in a vice to make cable carriers.

"There's no point in getting in a state," he said. "It's inflation. It was on the news again last night. It's nearly trebled. If things keep going like this, prices are going to go through the roof."

David was still muttering when we all met for lunch.

"How are we supposed to keep to the budget if prices keep changing?"

"Maybe we should go ahead and buy the materials we know we're going to need now," Mum suggested.

"You're right," Bob agreed. "It seems everything is going up. Which means we need to decide if we want a computer."

We had discussed the advantages of owning a computer, and now we looked at each other and nodded.

"Can you get some up-to-date quotes?" I asked.

It was a week before Bob brought the subject up again. I could tell from his face it was not good news.

"So, what's it going to cost?" David asked eagerly.

"The thing is, it's not just the computer," Bob began. "We'll need a monitor and speakers, a base unit, a printer, a keyboard, cabling, a special stand to put it all on, and then, once it's installed, we'll have to go on a training course."

"That makes sense," Mum said. "Operating a computer is not the sort of thing you can learn from an instruction book, is it?"

"But how much is it going to be?"

David's expression when Bob revealed the total cost was comical.

"How much!" He exclaimed. "Bloody hell! I could buy a car for that."

"It is a lot," Bob admitted. "but we need to see it as an investment. If we can send out personalised letters and attract more business, it will be worth it."

*****

Claire's sixth birthday was at the beginning of December, so we invited some of her school friends over for a party.

"Can we have our Christmas decorations up by then?" she asked.

"Of course, darling," I answered while trying to remember where I had put them.

Our flat had very little storage space, and I vaguely remembered putting a box of baubles and tinsel somewhere safe, but it took me days to track the box down to a disused cupboard at the back of a storeroom.

As I draped bright streamers across the tearoom walls, I noticed how welcoming it looked with an extra splash of colour.

"It's lovely in here now, isn't it?" I asked Bob.

"Yes, it's very festive," he agreed.

"This is what's missing in the restaurant," I said suddenly. "Even with the new arches, it's still all one colour. We need to do something to liven it up."

"We can get some pictures easily enough," Bob suggested, but I knew that wouldn't be enough. It needed something more dramatic. I just didn't know what.

Claire's party was planned for a Saturday and we had arranged for Liza Berlin, our resident entertainer, to give a special performance with Roly the

Wonderdog.

Claire and Michael were dressed in their party clothes and racing excitedly around the house long before the other children were due to arrive.

"Mummy! Mummy!" Claire squealed.

"What is it, Honey?"

She pointed at the window and as I looked across, I was surprised to see white flakes fluttering down outside.

The children were ecstatic. As their friends arrived, they ran in circles on the lawn, catching the snowflakes on their tongues and giggling together.

When everyone was there, I rounded them up, and they rushed into the house with flushed pink faces and snow-covered shoes.

For an hour, we organised games and watched as the children passed balloons from chin to chin and played musical chairs, then, once they were tired, we told them to sit on the floor in a circle.

Bob gave a theatrical introduction and, right on cue, Liza burst into the room in a full clown outfit followed by Roly.

The children adored the little dog and clapped wildly, but as I watched, I noticed Liza had missed out several of Roly's most popular tricks.

When the show finished, the children rushed to the tables at the back of the room and helped themselves to pizza and sausage rolls.

"Is Roly all right?" I asked Liza. "He doesn't seem as bouncy as usual."

For a moment, she hesitated, then she leaned close to me and whispered. "No. He's not as young as he used to be. I think he's got arthritis."

"Oh dear. I'm sorry to hear that."

Suddenly, Liza's eyes welled up.

"I took him to the vet last week but there's nothing they can do for him."

"How serious is it?"

"It's not too bad at the moment, but it's only going to get worse. The vet said that as long as he enjoys it, there's no reason why he shouldn't go on performing, but I don't know how long that will be. It might be months or it might be years."

A tear crept down her cheek, leaving a pink trail through the white makeup. She wiped it away and sniffed.

"I'm sorry. I shouldn't be talking about this now. It's very unprofessional of me."

She arranged her face into a smile and clicked her fingers at Roly.

"Come on, boy. We'd better say goodbye to the Birthday Girl."

*****

The next day I was sweeping snow off the drive when I heard the crunch of footsteps behind me. Turning around, I found Tom the Potter from the craft workshops was approaching.

"Good morning. Beautiful, isn't it?" I said.

Tom wrinkled his nose.

"No, not really. I prefer summer. Can I have a word with you?"

"Sure. Do you want to come inside?"

"No. I'd rather keep it private."

There was a tone to Tom's voice that I had not heard before.

"Is it something confidential?" I asked.

"Not exactly, but it's a bit embarrassing. I'm afraid I'm not going to be able to pay this month's rent."

I stared at him in surprise.

"It's my kiln. I'm afraid it's unsafe. I had hoped I would be able to have it repaired, but it seems that isn't going to be possible. I have to replace it straight away or I won't be able to finish my orders. I will make up the rent, naturally, but I'm afraid I can't guarantee when."

I nodded.

"OK. Well, thanks for letting me know."

"Perhaps you can explain to Bob."

"Yes, of course I will. Don't worry, Tom. These things happen."

Bob was in the kitchen when I found him.

"Tom had better not tell the others," he grumbled. "If they think they can all stop paying their rent whenever they feel like it, we're going to be in even more trouble."

"I don't think there's any chance of that. He was really embarrassed."

"So he should be. Can't we get him doing something? He helped with the decorating when we first moved in. Isn't there anything he could help with now?"

A flash of inspiration dazzled me.

"That's it! Two birds with one stone! You're right. It's perfect!"

"Slow down. What are you gabbling about?"

"Tom. He's not just a potter. He's an artist. He showed me some of his landscapes once. They've been in exhibitions."

"And....?"

"And he could paint a mural for us. Just imagine if one whole wall in the restaurant was a vast painting of Dartmoor. Wouldn't that be incredible?"

Tom was delighted when I asked if he would paint a mural for us.

"It would be a pleasure, my dear. Did you have a particular scene in mind?"

"Not really. I was thinking of the moors. Open skies and distant hills. That sort of thing."

He nodded thoughtfully.

"Leave it to me. I will create something especially for you. Can I see the wall?"

"Yes. I can show you now if you like."

Tom followed me into the restaurant and surveyed the room with a critical eye.

"I'm afraid it's still a bit of a mess but it will be very different when the new ceiling is put in and the walls are finished and the carpet's down..." I said but Tom cut across me.

"It's perfect. The light is excellent. When do you want me to start?"

"I suppose we'd better wait until the building work is finished. We don't want dust getting on the wet paint, do we?"

"Certainly not. Let me know when everything is ready for me."

With that, he turned on his heel and marched out of the room.

*****

The work on the heating system was due to be completed before Christmas, but there was a last-minute problem.

"They've sent us the wrong connection, but don't worry, we'll still get everything done in time," the plumber assured me.

Christmas Eve fell on a Monday and the work was supposed to have been finished by the previous Friday.

"I've spoken to the suppliers and they've ordered the right connection this time, but it won't arrive until Monday," he went on. "If you don't mind the heating system being off over the weekend, we can get everything else done. Then I'll collect the connection from the warehouse on Christmas Eve and call in to fit it myself. Is that all right with you?"

"I don't suppose we've got much choice, have we?" I grumbled.

I was dressing the children in gloves and extra jumpers when the plumber phoned on Christmas Eve.

"I'm sorry, but I'm afraid they've sent the wrong part again," he said.

"No! You're joking. Please say you're joking..."

"I'm sorry..."

"We've coped without heating over the weekend. Are you telling me we're not going to have any heating over Christmas either?"

"I really am very sorry..."

I put the phone down.

When he had finished shouting, David went off to search for alternatives. He found a small electric fire and stood it at one end of the tearooms and the glass engravers loaned us a Calor Gas heater, which we stood at the other end.

"I guess it's better than nothing," David muttered.

On Christmas Day, a storm raged outside, but we wrapped ourselves in coats and woolly scarves and pushed the children around the corridors on their push carts.

Bob cooked a magnificent dinner, and we ate it in the tearooms as heavy rain lashed against the windows.

"Let's drink a toast to us," Bob said as he raised his glass. "This time next year we'll have a banqueting hall of our own."

"With magnificent French windows and an indoor garden," I said.

"And Tom's mural," Phil added.

"And heating," Mum sighed.

The New Year brought more stormy weather. The temperature dropped and by the end of the first week the whole country was buried under a blanket of snow.

There was widespread disruption and British Rail made the legendary excuse that the chaos was caused by the wrong type of snow.

Claire and Michael were delighted that they couldn't go to school because the roads were impassable and spent days building snowmen. Their parents were only delighted when the plumber arrived with the elusive part and we were finally able to turn the heating system back on.

*****

On the seventeenth of January, a coalition led by the United States launched a campaign of air and missile attacks on targets in Iraq and Kuwait. The operation was codenamed Desert Shield and continued for weeks. Every day, the news was filled with images of bombing raids and burning oil fields.

"It's terrible. I can't believe we're at war again," Mum said sadly.

I understood how she felt. It was hard to concentrate on creating happy family fun when so much suffering was being inflicted in another part of the world.

*****

By the end of January, the weather improved, and the building work in the restaurant was finished.

"That's great news," David said when I told him. "How long until the shopfitters start?"

"Three weeks. The suspended ceiling people start tomorrow so they will be finished long before then."

"Excellent. After that, it will just be the carpet, won't it?"

"Yes." I grinned. "It's going really well."

The shopfitters were due to build the counters, shelves and display units in the restaurant and install the hot trays, boiling water dispenser and hand-washing sinks. They were also going to provide the tables, chairs, crockery, cutlery and the extra kitchen equipment we would need.

Their bill was the single largest item in our budget, but we were all looking forward to seeing how they would transform a large, empty space into a magnificent restaurant.

A few days later we received another letter.

"No!" I howled as I read it.

"What's the matter this time?" Bob asked as Claire looked up from her breakfast and Lucy's eyes opened wide.

"They can't do it," I gasped. "They just can't."

Bob grabbed the letter from my hand. The shop fitting company had increased their quote by almost fifty percent.

"I'll talk to them. There must be something they can do to bring it down," he said.

But there wasn't.

As soon as Phil got back from taking the children to school, I called a meeting and Bob repeated his phone call.

"They say the only way they can lower the quote is if we cut something out."

"But we've cut it to the bone already," David reminded us. "What are we supposed to cut out now? Table? Chairs?"

"Calm down. There has to be an answer," Dad said.

"Not this time. We're stuffed," David retorted.

I didn't want to agree with him, but my mind was numb. It felt as though we had run into a brick wall.

"Let's look at it logically," Mum said. "The things on the shopfitters' quote split into two different types. There are things they are going to supply and things they are going to do."

"Yes, I suppose so," I agreed.

"It was easier for us to let one company handle everything, but there's no reason why we can't buy things like tables and chairs ourselves."

"I suppose that's true," Bob agreed, "but it will mean a lot of work to track down the right suppliers."

"I don't see why we can't do the building part, either," Dad joined in. "We built everything in the tearooms, didn't we? And that worked out well enough."

"But the restaurant was supposed to be stylish. I thought we agreed we needed professionals to give it the right look?" I protested.

"Hold on a minute," Bob interrupted us. "You're forgetting something. When the shopfitters sent us their first design it was far too expensive, remember? The only way we could afford it was if we did the basic decorating, the walls, the floor covering and so on and left them to build the bespoke fittings like the counters."

"Yes..."

"And we've been working from the original drawings they sent us."

"Yes..."

"Well, haven't you noticed what's happened since then?"

I looked at the others, but they only stared blankly back at me.

"We've changed everything, haven't we?" Bob said in an exasperated voice. "Think about it. David said their design looked like a motorway services. You thought it was bland. Since then, we've opened up the windows, built a row of arches, commissioned a massive mural and made a feature of the indoor courtyard. Not to mention the mobile dividers. How much of their original design is left?"

"I hadn't thought of it like that," I said slowly.

"Bob's right. The shopfitters are really only acting as middlemen. There's no reason why we can't go ahead without them," David agreed.

"Except that it will be a huge amount of extra work," I protested.

Dad climbed to his feet.

"Then we need to get started," he said. "There's nothing to be gained by sitting here talking, is there?"

The others stood up and followed him, leaving Lucy sitting beside me in her high chair.

"But we haven't decided anything," I called out as the tearooms' door banged shut. "Who's going to do what?"

Lucy held out a chewed rusk to me.

"Thank you, sweetie," I said with a sigh. "Here we go again."

*****

The next weeks were manic.

Bob researched catering equipment and found there was an exhibition taking place at the National Exhibition Centre in Birmingham. Mum offered to look after Lucy for the day so Bob, David, Dad and I left home in the early hours of the morning and arrived at the NEC in time for breakfast.

We had listed down all the things we needed and everyone had a clipboard so they could write down details of anything they thought would be suitable.

By the end of the day we were all exhausted, but we found suppliers for everything from hot trays to napkin dispensers.

"That was hard work," I yawned as we drank tea out of plastic cups from a vending machine.

"True, but it was worth it. We've found some real bargains," Dad smiled.

"I think we'd better take it in turns driving home," David suggested, and I nodded.

"I'll go last. Wake me up when it's my turn."

*****

"I don't want to keep on about it, but we need to decide whether we're going to get a computer or not," Bob reminded me.

I was torn. I wanted a computer as much as Bob did, but it was another big investment.

"Let me have one last look through the budget," I said.

We had done well sourcing the things we needed for the restaurant and our total expenditure was back within our original budget level. We had just enough margin to buy the computer, but if we did, we would be back up to our limit with no room for manoeuvre.

Which way should we go?

The vote was unanimous. I looked around at the raised hands and hoped we had made the right decision.

"That's settled then," Bob said. "I'll arrange the dates for the training."

The course was called An Introduction to Computer Basics and was held in Torquay. It lasted three days, and the leaflet promised it would cover essentials such as word processing, formatting, data preparation and configuration.

"I hope we're not supposed to remember it all at once," Phil said.

"Don't worry," Bob reassured her. "We'll be given textbooks and worksheets we can take away with us afterwards."

"I should hope so," I muttered, "for what they're charging us, I was expecting a five-star lunch thrown in each day. The least they can do is give us a few books. It doesn't cost this much to go to university."

"Don't keep on about the money," Bob scolded me. "We'll never be able to use the computer if we don't get trained, so let's make the most of it, shall we?"

By the end of three days, my mind was numb. Before we left, everyone was given a written test to check we understood the new terms we had been taught and the procedures we would be using. I was relieved when we all passed.

"Congratulations!" Our tutor beamed at us. "Before you go, I would like to show you that computers are not just for business. They can be fun too. Look at this."

We crowded behind him and watched the flickering green glow of his screen as his fingers flew across the keyboard. A vertical line appeared dividing the screen into two and a cursor blinked on one side.

The tutor plugged two controllers into the base and handed one to Bob and the other to Phil.

"What do we do with these?" Bob asked.

"You play tennis. All you have to do is move this little wheel up or down and click here and you can make the cursor move."

"Really?" Phil experimented with her controller, and the cursor shot across the screen and disappeared.

"Brilliant!" the tutor exclaimed. "That's fifteen love to you."

As another cursor appeared, he turned to Bob. "Your turn. All you have to do is move your wheel up to hit the cursor back before it goes off the court."

Bob frowned. He fiddled with the wheel, and the cursor jerked across the screen. At once, Phil spun her wheel and the cursor shot back and disappeared.

Bob put his controller down.

"Right. Thanks for showing us that, but we won't be using our computer for games, we just need it for business."

"You might be surprised what you can do with it in the future," the tutor said. "In America, they've begun a thing called the World Wide Web. It links computers together. Some people say that one day we'll be able to play games with other people even if they're not in the same room as us."

"I can't imagine how that would work," I laughed.

"No," Bob agreed. "I'll be happy if we can just get our mailing list sorted."

*****

While we had been away, Dad and David had been busy with Steve on the designs for the restaurant.

Our original plan had been for the shop fitters to install a counter with hot trays, cold trays, and a self-service display where customers could help themselves to cakes and salads. There was also going to be a section with bar fittings and beer pumps.

We had selected the fittings we wanted from their brochure and everything was to have been prefabricated in a factory and assembled on site. Now we would have to build everything from scratch.

"The counter itself is easy enough," Steve told me, "but you will have to decide what you want above it."

He showed me the design the shop fitters had submitted.

"As long as it has a shelf so we can store glasses I don't suppose it matters too much," I said.

"That's easy enough. We can put some lights in it too to shine down on the counter if you like."

"Yes. That sounds good." I agreed.

"So, you'll be happy if we put a straight section of shelving across above the counter?"

I didn't have a chance to reply before Dad cut in.

"Hang on a minute. Are you sure that's what you want? This is the first thing people will see when they come into the restaurant. Don't you want it to look as attractive as possible?"

I sighed.

"You know, I do, but we can't afford anything complicated."

"Creativity doesn't cost anything. We can use the same materials."

I was intrigued.

"What do you have in mind?"

"A row of arches to match the ones at the other end of the room."

"Really? Is that possible?"

"I don't see why not? David and I can handle it. Do you like the idea?"

"It sounds great."

"Good. Then leave it with me."

A few days later, the frame for the new counter was in place. Dad had extended it to cover the full width of the room, which gave a lot of extra space and would make it much easier to serve large numbers of customers.

Above it, a row of elegant arches supported a wide shelf that was filled in on the customers' side to match the existing walls.

"That's perfect. It looks fabulous and we're going to have so much storage space," I beamed.

"And there will be more shelves and cupboards underneath," Dad told me.

I was delighted.

"I'm so glad it's worked out this way. It's much better than the original design."

"The electrician's coming in tomorrow to plan out the lighting. Obviously, there will be strip lights in the ceiling and wall lights lower down, but there's no reason why we shouldn't add some lighting behind the arches at the far end to shine down onto Tom's mural."

"That would be great." I grinned.

"And we could put some coloured spotlights in the courtyard to shine on your plants if you like the idea."

I did.

Suddenly, I bounced with excitement as a new idea arrived.

"Now what?" Dad asked.

"A glitter ball! You remember what we said? About keeping the far end of the room for dancing when we have smaller parties?"

"Yes..."

"Then we have to have a glitter ball! It will be awesome!"

Dad laughed as I twirled around to imaginary music, but I didn't care. In my mind, I could already see our function room in all its glory.

*****

The early part of February was much colder than usual for Devon, with snow showers and freezing fog. But as soon as the temperatures started to rise, a new team of contractors arrived to extend the car park.

I knew there would be serious earth shifting involved, but I was astounded by the size of the vehicles. Michael caught sight of them as Phil brought the children home from school and ran into the house shouting.

"Daddy! Daddy! There's great big yellow things outside. They're HUGE!"

We could only agree with him.

The next day, one of the Great Big Yellow Things ripped the topsoil from the field next to the existing car park until a gash of red clay was exposed like a gaping wound.

Another enormous machine clawed the ground and dragged piles of earth from one place to another. In no time, the gentle, grassy slopes of the field were transformed into a series of vast, muddy levels. As the short winter day drew to a close, the foreman reported to us.

"That's us finished for tonight. We'll be starting on the hardcore tomorrow."

"Great. It seems to be going really well," Bob replied.

"Yes, at this rate we'll have everything finished by Friday."

He was as good as his word. The excavators, bulldozers and dumper trucks worked tirelessly and by the end of the week the new car parks were topped with crushed stone and edged by neat banks of soil.

The planning department had suggested we plant around the edges of each level to make the car park less visible, and I had a lovely time deciding which trees and bushes to choose.

With the car parks complete, the contractors moved on to the access road. It was supposed to be suitable for two-way traffic, but there were several narrow sections which needed to be widened.

One problem point was at the bottom of the hill where the road joined the drive that led up to Norbrook caravan park.

I knew that Duncan Matthews, the owner of Norbrook, was likely to object to anything which delayed traffic going up the hill to the park, so I asked the contractors to be particularly careful not to cause any obstructions while they were working. However, I was not surprised to get a call from the foreman on Monday morning.

"Sorry about this, but we've got a bit of a situation here. Can you come down?" he asked.

Bob had gone into Newton Abbot, so I hurried outside. The contractors were standing in a row in front of their vehicles, and opposite them I recognised the bulky figure and straw-like hair of Duncan Matthews. His voice floated across to me long before I reached the entrance.

"And I say No! If you don't reinstate this mess, I'll have my solicitors after you. No one has the..."

He trailed off as he saw me approach.

"Why, look who it is. I should have known you'd turn up."

"What seems to be the problem?" I asked as politely as I could.

"Are you in charge of these goons? They've no right to interfere with my road. I didn't give permission for this..."

I held up a hand to interrupt him.

"We don't need your permission. We have a legal right of access over the drive. You know that. All we're doing is widening our road."

Matthews' lip lifted in a sneer.

"We'll see about that. You can't go around altering roads whenever you feel like it. You have to get planning permission."

"I know. We have."

He stepped closer until he towered over me.

"Don't lie to me, Missy. The planners wouldn't grant a new application without notifying the landowner."

I glared up into his watery blue eyes.

"They didn't have to. I explained what we wanted to do, and it's covered by the original application. Ask them if you don't believe me."

Matthews glared back at me, but his shoulders slumped.

"You're going to pay for this. You mark my words," he snarled as he stormed away.

I watched him go, then wiped my sweaty palms on the sides of my jeans and turned to the contractors.

"Sorry about that. Please carry on."

*****

From the first time I visited Silverlands, I had always wanted to cover the ugly concrete bunkers at the back of the house with flower beds. Now I finally had my chance.

A disused tennis court at the top of the property had been used by a training scheme the previous year, and the trainers had left behind a huge stack of old bricks. It was just what I needed.

I borrowed a wheelbarrow from Phil and trundled the bricks down from the tennis court. Once I had cleaned them, I was ready to start work. Originally, I had hoped the men on the training scheme would lay the walls for the flower beds, but now I would have to lay them myself.

The thought didn't worry me. Dad had taught me many useful skills when I was younger, and I was sure that I could lay bricks as quickly as our builders even if they weren't perfectly straight. My abilities were certainly good enough for flowerbeds.

As I shovelled sand and cement into a mixer, I thought how lucky I was to have Dad as my father. He might be a little eccentric, but he had always treated David and me equally. He was an old-fashioned gentleman and believed in opening doors for ladies, but in other, more practical ways, he could have been described as a feminist. He believed in treating all people equally and giving everyone the same opportunities.

After several days of bricklaying, I plastered the outside of the walls with render to give them a smooth surface and painted them. Then I arranged for several lorry loads of topsoil to be delivered and settled down with a catalogue to order enough plants to fill the beds.

The thought of seeing the area bright with flowers made me smile. I couldn't wait for the plants to arrive.

*****

"Have you heard the news?" David demanded.

"No. What's happened?"

"The ground assault in Kuwait. It's started. Our troops went in before dawn."

The whole country had been anticipating this moment, and yet it still came as a shock.

For weeks, the news had been full of reports of the Allied air raids on Iraq and Kuwait that had begun in the middle of January. The television and newspapers showed hazy images of burning oil fields and plumes of smoke rising from devastated buildings, but it had all seemed distant and unreal.

Huge demonstrations had taken place in London and around the country as protestors demanded another way to resolve the conflict, and even after the bombing campaign began there was a lingering hope that Saddam Hussein might back down and accept the Allies' demands.

Now that hope was finally extinguished. We were at war.

"But what does it mean?" I asked. "How long is it going to last?"

David shook his head.

"There's no way of knowing. Saddam can't win on his own. It depends on whether other countries are willing to get involved. If they do, God only knows how long it might drag on."

After that, it was hard to concentrate. I kept the radio beside me as I shovelled soil from a wheelbarrow into the new beds. The only subject was the progress of the invasion, and there were more questions than answers. How far had our troops advanced? How many casualties were there? How many oil wells had been set ablaze by the Iraqi troops as they withdrew?

I kept working, but flowering shrubs didn't seem important anymore.

*****

Once the builders finished renovating the last two craft units, Penny arrived to view them. Bob introduced her to the craftspeople and Penny explained how she could help promote their products and sell them when their units were closed.

I was pleased to hear the craftspeople thought that having a communal shop was an excellent idea. I was particularly relieved to hear that Tom was eager to be included.

Penny decided she preferred the unit at the far end of the building, as it had enormous windows with magnificent views across the Animal Meadow to the woods and fields in the distance.

"The builders have done a great job," she said when she came over to the main house to find us. "As soon as I've decorated it, I can get everything set up."

After that, she could be found painting the walls or stripping varnish off display stands whenever she had a day off work.

One evening, I noticed Bob was unusually quiet as we ate our evening meal. Claire described what she had been doing at school and Lucy dropped chips on the floor for Dino whenever she thought I wasn't looking, but Bob didn't notice either of them.

"Is everything OK?" I asked once the girls were in bed.

"Yes, it's all fine," he replied, but his usual smile was missing.

I sat on the sofa beside him and curled my feet under me.

"You seem a bit quiet."

He put an arm around my shoulders and pulled me closer.

"To be honest, I was hoping the advance bookings would be going better than they are. We've had lots of enquiries about functions but only two actual bookings so far."

I tried to hide my disappointment.

"Never mind. At least it's a start. It will be easier once everything's finished and you can show people around."

"Yes, I suppose so," he agreed.

Dino had been watching us, and now he walked across and dropped a well-chewed sock on Bob's lap.

"Urgh! That's disgusting," Bob muttered.

"Don't be like that," I laughed. "He's only trying to cheer you up."

*****

As the end of February approached, we were able to tick more things off our To Do List, but there was still a lot left. Steve had run into unexpected problems and the extra labour costs cut into our budget.

I juggled the figures as best I could, but the bottom line kept turning red.

"I'm sorry," I said to the others. "I've been trying to avoid it, but we're going to have to make more cuts."

"It's a bit late, isn't it?" Phil asked. "Aren't we committed to everything now?"

"Yes, we are," I agreed. "In fact, there's only one thing left we can cancel."

"And what's that?" David asked gloomily.

"The activity equipment for the entertainments room."

"No! You can't cut that," he objected.

I felt guilty. Without the equipment, the room would just be a big empty space.

"I'm sorry, but we don't have any choice. It's just for this season. We can add things in next year."

But David persisted.

"No. I mean it. You can't cut it. It's included in our leaflets."

A knot gripped my stomach. He was right.

"Does it say exactly what the activities are going to be?" Dad asked.

I hesitated as I tried to remember the words we had put on the leaflets.

"No, I don't think so. It just says there will be exciting surprises, or something like that."

"Then we'll have to find alternatives, won't we?"

"That's easy to say, but we can't just magic things out of thin air," David protested. "If we can't afford to buy the equipment we had in mind, how are we going to afford anything else?"

"We'll have to use our imagination, won't we?" Dad said stubbornly.

"And use imaginary materials too?" David retorted.

"Let's keep this constructive, shall we?" Mum broke in.

"But there's no point in saying we have to do something if there's no way to do it."

"There's always a way," Dad insisted.

"Please!" I cut across them. "Let's not waste time arguing. We should be getting back to work now. If anyone can come up with a sensible idea, let's hear it tomorrow."

The following day we gathered as usual for a morning mug of tea.

"Has anyone got any suggestions?" I asked hopefully.

"No," David replied.

Everyone else was silent.

"Then perhaps we'd better give it another day."

The following morning, I didn't get a chance to ask for suggestions. David gathered everyone together after breakfast and dragged us up to Dad's workshop.

"Take a look at this," he said proudly.

A wooden packing case was standing in the middle of the floor.

"What is it?" I asked.

"That's the point. It could be anything. I can get hold of loads of them. For nothing. They're really solid, so kids can't break them. All we have to do is make them interesting."

"And how do we do that?" Phil asked.

David pointed to the top of the case.

"If that panel had 'DON'T LIFT ME' written on it, what would kids do?"

"Lift it?" I replied.

Phil lifted the panel, and a siren blared out. Everyone jumped and we all burst out laughing.

"I wasn't expecting that!" Mum giggled.

"That's the point," David beamed. "Each case can do something different. One can play music, another can have a bright blue light that flashes out like a police car...."

"I've got an idea," I said. "If you make a hole in the side and paint a circle around it, the kids would be sure to look through it. I've still got some motion sensors somewhere. You could set them so that a light goes on inside the box when people get close."

"What would they see?" Mum asked.

"Anything we like. A giant snail eating cabbage leaves, maybe?"

"Why a snail?"

"Why not?"

"I've got a better idea," David grinned. "I could make up a great big eye ball. That way, when the kids look inside, they'd see it looking back at them."

"Ooh, yes! I like that!" I grinned.

"And there's something else," David went on. "I know a guy who's setting up his own business, making electronic systems. Do you remember the film Big with Tom Hanks?"

"Yes."

"Do you remember the giant keyboard they danced on?"

"Yes, that was the best bit of the film."

"Well, my friend's got a licence to make them. Wouldn't it be awesome to have one of those keyboards so the kids could dance on the keys and play a tune?"

"It certainly would be, but I don't suppose your friend's going to be giving them away free," Dad said.

"Not exactly." David was looking smug. "But he needs to advertise them. He says that he will supply us with one free-of-charge if we put up a sign beside it saying where people can buy their own."

"You're joking! That would be awesome."

For the first time in days, I allowed myself to feel excited. Suddenly, I knew our visitors were going to love the entertainments room after all.

*****

On the third of March, Iraq surrendered and accepted the terms of a cease-fire agreement. Saddam Hussein was still at large, and his retreating forces were setting fire to entire oil fields before abandoning them.

News reports showed hundreds of oil wells burning uncontrollably and vast clouds of black smoke drifting across the entire region. It was feared the fires would take years to extinguish.

"What's happening is terrible, but at least the war is over," Mum said sadly. "Perhaps, one day, the world can get back to normal."

I nodded.

"I hope so. But it doesn't feel as though there's much to celebrate right now. It's all such a mess."

"That's true. And I'm afraid we've got this."

She handed me a letter from the bank.

"What is it?"

"Read it and you'll see. They've put the interest rates up."

There had been a lot of speculation that the crisis in the world oil supply would affect bank rates, but I hadn't expected anything to happen so quickly.

My eyes widened when I saw how much the monthly repayments on our loan would be.

"That's all we need," I sighed.

"Let's not tell the others yet," Mum suggested. "We can break the news once we're open."

There were only four weeks left until Easter, and there was still a huge amount to do. We still had to assemble the model circus, build the features for the entertainments' room, reorganise the kitchen and finish the restaurant. It wouldn't help if everyone started worrying about money.

In the restaurant, Tom was still only half-way through his mural. Some days he would spend hours perched on a ladder flicking a paintbrush across the wall with an intense expression on his face, but on other days he didn't turn up at all.

"How long is he going to take to finish it?" Dad frowned.

"I've no idea. Why don't you ask him?"

Dad chuckled.

"Not likely! That's your department."

"All right. I'll ask him next time I see him," I said reluctantly.

I bumped into Dad in the corridor later.

"You'll be pleased to know I asked Tom about the mural," I told him.

"And what did he say?"

"Not much. The gist of it was that you can't hurry an artist."

Dad's eyebrows shot up, and his mouth curved into a grin.

"I see. Then tell him we don't mind at all if he doesn't finish before Easter. We'll put a barrier up around him and the customers can watch him working while they eat."

I passed the message back and was amused to see Tom perched on his ladder for the rest of the day.

I was itching to fill the flower beds with plants, but the delivery from the nursery had not arrived. I phoned to chase the order and was relieved to hear that it was on its way.

We were also waiting for a delivery of tables and chairs.

"They were supposed to be here by the end of February," I complained.

"Don't worry," Bob said calmly, "it might be a good thing. The carpet layers are coming in next week. It will be much easier to get them out of the way before the furniture arrives."

"I suppose so," I agreed. "I just can't face any more problems."

As the opening weekend approached, each day brought new excitement.

David finished making the dividers for the restaurant and we wheeled them carefully from the workshop at the back of the building down the hill and around to the front entrance.

I painted them glossy white, filled the bottoms with ferns, and they looked wonderful.

As the hot trays, cold trays and jacket potato baker arrived, we put them in place on the counter and tested them out. Everything worked beautifully.

The men from the brewery arrived to install the pipes and pumps for the beer on the same day the fitters arrived to lay the carpets.

"It's all going like clockwork, isn't it?" Bob beamed. "By tonight we'll be able to pull ourselves a pint to celebrate."

I laughed.

"I thought we were supposed to be selling the beer, not drinking it ourselves?"

"We have to check the quality, don't we?" Bob grinned.

As I painted the shelves above the counter, I listened to the brewery men explaining to Bob how important it was to clean the pipes and check the pressure of the gas cylinder each time the pumps were used.

Bob was listening intently to all the instructions, and I couldn't help but smile at his serious expression.

*****

The week before Easter, Abbie and Martha returned to help us clean the kitchen and prepare the tea rooms for opening.

"I'm not a teenager anymore," Abbie announced as soon as she saw me. "Can you believe it? I'm twenty!"

It certainly was hard to believe. Abbie's face still had a child-like innocence, but the tips of her hair had been dyed red.

"Do you like it?" she asked earnestly as she flicked her head from side to side. "I had it done to remind me that I'm an independent woman now and I don't have to please anyone."

Behind her, Martha raised her eyes to heaven.

"You'd better remember to please me, young lady, or I'll have you chained to the dishwasher from morning to night."

"I didn't mean you. I meant men."

"I take it things didn't work out with Jaz then?" I asked, remembering the young man Abbie had introduced to me the previous year.

"No. He was too immature. I'm better off without him."

She sniffed, and I decided not to ask any more questions.

"Never mind. I'll give you both a tour to show what we've been doing."

Martha and Abbie were impressed by the new facilities.

"It's awesome! I love the restaurant! It's the best thing ever. It's so light, and it's all new, and we can see out into the grounds, and it's going to be so great!" Abbie gushed.

"Yes, very nice," Martha nodded, "but we'll need more staff."

"Don't worry," I reassured her. "The restaurant will only be open over lunchtime and we've taken on more girls to cover it. They're coming in on Thursday to go over everything."

"Good." Martha nodded briskly. "In the meantime, I'd best see if our independent woman here remembers where the mop and bucket are kept."

*****

I phoned the nursery to complain the plants still hadn't arrived. After a long delay, an apologetic woman told me the delivery had been sent to the wrong address. She assured me she would sort out the problem and make sure we received the plants the next day.

As promised, the delivery arrived the following morning, but sadly, nearly all the plants were dead.

This time I spoke to a man who seemed convinced that if I gave the plants enough water, they would miraculously recover.

"They're dead!" I protested. "They've shrivelled up and their leaves have fallen off. If I plant them out, it will look as though they've been sprayed with weed killer."

Eventually he realised I was not going to be placated and agreed to send a new delivery.

Bob was also spending a lot of time on the phone. We still didn't have any tables or chairs.

"Don't worry, as long as they arrive before we open it will be fine," he said.

"But what happens if they don't?" I asked. "We can't expect people to sit on the floor, can we?"

"Perhaps we could get some rugs and say it's a new style of indoor picnic."

"It's not funny!" I pouted. "It's going to be a disaster."

"No, it's not. The manufacturers have promised me everything will be here by Friday and I believe them."

Bob was right. Forty tables and one hundred and sixty chairs arrived on Friday morning. He spotted the delivery van driving in through the gate and hurried outside to direct them to the restaurant.

What he hadn't expected was that everything would arrive in cardboard boxes.

"They're flat-packed!" David howled when he saw the huge pile standing in the middle of the restaurant. "Bloody hell!"

Dad, David, Phil, Abbie, several of the craftspeople, Bob and I spent the rest of the day screwing furniture together.

"I think my wrists are going to fall off," Abbie said half-way through the morning.

Mum was looking after Lucy.

"I can make you all a cup of tea if you like," she offered.

"Great idea," Bob said, "but we'd better have it while we're working. No time for tea breaks today."

By the time we finished, the sun was touching the horizon, but the restaurant was full of tables and chairs and looked ready to welcome its first guests. We should have celebrated, but we were too tired.

At the end of the room, Tom climbed down from his ladder and wiped his brush on a rag.

"There, it's done," he said proudly.

I stood back and admired the mural. A country scene stretched from wall to wall, rich with the warm tones of Dartmoor. It was exactly what I wanted.

"Thank you, Tom. It's beautiful."

*****

We spent the evening catching up on the jobs we had abandoned to put the furniture together.

"How much more is there to do?" David asked me soon after midnight.

"I don't usually say this, but we seem to be up to date."

"Does that mean we can call it a night?"

"I don't see why not. We've still got tomorrow to do the last things. You and Phil have the stock to put back into the gift shop. Mum has the ticket box to get ready. Bob has the stock for the bar to sort out and Dad's finishing off the last things in the entertainments room."

"That doesn't sound too bad."

"My only concern is the plants. It will take most of the day to get them into the flower beds, but I've been promised they'll be here first thing in the morning, so as long as they turn up on time everything should be OK."

By lunchtime the next day, I was panicking. There was no sign of the delivery. I had already phoned the nursery twice, but it was clear the man on the other end of the line had no more idea of when the plants would arrive than I did.

It was nearly four o'clock when a truck blared its horn at the entrance.

"Hello, there," the man said cheerfully. "Sorry, I'm a bit late. Where do you want me to put these?"

I wanted to tell him exactly where to put his delivery, but I controlled myself.

"You were supposed to be here this morning," I complained.

"Is that what they told you? Never mind. We'll have everything unloaded in no time and I'll be on my way."

By the time I had helped him unload the truck, the sun was nearly down to the horizon. The truck drove away, and I was left with seven hundred plants in black plastic pots.

My arms still ached from screwing the furniture together, as I bent down and picked up my spade.

"Are you going to put all those in tonight?"

It was Tom's voice.

"Yes."

"My goodness. You'll be busy."

I was not in a mood to be polite, so I said nothing. I hoped he would go away, but instead he stood and watched as I dug the first hole.

"That's a Willmottia, isn't it? They have lovely blue flowers."

"Mmm," I grunted.

I prized the plant from its container and lowered it into the hole.

"Make sure you firm the soil down around its roots. It won't grow properly if it's got air pockets," Tom instructed me.

Ignoring him, I began on the next hole.

"And that's an Acer, isn't it? Very nice. But they don't like too much sun. You might want to put it at the end so that it gets a bit of shade."

My patience was fading fast.

"I don't need any advice, thank you."

Tom sniffed disapprovingly.

"Fine. If you don't need my help, I'll leave you to get on."

"But you're not helping, are you?" I snapped.

"Charming!" Tom turned on his heel and marched away.

I felt guilty at once and promised myself I would make peace with him in the morning.

I went on digging holes and jumped when a voice spoke behind me.

"So, what do you want put where?"

It was Tom. He had changed into wellington boots and was brandishing a trowel.

"I'm sorry..." I began, but he waved his hand to stop me.

"Never mind. Tell me where they have to go or we'll still be here in the morning."

Chapter 3

I woke with a start as the alarm clock rang.

For a moment, I struggled to escape my dreams, but then I remembered that today was Easter Sunday. In a few hours we would open our new, improved version of Silverlands to the public.

After all the struggles of the previous months, we had completed the building work on time and on budget. What was more surprising, I had been in bed before midnight. Bob and David had arrived with torches and helped Tom and me plant the last of the flower beds.

I yawned contentedly and felt pleased with myself.

"Come on, you can't go back to sleep."

Bob prodded me and my eyes flew open.

"I wasn't…" I mumbled.

"Good, because it's going to be a busy day." Bob grinned as he whipped away the duvet.

The next few hours were a whirl of activity. The weather was kind to us and visitors were waiting at the gate by ten o'clock.

"Here we go again." Mum smiled as I carried her bag to the ticket box. Through the entrance gate I could see vehicles passing along the newly widened road.

"At least we don't have to worry about running out of parking space this year," I said.

"That's true," Mum agreed. "In fact, I'm not going to worry about anything this morning. I'm just going to enjoy the day."

"Excellent plan. Doesn't the Judas tree look beautiful now all its flowers are out?"

It was true. The tree was smothered in tiny purple flowers, and the grass beneath it was speckled with blue wood anemones. The grounds always looked their best in spring when wild flowers blossomed everywhere.

I helped Mum settle herself in the ticket box, opened the gate, smiled at the first visitors and made my way back to the house. The Tulip tree by the kitchen yard was laden with as much blossom as the Judas tree and a delicate fragrance filled the air. For a brief moment, I felt at peace.

The kitchen door was the portal to a more frantic world. Martha bustled past with trays of cakes for the servery. Abbie stabbed potatoes, Millie grated cheese and Pam sliced cucumber so fast green flakes flew across the worktop.

"Morning, everyone, I hope you're ready for lots of visitors."

Abbie grinned at me.

"Bring them on! We can feed thousands now."

I laughed.

"Good, let's hope we have to."

The day went well.

The restaurant had a wonderful atmosphere with queues at the counter and families filling the tables. In the kitchen, the girls kept a constant supply of meals flowing and no one had to wait long for their orders.

I had been worried there would be confusion with orders coming from both the tearooms and the restaurant, but in practice our systems worked well. The menus in each servery were completely different, and we used coloured paper to identify the orders from each side.

By the end of the day, everyone was exhausted but happy. Martha made sure the girls left the kitchen spotless, and I thanked everyone for their hard work before they left.

Once we had done our customary search to make sure no visitors had been left behind, the family gathered as usual. For the first time, we met in the restaurant.

"That was awesome," David said as he leaned back in his chair.

"Let's hope every day is like that," Phil agreed.

Mum was still counting the day's take.

"Yes, indeed. It's very promising." She nodded as she licked her finger and counted twenty-pound notes.

"I think we should celebrate," Dad said happily.

"What do you have in mind?" David asked.

"Nothing much, I thought we could have a meal together. The customers like our restaurant. We ought to try it ourselves."

"Why not? I really don't feel like cooking," Mum smiled.

"There was a whole steak and kidney pie left over. We can finish that up if everyone's happy?" I suggested.

"Excellent. With some cheesecake afterwards," Bob said.

"But we can't do this every night," Dad frowned suddenly.

"Of course not. This is a special celebration," I assured him.

"Good. Because we can't start eating all the profits."

"Hold on. It was your suggestion!" Mum reminded him, and we all laughed.

I made sure the kitchen was spotless again before Martha arrived the next morning.

Easter Monday brought a few clouds, but we still had lots of holidaymakers. A family of regular visitors arrived and made a point of telling us how much they loved the new facilities.

"Your model circus is always the best thing," the father told me. "Nothing can equal that, but there's so much more for the kids to do now. We'll be back again soon, that's for sure."

Later in the morning, while I was filling jacket potatoes with coleslaw, Abbie stopped beside me.

"I meant to ask, have you had any problems with Fred recently?"

"No. In fact, I haven't even thought about him for a while. That's strange, isn't it?"

"That's good. Maybe he's moved on."

I put some garnish beside the potatoes.

"Here, can you take these out for me?"

Abbie disappeared with the plates and I thought about what she had said.

Maybe she was right. Maybe Fred had gone. I was surprised to find I didn't like the idea. If Fred wasn't here, where was he? Was he happy? Did ghosts feel happy? Did they feel anything? I was still lost in thought when Abbie burst back into the kitchen.

"You'll never believe what's on the lawn," she gabbled.

"What?"

"A cat! It's with a family. They've brought their cat with them. It's on a lead and everything."

I couldn't resist slipping into the servery and peeping through the window. It was true. A large grey cat was sitting on the grass. It wore a sparkling collar and its lead was held by a teenage girl. A small bowl of meat had been put on the grass beside it, but the creature seemed happy to survey the world with contented, half-closed eyes.

"I suppose there's no reason why people shouldn't bring their cats with them," I said to Abbie when I returned to the kitchen.

"It seems a bit weird, that's all."

"True, but weird fits in well here, doesn't it?"

*****

Once the Easter weekend was over, the number of visitors dropped dramatically. In the past, our numbers had stayed steady until the children went back to school at the end of the holidays, but this year was noticeably different.

"Where is everyone?" David asked as he came into the empty tea rooms one afternoon.

"Maybe they've gone to the beach. It's very hot for the time of year," I suggested from behind the servery counter.

"Perhaps you're right. Phil's worried it's too hot for Snuffle and Snout."

"Really? I thought they liked the hot weather."

Snuffle and Snout were a pair of Vietnamese pot-bellied pigs. They had been among the first residents in the Animal Meadow and had been popular with the public from the moment they arrived.

When they were piglets, they ran around frantically, chasing each other with their tails held high in the air, letting out continual grunts and squeaks of excitement. Now they were mature adults, they had developed their characteristic pot-bellies. Their faces were endearing with deep wrinkles and bristly chins but they still had the same playful personalities. They loved to burrow into the soil and flick dirt at visitors with their noses.

Phil left the hose running in their enclosure for a while each day to create a mud hole for them to roll in. The vet had advised her it was the best way to keep their skin in good condition but now, when I visited the Animal Meadow, Phil told me she had noticed Snuffle, the smaller of the pair, had fine lines appearing across her shoulders.

"I don't know what's causing it," she told me, "but it's getting worse. I've asked the vet to call in."

"It looks as if it's cracking, doesn't it?" I said as I studied the pig's skin.

"That's what I thought. I hope it's not some sort of disease."

Later that afternoon, I noticed the vet walk past the tearooms and, a little later, Phil called in.

"We were right. The skin is cracking," she said.

"What did the vet suggest?"

I was already worrying about how much the bill would be.

"Well... There's good news and bad news."

"Oh?"

"The good news is that it's not going to cost us anything..."

"And the bad news?"

"The only treatment is to stop the skin drying out, so I have to massage both the pigs with baby oil. Every morning."

I tried to keep a straight face, but it was impossible.

"Can I come and watch?" I giggled. "Or can we add it to the entertainment list? I'm sure the visitors would love it!"

"No way! I'm not having people watch me wrestling a slippery pig," Phil pouted.

"Oh, go on!" I teased. "We could charge extra for that."

CHAPTER 3

*****

One morning Mum phoned me from the ticket box.

"I don't know what's going on, but there's a bit of a commotion outside. I think someone had better come down and see what it's about."

I hurried down to the entrance and found Duncan Matthews with a team of men putting barriers across the newly widened approach road.

"What's going on?" I demanded.

"I'm reclaiming my land," he barked pompously.

I had no idea what he was talking about.

"You can't just change the road," he went on. "I've looked at the plans and your land ends three feet from the drive. That means you've built your extension without the landowner's permission."

"Are you saying our road encroaches three feet onto your land?"

"Now you're paying attention," he sneered.

"But why would you even care? What's the point? We widened the road to give better access to the car park. If the cars can't get through, they back up and block the traffic trying to get to you. Surely it's in your interest to widen the road as much as ours?"

"Don't you tell me what's in my interest, Missy," he snarled. "You'd better run along and call your lawyer because I'm going to see you in court this time."

"Over three feet of grass?"

Behind him, a man began marking a white line across the curve of the new road.

"What's the line for?" I asked.

"That's how much we're digging up."

"What? Seriously?" I was too amazed to be outraged.

"And there's nothing you can do to stop me."

A car had been waiting patiently behind the workmen, but now the driver honked his horn.

"Piss off!" Matthews bellowed across at him.

The driver's eyes opened wide in surprise and a small face peered out of the back window. A wave of embarrassment flooded me and I hurried over.

"I'm sorry about that. I'm afraid we're having a discussion with our neighbour. Would you mind driving over the grass? It's dry so it shouldn't be a problem."

"I can drive over your neighbour instead if you'd like," the man said.

I smiled.

"That's a kind offer, but no, thank you."

Turning back, I took a deep breath and marched up to Matthews.

"Listen to me," I said, raising my voice. "Right now, I'm going to call my solicitor. After that, I'm going to call the Land Registry and arrange for a surveyor to come out and mark the exact line of our boundary. If you damage our road before the surveyor arrives, I will call the police and have you arrested."

I turned away before he could answer and closed my ears to the insults that followed me as I walked back to the house.

David was in the shop and I joined him behind the counter and told him what had happened.

"The man's an arsehole," he scowled.

"I know, but why? What's the point? Why does he hate us so much?"

"I don't know. My friend, Mark, is one of the maintenance team at Norbrook. He asked me the same thing. He said Matthews talks about Silverlands all the time and he's got a particular thing about you. He calls you the Ice Queen or the Wicked Witch of the West, so it does seem a bit personal. "

"But why? What have I done to him?"

"To be fair, you have made him look an idiot in front of his men a few times. And you do keep ordering him off our land."

"True, but I wouldn't have to do it if he wasn't such an idiot," I muttered.

*****

The first function in the new restaurant was to celebrate a golden wedding anniversary. It sounded simple enough. The family wanted a three-course dinner with a disco afterward. Bob had hired a local DJ to set up the disco and had agreed on a menu that sounded exciting but was reasonably easy for us to prepare.

He had even arranged golden balloons and table decorations to suit the occasion. It was only on the day itself that I realised how little time we had to transform the restaurant into a function suite.

In theory, Silverlands closed at six o'clock and the function began at seven-thirty. In reality, it was often nearer six-thirty before we finished our search of the house and I knew the couple who had booked the evening would be arriving at seven with the cake because they wanted to be ready to welcome their guests.

It gave us very little time to clean the restaurant, blow up the golden balloons, arrange the table decorations and change into fresh clothes.

We also had three small children to feed and get ready for bed, and three large dogs who needed to be taken out for a run in the grounds.

"I'm sure doing functions will get easier once we get the hang of it," I said to David as we rushed around laying tablecloths and distributing cutlery.

"Of course, it will," he agreed. "Are we supposed to be putting glasses on the tables? Or do they have to get drinks from the bar?"

"I've no idea. I'd better check with Bob."

When we first thought about holding functions, we anticipated bringing in staff to serve the meals and provide extra help in the kitchen but, after the first few weeks of the season, our figures were already well below our projections. We needed to cut expenses wherever we could, so it made sense to do as much as possible by ourselves.

But we couldn't do everything.

Marion and Elliott, the glass engravers from the craft block, had asked if we needed extra staff for the functions. Elliott had worked in restaurants in the past and we knew Marion would be brilliant in the kitchen. She was a lovely, large lady and was always full of energy.

We decided to take them on. We knew the figures in the craft block were down too, and it made sense to support our tenants if we could.

I looked around for Bob to ask about the glasses but found that he was ahead of me, polishing champagne flutes and placing wine glasses on the tables.

He was in his element. He loved hosting events and had been looking forward to the evening from the moment he took the booking. He was determined everything would run smoothly and had planned every detail.

The meal would be served to people at their tables, so he had converted the restaurant counter into a bar. At one end, there were beer pumps and optics, but now he had removed the hot and cold trays that usually sat on the counter, leaving a long, clear space where people could order their drinks. Behind the counter, the shelves that held crisps and snacks during the day had been cleared and now held a selection of wines and bottled beers.

The guests would be offered a glass of champagne as they arrived but Bob knew some would prefer other drinks so he had checked and double checked that he had enough glasses, spirit measures, ice cubes, lemon slices, bottle openers and bar mats ready to go.

The beer barrels had been changed, and he had cleaned the pipes and made sure the gas cylinder was full earlier in the afternoon.

When the first guests arrived, Bob was standing at the door to welcome them.

Cheerful music drifted back into the kitchen as Phil and I laid out plates and prepared garnish for the starters. Butterflies were fluttering in my stomach, but I was pleasantly surprised that everything seemed to be under control.

Upstairs, Mum was getting the children ready for bed, but Dad was beside me in the kitchen waiting for instructions.

Suddenly, the door from the restaurant crashed open, and Bob rushed in. Without stopping to explain what was wrong, he ran to the gas cylinder in the corner and frantically turned the wheel on the top.

Without a word, he ran back to the door, stopping only to collect himself before stepping out into the restaurant.

"What was that all about?" Dad asked.

"No idea." I shrugged.

The evening went well.

I spent most of my time in the kitchen, but whenever I carried plates of food through and placed them on the tables, I felt a rush of pride. Everyone was happy. The guests were chatting, laughing and enjoying the food. It was just how I had hoped it would be.

As the sun set outside, the wall lights gave the room a golden glow and the coloured spotlights gave the indoor garden a magical quality.

When the meal was finished, the guests moved to the far end of the room where the DJ had set up a disco beside Tom's mural. It was obvious that everyone was enjoying themselves.

"That was brilliant," David said as Bob shut the door behind the last guests.

"Yes, it was," I agreed as I collected stray glasses and brought them back to the counter.

Bob locked the door, and his smile was wide.

"Well done, everyone, that couldn't have gone better," he beamed. "I can't believe how much we took on the bar. I'm going to have to reorder tomorrow. They never stopped drinking."

"They seemed a happy bunch," I said.

"Yes, they were lovely, really lovely," Bob agreed.

Suddenly he laughed.

"There was only one problem. Did you notice? As they were arriving, I went to pour a pint of beer and nothing happened. I kept pulling the pump, and all I got was froth."

"No! Why was that?" Phil asked.

"I must have forgotten to tighten the valve on the gas cylinder."

"I wondered why you came rushing into the kitchen." I laughed.

Bob made a face.

"It was a nightmare! I had a counter full of customers and no beer. It couldn't have been worse timing."

"Never mind. You won't do that again," David grinned.

*****

Bob insisted on inviting Duncan Matthews down to meet the Land Registry surveyor. I wanted to send him a written report afterwards, but Bob was convinced Matthews would claim we had moved the stakes unless he saw the surveyor place them himself.

"You're probably right," I grumbled, "I just don't want to be anywhere near the man."

"Then let me deal with him."

I shook my head.

"No. I won't let him think I'm afraid of him."

Matthews was already sitting in his Range Rover at the side of the road when the surveyor arrived. He drove up to the house to park and Bob and I walked back to the entrance with him.

As soon as the surveyor opened his case and took out his equipment Matthews climbed out of his car and strolled over.

"You're wasting your time," he said and pointed to the white line on the tarmac. "My men have already marked the boundary."

The surveyor looked up.

"And you are?"

"Duncan Matthews. I own all the land from the main road up to Norbrook park."

The surveyor's voice was cold.

"I see."

He handed Matthews a business card.

"Steven Phillips. I'm an independent surveyor working for the Land Registry. I'm here to mark the correct position of the boundary and I would appreciate it if you let me get on with my work."

There was silence as the surveyor lined up his equipment and consulted his charts. After a long time, he took some steel poles and drove them into the ground. Then he took a length of cord and tied it between the poles.

I fought back a smile as the cord skimmed the edge of the tarmac.

"Just to be sure, that means the road is built entirely on our land, doesn't it?" I asked.

"Yes, that's correct," the surveyor agreed.

"Thank you. That's all we needed to know."

Behind me, I heard the slam of a Range Rover's door.

*****

Once the children went back to school our visitor numbers dropped even further. On some days we didn't see a single family until eleven o'clock in the morning.

"Why is it? What have we done wrong?" David asked.

"It's not just us," I said. "Dad's been up at the Motor Museum talking to Eric and his figures are as bad as ours."

"Really? I don't know if that's good news or bad."

"And it's not just the visitor numbers. Our take-per-head is down too. Even when we get visitors, they're not spending as much on food and in the shop as they did last year."

"I had noticed there are a lot more families bringing picnics, but I thought it was because we've been advertising the indoor picnic area."

"It's just the way the world is at the moment. Bob thinks we should do another Outdoor Shakespeare this Autumn. The last one went well."

David nodded.

"I wish we had more functions lined up. The first one was brilliant."

"Yes, that would certainly help our bank balance. I still can't believe how much they spent on the bar."

"When is the next one?"

"A week on Friday. And we've got more people coming this time."

"Great. At least that will keep us busy."

The next function had been booked by a local Gardening Club. They wanted a finger buffet instead of a sit-down meal and asked for a sound system with a microphone as they were going to have speeches.

"From what Bob told me, they're going to be an elderly lot so I don't think the bar takings are going to be very high this time," David said sadly.

"Never mind. There are eighty people coming so it will still be worth doing," I replied.

This time we closed the doors to the restaurant as soon as we stopped serving lunches and laid out the tables and chairs and rearranged the bar during the afternoon.

Abbie helped me and was very excited at the idea of having an event in the evening.

"It must look lovely at night," she said wistfully. "I can imagine it with the lights on and the music playing. In the summer, if you have a disco, people can dance outside under the trees, can't they? You don't have to worry about disturbing the neighbours here."

"Yes, I suppose that's true," I agreed.

By the time we closed, most of the preparations for the function had been done. I looked around the restaurant and smiled. We wouldn't have to rush so much tonight.

"Testing, testing. One, two, three... Can you hear me?" David's voice came over the sound system.

"Loud and clear," I called back. "Let's go and search the house before we do the last touches."

An hour later, I was in the kitchen when Bob came in and twisted the valve on the top of the gas cylinder with both hands.

"There. That's definitely connected this time."

I smiled, and he gave me a quick kiss as he passed on his way back to the bar.

Dad was helping me lay out platters of food for the buffet when we heard the first guests arrive.

There was a sudden buzz of chatter, and Bob's voice sounded loud and friendly as he welcomed them. Glasses chinked as they were taken from the shelf, and I heard a voice asking for two whiskies and a pint of beer.

A moment later, the door crashed open, and Bob rushed in.

"I don't believe it!" he gasped as he ran to the gas cylinder. "I tightened it! I know I tightened it! There's a queue of people out there and no beer! It's a disaster!"

I should have panicked, but Bob was panicking enough for all of us. His mouth was wide and his eyes were enormous.

"I tightened it! I know I did!" he shrieked as he wrestled with the valve.

"Get on, you stupid thing! There! Fixed it!"

He ran back to the door, stopped, ran a hand through his hair, then walked calmly back into the bar.

I caught Dad's eye and the two of us burst out laughing.

The next time Bob rushed into the kitchen, it was because he had run out of gin and needed another bottle from the storeroom. The time after that, he had run out of whisky. Then vodka.

"I can't believe how much they drank," he said when all the guests had gone. "It was incredible. And we'll have to have a bigger float next time, I kept running out of change."

"Yes, I can see why the other attractions like doing functions." I grinned as I took the notes out of the till.

*****

"It seems a strange choice for a twenty-first birthday party. That's all," I said.

Bob had just told me that our next function, a large, family birthday party, would include a jazz band playing all evening.

"It's not that strange. Lots of people love jazz," he retorted.

"Fifty years ago, maybe. Do you think it was the parents' choice?"

"Possibly. They are the ones who are paying for it, after all."

I was changing into a tube-like, flapper dress and I wasn't happy.

"It's ridiculous wearing this in the kitchen. What happens if I spill something all over it?"

"I told you earlier. You don't have to wear it if you don't want to..."

"But if I don't, I'll be stuck in the kitchen all night and we won't have enough people to serve the tables," I grumbled.

"Then wear an apron in the kitchen. They're paying a lot extra to make this into a Theme Night. I thought you'd be pleased."

"Money isn't everything," I sniffed.

"Really? Then why are you spending so much time poring over the books every night?"

I didn't answer. Instead, I frowned at my reflection in the mirror.

"OK. I'll wear an apron."

I felt better when I saw the others in equally dramatic outfits. Phil looked demure in a beaded dress with long tassels hanging from the hem, and Marion was eye-catching in an Egyptian-style silk kimono.

"It was the only thing the hire company had in her size," Bob whispered to me.

"Well, they can't say we haven't made an effort." I sighed.

The restaurant looked wonderful. David had found a collection of Art Deco lamps to spread around the tables and had borrowed a hat stand complete with fedoras and cloche hats that we stood by the entrance.

"I think it looks brilliant," Phil smiled as she brought in a tray of glasses and stacked them behind the bar. "Is there anything left to do?"

"Just one thing," Bob said, and I noticed a large spanner in his hand.

"What's that for?" I asked as I followed him into the kitchen.

"I'm making sure there aren't any problems tonight," he said as he grasped the wheel of the gas cylinder with the spanner and twisted it.

"There! There's no way that's coming off."

David hurried in with a black bin liner.

"Some horrible child's dropped a mountain of confetti by the entrance. God only knows where they got it, but it's taken me ages to clear it up. Bob's not booking any wedding receptions, is he?"

"I don't think so. Go and get changed. They'll be arriving any minute."

Dad was looking out of the window.

"This must be them now," he said as a row of vehicles drove past.

I looked out and saw a group of flappers and gangsters climbing from the cars.

"Wow! They really have taken the theme thing seriously, haven't they?"

"They look fantastic!" Phil gasped. "This is going to be fun."

One of the guests was wearing a wide-striped suit with an Al-Capone hat pulled down over his eyes and carried a violin case.

I smiled. Suddenly I didn't feel so overdressed.

The pulsing rhythm of the band filtered through to the kitchen as I checked the mighty saucepan of soup simmering on the stove. Above the cheerful babble of voices at the bar, I recognised a familiar gasp.

A moment later, the door crashed open. Dad jumped out of the way as Bob charged through to the gas cylinder, his hands grasping the air in exasperation as he mouthed silent expletives at the ceiling.

"This can't be happening!" He reached for the spanner, but as he touched the connector it fell off in his hand.

"No!" he howled. "It's not possible. I checked it myself..."

"Can I help?" I offered, but he batted my hand away and struggled to fit the connector himself.

"This can't be a coincidence! Every time! Just as I pull a pint!" His voice was sharp with frustration as he screwed the connector into place and attacked it with the spanner.

"There." He heaved until his cheeks turned scarlet and perspiration ran down his face. Then he turned and glared suspiciously around the kitchen.

"No one... touches... it..." He gasped, jabbing a finger at each of us, then grabbed a kitchen roll, wiped his face, and darted back into the restaurant.

For a moment, no one moved.

"Well, that was interesting," Dad said at last. Looking across, I caught the twinkle in his eye, and my shoulders heaved with suppressed laughter.

"Don't make me laugh," I pleaded. "If he hears, he'll think it was me..."

But Dad's grin widened, and I couldn't control myself. The anxiety of the last weeks flooded out, and I laughed until tears ran down my cheeks.

Phil and Marion were laughing too, and Dad was doubled up.

"What did I miss?" David demanded as he appeared in the doorway, but I pulled myself together.

"No time to explain," I said as I wiped my eyes. "They'll be ready for the soup any minute."

*****

Once the party was over and the guests left, I expected Bob to bring up the subject of the disconnecting gas supply, but he never mentioned it.

I'm sure Marion was thinking the same thing because I saw her staring at him, but Bob behaved as though the incident had never happened.

"Thank you, everyone, that went really well," he said as we stripped the cloths from the tables. "I had some lovely comments about the food. Great work."

It wasn't until we were getting ready for bed that I asked him what had happened.

"It has to be a faulty connection. There's no other explanation. I'm going to ring the suppliers in the morning and ask them to replace it."

The next day I escaped from the tea rooms for a quick lunch break and took the opportunity to find Dad in his workshop.

"You were there yesterday," I began. "Do you have any idea how the gas connection came undone."

"No," he said simply. "It doesn't make sense."

"There were only four of us in the kitchen and nobody touched it, did they?"

"No. I would have seen them. Do you have any theories?" he asked.

"No. At least, no sensible ones."

I munched my sandwiches and Dad watched me.

"You think it was your ghost, don't you?" he said at last.

"He's not my ghost."

"Fred. Isn't that what you call it?"

I couldn't tell from his tone whether he was teasing me, so I didn't answer.

"What I don't understand is why it's doing it. What's the point?" he asked.

I took another bite.

"Is it trying to tell us something? Is it some kind of message?"

"No," I said at last. "I think he does it because it's funny."

*****

It was the end of June before we had another function. This time the guests were members of a Country and Western group from Plymouth.

"Does that mean we have to wear cowboy outfits?" I asked.

"Yes, I'm afraid so," Bob said. "They meet up every month in a pub, but they want to have a bigger event where they can bring their families. They want burgers and chips with line dancing and an entertainer."

"Burgers and chips? Really? You mean we're competing with McDonalds now?"

"It seems like it. They're hiring coaches to drive them here, so I think they'll be drinking a lot. I'm going to order extra everything for the bar."

As the summer weather arrived, we had been selling more cold beers at lunchtimes and there had been no repeat of the problems with the gas supply. Bob had insisted the connection to the cylinder was replaced, and he seemed confident there would be no repeat of the earlier dramas as we prepared for the evening.

Dad and David were wearing jeans with checked shirts and bandanas around their necks as they helped in the kitchen. I had a black miniskirt and a flamboyant black shirt with white fringe across the shoulders and white piping around every seam.

I still felt self-conscious, but I was getting used to wearing fancy dress. If my skirt had been a little longer, I would have felt comfortable.

This time, the restaurant was decorated with American flags, Stars and Stripes beer mats, and Budweiser posters.

A few minutes before the coach was due, Bob strolled into the kitchen and walked over to the gas cylinder. I watched him take a spanner from his pocket and heave on the connector. As he turned around, he noticed me watching him.

"Just checking," he said evenly as he laid the spanner on the shelf above the cylinder.

"They'll all be arriving at the same moment tonight. It's going to be manic. I'm really glad I'll have Duncan behind the bar with me."

Kate and Duncan were friends of ours who both had experience working in bars. I was glad to have them too. This would be the biggest crowd we had served so far, and I was sure they were going to be lively.

Country music blared through the building as the coaches arrived and the kitchen was rich with the smell of burgers and frying onions.

I had plates warming in the ovens and tubs of ingredients lined up ready to create 'Silverland's Special Burgers.'

"Has Bob checked the beer pumps?" David asked me.

"Yes. Everything's fine," I said.

"Good. It would be a disaster if anything happened now..."

He hadn't finished his sentence when the door flew open and Bob charged through.

"Out of my way!" He bellowed. "The spanner! Where's the spanner?"

I should have felt sorry for him. I did feel sorry for him. But as he fumbled for the spanner, his agitated expression was so comical I couldn't keep a straight face.

"This isn't funny!" he exploded. "There's no beer! All those people! No beer! Just froth!"

He yanked the connector tight with the spanner and was about to put it back on the shelf when he changed his mind and dropped it into his pocket.

Confusion turned to anger as he glared around at us.

"We'll talk about this later," he scowled and ran back into the bar.

"It's Fred, isn't it?" David said as the door clattered shut behind him. "It has to be."

"Not now," I hissed. Kate was staring after Bob with her mouth open.

"But it has to be..."

"Shh! We have to concentrate. Think burgers."

Reluctantly, David began piling onion, lettuce and sliced tomatoes onto buns while I shovelled chips into the deep fryer.

It was a long evening.

I had never seen line dancing before and was intrigued to see so many people performing intricate steps in perfect synchronisation while taking no notice of each other whatsoever. It seemed peculiar to me. I had always thought of dancing as a group activity, and there was something perverse in the way each individual seemed oblivious to the people on either side of them.

When the guests left, Bob marched into the kitchen with a face like thunder.

"Right. I've had enough of this. Who's responsible?"

Red patches were burning on his cheeks and I knew that this time it wasn't funny.

"It wasn't anyone," I said quickly.

"Don't be ridiculous. Someone disconnected the gas. I spent hours preparing everything, making sure we were ready. How do you think it makes us look when people arrive and we can't serve them? It's unprofessional. It makes us look stupid. I'm not having it. I want to know who did it!"

We stood like naughty children as his voice boomed around the room.

"No one touched the connector," Dad said calmly. "I was beside it the whole time."

"Then how did it happen?" Bob challenged him.

"It was Fred," I said.

"For Christ's sake!" Bob exploded. "I don't want to hear that again! Never! Someone did this. And if it ever happens again, there will be consequences."

There was silence as he marched out of the room and slammed the door behind him.

"Sorry about that," I said awkwardly.

Kate looked shell-shocked.

"What was that all about?" Duncan asked.

"It's complicated..." my mind scrabbled for an explanation, but David couldn't stay quiet any longer.

"We have a ghost. It's called Fred, and it disconnects the beer pumps."

"Please, don't..." I began, but he ignored me.

"Diana pretends it doesn't exist, but it does."

"That's amazing. You're so lucky," Kate squealed.

"Lucky?" It was not what I had expected.

"I've always wanted to see a ghost. What does it look like?"

"I don't know. Look, I'm sorry, but I really don't want to talk about this right now."

Dad nodded.

"I think we'd better get on. We've still got a lot of clearing up to do."

By the time I went upstairs, Bob was in bed. I couldn't tell if he was asleep because he had his back to me, but he didn't move as I crawled under the duvet.

The next morning the sun shone, but I felt there was a huge cloud hanging over me.

"Are you OK?" I asked Bob, but he said nothing.

"Shall I get the breakfast this morning?"

"Do what you like," he replied. "I'm taking Dino for a walk."

It was nearly opening time before he returned. I tried to talk to him, but he merely turned away.

"Do you need a hand with anything?" I offered, but he ignored me.

"Is Bob all right?" Abbie asked.

"Yes, he's fine," I assured her. "He's just a bit tired. We had a big crowd in last night."

*****

By the end of the day, Bob had calmed down. We ate our evening meal after the girls had gone to bed and when we finished, he reached across and put his hand on my mine.

"You do still love me then?"

"You know, I do." He sighed. "But people have to take the functions seriously. It's not just a game."

"We do take them seriously," I said earnestly. "We all worked hard, didn't we? Everything went well."

"That's not the point. Someone was responsible for what happened, and I need to find out who it was."

I knew talking about Fred would only make the situation worse, so I changed the subject.

That night, as I lay in bed unable to sleep, I decided to try a different approach. If I couldn't talk to Bob, I would try talking to Fred. I had come to think of him as a naughty child. I didn't think he meant any harm. He just liked causing trouble.

The next time I was alone in the kitchen, I told Fred I needed to talk to him. I explained how important it was for us that the functions went well and how sad it made me when Bob was upset. Then, I asked him not to interfere with the beer supply again.

When I had finished, I looked around the empty room and wondered if I had finally lost my mind.

*****

"There's something I wanted to talk to you about," David said as we began our evening search of the house.

"What's that?" I asked.

"I think we're missing something..."

He hesitated, and I glanced at him. It was unusual for David to be lost for words.

"Our visitor numbers are down, aren't they?"

"Yes."

"And we need to do something to increase them?"

We had reached the split in the upstairs corridor and I waited while he went and checked the circus and entertainments room.

"Go on..." I said when he came back.

"I think we need to use any advantages we can to get extra attention."

"How do you mean?"

"I'm just saying that it seems a waste if we've got something special and we're not using it."

"I have no idea what you're on about."

"Yes, you do. I'm talking about Fred. We have a ghost. Other places would give a fortune for an opportunity like that."

"No!" The word popped out by itself.

"But think about it. We could get thousands of people here. All we have to do is put out a press release."

"No! We can't."

David frowned as he switched off the lights in the First World war exhibition.

"Why not?"

"Because it wouldn't be right. Anyway, it wouldn't work. Ghosts don't perform on cue. If you did get people here, what would you say if nothing happened? They'd just think you'd conned them. And even if something did happen, they'd think it was staged."

"So what? It wouldn't matter. It would still be great publicity."

"No, it wouldn't! This is a family attraction. Lots of people are scared of ghosts."

We reached the entrance to Devon Mysteries and David opened the control box and flicked off the power supply.

"But we've included lots of ghost stories in here and people love them."

"That's different," I protested. "Everyone knows they're just stories but you're talking about putting out a press release saying we've got a real ghost."

"And why not? It's true. You know it is."

I glared at him.

"No, I don't. I don't know what I believe."

David threw his hands in the air in exasperation.

"For Christ's sake, Diana! Why are you being so difficult?"

I didn't have the words to explain.

"I'm sorry," I said at last. "It would be wrong, that's all I can say."

We finished the search in silence.

Chapter 4

The plants in the flower beds outside the craft block had settled in well and were now a riot of colour. I had chosen a combination of perennial plants and annuals and was delighted with the results. Whenever I had a chance, I slipped away and spent a few happy moments watering them.

I was pleasantly surprised that I hadn't needed to visit the craft block to sort out minor squabbles between Tom and the other craftspeople this summer. It seemed that Penny was a calming influence. It was clear that her shop had become a focal point and had helped create a community atmosphere.

One morning, Bob popped over to see how Penny was getting on and found her deep in conversation with Liza Berlin, our resident entertainer.

"Liza made an excuse and left as soon as I arrived," Bob told me later. "She seemed upset, so I asked Penny about it. Apparently, Liza's worried about Roly. His arthritis is getting worse."

"Is that going to be a problem?" I asked. "With the show, I mean?"

Bob shrugged.

"I don't know. I hope not, but I suppose I'd better talk to her."

That evening, Bob had been on his way to Liza's flat when he spotted her walking around the edge of the Animal Meadow with Roly.

"I didn't need to ask her anything. The moment I went over it all came pouring out. The vet has started Roly on a new treatment but he's warned Liza that he mustn't do any tricks that involve standing up on his hind legs."

"But that cuts out most of his act," I said. "What a shame. I can't imagine her without Roly the Wonderdog."

"No, it's sad. They're inseparable, aren't they?" Bob agreed. "But she says she's going to develop a new act that Roly can do without standing up. It involves ducks."

"Ducks?" I said in surprise.

"Yes. Indian Runner ducks. They're the ones with long necks and tall, slim bodies."

"I don't think I've ever seen them."

"Well, you will. Liza's got six ducklings arriving tomorrow."

"Goodness. I hope Roly likes them."

"So, do I," Bob raised his eyebrows. "You know what they say about old dogs and new tricks."

The following morning, Penny phoned me from her shop.

"You've got to see this! Liza's brought her new ducklings over. They're adorable!"

The tearooms were quiet, and the restaurant wasn't due to open for another hour so I hurried across to the craft block. I had expected the hatchlings to be tiny balls of fluff sitting in a cage of some sort but they already had sleek white feathers and were running around between the displays in Penny's shop.

They were unlike any ducks I had ever seen. Instead of the dumpy shape I associated with waterfowl, these birds really were designed for running. They had long orange legs and their bodies were tall and sleek. They held their heads high and peered around like meerkats. Penny was right. They were absolutely adorable.

I couldn't stop smiling as I watched them follow each other in a long line like well-behaved children on a school outing.

Liza beamed with maternal pride. She was wearing her clown outfit and motley as she perched on a stool beside Penny.

"They're just how I imagined them," she said.

"Have you trained ducks before?" I asked.

"No, but I've trained everything else. Dogs, cats, parrots, pigs, sheep. I even trained a praying mantis once for a television advert."

"And not many people can say that," I laughed.

"The director wanted it to wave at the camera," Liza explained. "It took a while because insects can be very stubborn, but everyone was happy with the performance in the end."

Penny caught my eye and we both turned away to hide our giggles.

"I'm going to make little bow ties for them," Liza told us. "I want them to look smart. Roly has his ruffle around his neck but I can't make my mind up whether the bow ties should be a matching colour or something different."

"Black would be best. Then they would look like little waiters," Penny laughed as the row of ducklings raced around the base of a display stand.

"What does Roly think of them?" I asked.

The little dog was sitting quietly by Liza's feet and looked up at the sound of his name.

"He's not taking much notice of them at the moment, but they're going to be great friends. You'll see."

*****

A few days later, I was on my way to the Animal Meadow when I noticed a family bending over the flower beds. I was curious to know what they were looking at, so I waited for them to go and walked across.

To my surprise, a neatly typed label attached to a stick had been pushed into the ground next to a beautiful penstemon. The label read Scarlatina.

I couldn't imagine who would have gone to the effort of making the label, especially as the name was wrong.

Looking around, I saw that many of the other plants had similar labels with names such as Plaga, Anthracis, Botulinum and Nigrum Mortem. It was many years since I studied Latin at school, but I recognised Nigrum Mortem. Suddenly, the penny dropped.

"Tom, what is the point of these?" I demanded, holding out the labels as I marched into his workshop.

The Potter wiped clay from his hands and looked me straight in the eye.

"I beg your pardon. What makes you think it was me that was responsible for those?"

I glared back at him.

"Who else would go to the trouble of writing these out and putting them next to my plants?"

Tom sniffed and turned away from me.

"There were too many old ladies asking me what the names were. I was merely being helpful."

"No, you weren't!" I snapped. "These aren't plant names. They're Latin names for diseases. Anthrax, Botulism, Black Death. What were you thinking?"

"I was thinking that if they waste my time, I'll waste theirs," Tom said sweetly. "I like to imagine them at a nursery asking if there are any Bubonic Plagues in stock."

I had expected him to be ashamed of himself, but instead he looked smug.

"I am confiscating these labels. Please do not do it again." I said in my best headmistress voice and walked out.

Penny was at the entrance to her shop.

"How do you put up with him?" I asked, but Penny only grinned.

"You mean Tom? He is a bit of a character, isn't he?"

"A character?" I sighed. "He's impossible!"

Later that day, I took a delivery over to Phil and found her grooming the donkeys.

"Hello, old fellow," I said as I stroked Victor's velvety nose.

A sudden movement in the top field caught my eye.

"Is that Liza with Roly?" I asked.

"Yes." Phil nodded. "They've been up there for hours, but I don't think the training's going well."

As I peered up, I could see Liza's arms waving dramatically and a row of white dots following each other across the field, but Roly was staying stubbornly in one place.

"Oh, dear," I sighed. "It doesn't look as though they're going to be such great friends after all."

*****

As the date of our next function approached, I grew anxious. I considered having another talk with Fred, but told myself I was being ridiculous.

We were only expecting a small group of people for a carvery meal with no entertainment. After the last events it was something of an anticlimax.

Marion & Elliott had a family celebration of their own but Kate and Duncan were going to be helping us and I prayed the evening would go smoothly.

I pretended not to notice when Bob walked through the kitchen and checked the connection on the gas cylinder. He put the spanner into his pocket and moved to the centre of the room.

There was a moment of awkward silence as everyone stopped what they were doing and looked at him.

"I don't want to talk about anything that's happened in the past," Bob said in an even voice, "but I do want to talk about tonight. It should be an easy event. Everything is straightforward. Let's all enjoy it without any distractions, shall we? Let's concentrate on being professional, and doing the best job we can."

There was a murmur of agreement, and Bob went back into the restaurant.

"Have you got the spare spanner?" I asked David as soon as Bob had gone.

"It's here," David said, and held it out towards me.

"Good. I can hear people arriving now. You'd better be ready."

David hurried over to the cylinder, fitted the spanner onto the connector and braced himself.

I listened at the restaurant door as Bob welcomed the first arrivals and took their orders. There was the familiar sound of a pint being pulled and I drew a breath of relief.

"It's OK. It's working," I said to David.

"Thank God for that, but I'd better stay here for a while just to be sure."

The rest of the evening ran smoothly, and we were finished and up in our flat well before midnight. Bob had made mugs of chocolate and we curled up on the sofa to drink them.

"I enjoyed tonight," Bob said as he relaxed. "It might only have been a small group, but they enjoyed themselves and it was a great atmosphere."

"Yes, it was good."

"And it was a relief that there was no silliness this time. I think my little talk before we started must have done the trick."

*****

At the beginning of July, our visitor numbers went up dramatically. Although we still weren't as busy as we had been the previous year, it was a great to see the exhibitions full and, for the first time, the restaurant was working at full capacity. Everything was going well.

Abbie had perfected the art of carrying trays without leaving a trail of broken crockery behind her, and the new girls in the kitchen had had time to learn what to do.

"In some ways, it's been useful to have a few quiet weeks before getting into the peak of the season," Bob said.

"That's true, but it's left us a lot of catching up to do," I reminded him.

"Who knows, maybe we'll be packed every day from now on," Bob said optimistically.

I was in the kitchen preparing lunches when the fire alarms went off.

The rumble of fire doors slamming shut through the building made me jump even more than the wailing siren. We had practiced a fire drill, but it took me a moment to remember what to do.

"Abbie, you and the girls get everyone out of the restaurant. I'll help Martha in the tearooms."

I had expected people to panic when the alarms went off, so it came as a shock to open the fire door and see families sitting at every table. Martha was leaning down to an elderly couple, shouting to make herself heard above the siren.

"You can come back later, dear. You need to go outside until the alarms stop."

I couldn't hear the old lady's reply, but she remained stubbornly in her seat.

My heart was pumping. If there really was a fire, every moment counted.

I was desperate to find out what was happening, but I couldn't leave until everyone was out of the tearooms.

"Please, you have to go outside," I yelled.

A few families stood up, but others were still eating. Martha and I moved from table to table, urging the customers to leave.

"Take the food with you, but you really have to go!"

"You check the loos," I said to Martha when the room was finally empty.

Running to the front door, I found David scanning the flashing symbols on the alarm panel.

"Is it a fire?" I asked him.

"I don't know. Whatever it is, it's in the upstairs corridor."

He was racing towards the staircase before I could take in what he had said. I raced after him and bounded up the stairs two at a time.

Holding open a fire door, I directed a family down to the nearest exit, then ran to catch up with David. The emergency lighting had cut in and the corridor was bathed in an eerie blue glow. The Down in Devon Exhibition was to my right. I opened the fire door and was horrified to see it was full of people.

Panic gripped me. What if there really was a fire? How many other people were still inside? A siren was wailing near the ceiling and I didn't waste time trying to speak. Instead, I grabbed people's arms and pointed to the exit. To my relief, they began to move. I herded them to the top of the stairs and left them following each other down to the front door.

Racing back, I found David staring up at a smoke detector.

"It's this one!" he shouted, pointing to a flashing light on the side of the casing. "It's OK. It's a false alarm."

The relief was immediate. My shoulders sagged, and for a brief moment, I thought I was going to throw up.

"Are you all right?" David bellowed in my ear.

"I'm fine," I lied. "Does that mean we can turn these bloody alarms off?"

We headed back to the control panel and David flicked the switches, but although the sirens stopped, my ears kept ringing. It was as if my head was full of cotton wool.

I went back to the kitchen and found Abbie and the girls standing in the yard.

"It's all right. You can come back in now," I told them.

Suddenly, my heart raced again as the acrid smell of burning filled my nostrils. Spinning around, I saw smoke escaping from one of the ovens.

Abbie pushed past me.

"Oh, my God! The lasagne!" she wailed.

She pulled open the oven door and black clouds billowed out into the room. Before I could stop her, she grabbed a tea towel, reached inside and pulled out a catering-sized lasagne. Flames were leaping from the edges.

"Put it on the hob," I ordered, pulling a fire blanket from the wall. "Quick, get this over it before the alarms go off again!"

Abbie lifted the tray towards the hob, but the flames flicked sideways. She flinched violently and the foil tray crashed to the ground, splattering blackened lasagne across the floor.

"Are you all right?"

"No! It burned my fingers," she wailed.

"Well, don't stand there." I pushed her towards the sink. "Get them under cold water."

*****

Fortunately, Abbie's burns were only superficial. When we closed, we went back and looked at the offending fire detector.

"Can you see anything wrong with it?" Dad asked.

"It seems fine now." David shrugged. "As soon as I turned the alarms off, it went back to normal. It must have been a fluke. Let's hope it doesn't happen again."

The following day was rainy and visitors were queueing in the tearooms and restaurant when the alarms went off.

"I don't believe it," I groaned. I left Abbie and Martha to evacuate the visitors and hurried to the front door to consult the alarm panel. David was already there.

"Is it the same detector?" I asked.

"No. It's in the Enchanted Forest this time."

We hurried through the building, asking people to leave as we went. As soon as we reached the Enchanted Forest, I saw a red light flashing from the ceiling.

"That's ridiculous," I complained. "Why has it gone off? There's no smoke. There's nothing wrong at all. It must be a problem with the system."

This time we called the alarm company. They arrived quickly and tested every sensor.

"You'll be pleased to know there is nothing wrong with the system," the man said cheerfully. "I can't find any obvious reason for the alarms going off, but these detectors are very sensitive. Sometimes they get tiny cobwebs inside them and then the slightest draught can disturb the cobweb and trigger the sensor."

"Does that mean it's likely to happen again?"

"Not at all." The man reassured me. "I've cleaned every detector, inside and out, so you shouldn't have any more problems."

I had just drifted off to sleep that night when I was jolted back to consciousness. The alarms were screeching through the house and Dino barked in my ear in case I hadn't noticed.

Bob scrambled out of bed and I dragged my dressing gown on and hurried to the girls' room.

"What is it, Mummy?" Claire cried.

"It's nothing to worry about, Angel. It's only the alarms being silly again."

"They're so loud. Can't you turn them off?"

Lucy held her arms up to be carried.

"We will soon. But we have to go downstairs first."

"Why can't you turn it off now?"

"It's the rules, darling. We can't turn the alarms off until Daddy finds out what caused it."

I didn't want to tell her that we had to make sure the house wasn't really on fire.

Grudgingly, Claire climbed out of bed and took my hand. I already had

Lucy in my arms and together we made our way downstairs.

"Why does it look so strange, Mummy?" Claire asked.

I squeezed her fingers.

"It's the emergency lighting. It's rather blue, isn't it?"

"I don't like it."

"Don't worry, we'll soon have you back in bed."

The others were already by the front door. Phil was sitting on the floor cuddling a sleepy Michael and David was studying the control board.

"It's in the downstairs loo, this time," he said heavily.

Mum, Dad, Phil and I stayed with the kids until David and Bob returned and confirmed that it was safe to turn off the alarms.

We did the same thing the following night.

And the night after that.

On the fourth night, I couldn't go to sleep. Instead, I lay in bed listening. I was still awake at three in the morning when the silence was shattered by the wail of the siren.

"I can't cope with much more of this," I moaned as Bob and David set off to find the offending detector. But when they returned, David was elated.

"We've solved the mystery!" he announced. "It's bats. One flew past us in the corridor. I knew there were some in the attic, but there must be a hole somewhere that lets them into the house. They're triggering the alarms."

"I suppose it's possible," Dad agreed.

The next night we closed every door in the building in the hope it would stop the bats flying along the corridors.

"I think we've cracked it this time," Bob said as we climbed into bed. "I'm sure we'll get a decent sleep tonight."

"I really hope you're right," I said, but as I turned off the bedside light, an alarm pierced the darkness.

"No! Not again!"

I was so tired I wanted to cry, but instead, I climbed out of bed and fumbled with my dressing gown. I couldn't find the sleeve holes, so I draped it around my shoulders and plodded into the girls' room.

Lucy was waiting for me, but Claire was still asleep, oblivious to the ear-splitting whine.

"Come on, Darling."

Claire pouted and pushed my hand away, her eyes still closed.

"Please, Darling, we have to go."

This time, I carried Claire while Lucy trotted down the stairs beside me.

The dressing gown kept slipping from my shoulders, and the wailing alarm sliced into my brain. I didn't believe there was a fire, so instead of going to the front door, I sat on the bottom step and rocked the girls in my arms. Phil joined me with Michael.

My eyes were half-closed, but I heard Bob and David hurry off along the downstairs corridor.

"It's OK, nothing to worry about," Bob called a few minutes later as David turned off the alarms.

"Oh, my goodness, look at you!"

The wailing stopped, and I realised Mum and Dad were standing in front of me. Bob was beside them, laughing.

"If it's a new fashion, I don't think it'll catch on."

I frowned, not understanding the joke.

"She's exhausted, leave her alone." Mum said.

I looked down and realised the dressing gown draped around me was actually Dino's blanket. Bob and David were roaring with laughter, and suddenly my patience snapped.

"This isn't funny! It's not fair on the kids! Why should they be dragged out of bed every night?"

"I know. I'm sorry." Bob looked chastened, and I felt guilty for shouting.

The alarm people returned that morning and tested every part of the system. They were apologetic but still couldn't find anything wrong.

When we went to bed, I held my breath and waited, but all was silent. Eventually, I drifted off to sleep and heard nothing until the alarm clock rang the next morning.

The false alarms had stopped as unexpectedly as they started.

*****

Once the summer holidays began, our turnover finally matched our projections. I breathed a sigh of relief as I watched the visitors flooding in through the gates.

It was wonderful waking up each morning knowing the day would be filled with excitement and activity.

Families came to enjoy themselves and I loved to see them packing the exhibitions, exploring the woodlands, visiting the craft centre and cheering the entertainers on the lawn.

"This is more like it," Dad grinned one afternoon as he stepped into the kitchen.

We had finished serving lunches and there were piles of crockery everywhere waiting to go in the dishwasher.

"Are you busy?" I asked hopefully as Millie raced in with another tray of dirty dishes.

"I can spare an hour if you like." He grinned. "The kids are in the ticket box with your Mum."

"Will she be all right?"

"I think so. Lucy's asleep and the other two are colouring in books. She'll phone if she needs anything."

"Great," I threw him a tea towel and started stacking plates into the dishwasher. "You do the Outs, I'll do the Ins."

The dishwasher had three trays that worked on a sliding steel shelf. This meant that while one tray was being washed, the previous tray of clean china needed to be dried while a third tray could be stacked with dirty dishes.

It worked best with two people, and in the height of summer, the dishwasher never stopped.

"Where's Abbie? I thought she was here today?" Dad asked.

"She and Pam are cleaning up in the restaurant. We had another puker."

For some reason, there had been a spate of babies practising their projectile vomiting skills.

"Oh dear. I hope it wasn't anything we gave them."

"No. Nothing to worry about. They brought their own baby food."

"That's all right. The kids can puke as much as they like as long as it isn't our fault."

"I'm not sure Abbie would agree with that," I laughed.

The door to the kitchen yard was open and Zac, the juggler, appeared.

"Is it all right if I get myself a coffee?"

I signalled him to come in.

"Of course it is. I don't know why you even ask after all this time."

He grinned.

"I don't want to take anything for granted."

"You can make one for me if you like," Dad suggested. "This tyrant's got me working again."

"She's a nightmare, isn't she?" Zac laughed.

Abbie rushed in from the restaurant with a bucket and an armful of cleaning cloths. I noticed her eyes light up at the sight of Zac and she threw back her shoulders before walking past him.

"That's all done. What do you want me to do next?" she asked.

"Wash your hands, please. Then you can take over here while I get started on the afternoon teas."

"Right you are."

Zac had moved to the far end of the kitchen and was twisting a plastic tea tray between his fingers. He flipped it into the air and caught it on his head before letting it slide down past one ear and balance on his shoulder.

"He's so clever," Abbie whispered to me. "I could watch him all day."

*****

Donkey rides had proved popular the previous year, so now we included them in our daily timetable. Each morning, Phil led one of the donkeys over to the main lawn and our youngest visitors were lifted onto its back for a leisurely amble around the grounds.

Moses and Victor were both gentle creatures and it was clear they enjoyed the experience. They waited patiently as each child was settled and were never in a hurry to return to their field at the end of the session.

Moses, the older of the two, had a soft grey coat and patient eyes. Victor was a dark, chocolate brown with a creamy muzzle and ears that rotated like radar detectors to make sure he never missed a thing. He was eternally curious and delighted in chewing anything which was left within his reach.

Despite his docile appearance, it was Moses who sometimes caused Phil problems. Both the donkeys had regular visits from the farrier to make sure their hooves were kept in good condition, but Moses did not appreciate the attention.

He was never aggressive, but the moment the farrier arrived Moses planted his feet firmly on the ground, a little more spaced out than usual, and refused to lift them. When the farrier touched his leg to indicate he wanted Moses to lift his foot, the donkey shifted his weight onto that leg.

If the farrier took hold of the hoof and tried to lift it off the ground, Moses simply leaned on him. The farrier was a tall, solidly built man, but there was no way he could support the weight of a fully grown donkey.

The first few visits had ended in defeat. Moses' hooves were growing longer and Phil had been worried she would have to report the problem to the donkey Sanctuary when the farrier suggested another approach.

"He said he wanted to try something different," Phil told us later. "Moses was wearing a head collar with a leading rein and the farrier grabbed the rein and pulled it down to the ground."

"How did Moses react?" I asked.

"I thought he was going to object, but he didn't. He laid down on the ground without any fuss."

"Then what?"

"That was the amazing bit. The farrier touched his shoulder and Moses rolled over onto his back. He lay there with his feet up in the air. It was incredible. He didn't care at all. He stayed there all the time the farrier was filing his hooves. You should have seen the looks we got from the visitors. They thought it was hilarious."

"Maybe we should put it on the entertainments list," Bob suggested. "Come and see Moses, the reclining donkey, having his toenails clipped."

"Yes, the visitors would probably pay extra to see that," Dad laughed.

CHAPTER 4

*****

One morning I noticed the donkeys had not been giving rides.

"Is there a problem?" I asked Phil when I saw her.

She nodded and looked worried.

"I thought there was something wrong with Moses yesterday, but I couldn't tell what it was. He was eating, but he seemed tired. I thought it was because the weather's been so hot, but this morning Victor seems off-colour too."

"What do you mean, exactly?"

"It's strange. They're wrinkling their skin as though something's irritating them. I've had a good look, but I can't see any mites or anything like that, but I don't want to do any rides until I know what's causing it."

"Can I take a look?"

"Of course."

I walked across to the Animal Meadow with Phil and saw the two donkeys standing together at the far side of the field. Normally, they would come trotting across as soon as they recognised us, but now they stayed still with their heads down.

"You see what I mean? Something's wrong."

I nodded. As we got closer, I could see the donkeys were twitching their shoulders and sending little ripples through their coats right down to their tails.

"Something's bothering you, isn't it?" I said as I patted Victor on the neck. He shivered at my touch and I frowned. "What is it, old boy?"

He stood patiently as I parted the thick hair on his shoulder until I could see the skin. It looked pink and irritated, but there was no sign of bites or insects.

"We're going to have to get the vet in, aren't we?" Phil asked.

"Yes."

I smoothed Victor's coat back into place and noticed my hands were covered in dark brown hairs.

"Are they supposed to be moulting?"

"They always do a bit, but I did notice that a lot of hair came out when I groomed them this morning."

The vet arrived late in the afternoon. I saw him walk past the window and waited curiously until Phil appeared in the kitchen. I could tell at once it was bad news.

"What did the vet say?" I asked.

"You're not going to believe it, but they've got buttercup sunburn."

"What on earth is that?"

"It means they've been eating too many buttercups. There's something in the plants that upsets the donkeys' skin and makes them sensitive to sunlight."

"Even with their thick coats?"

"Yes, it's weird, isn't it? If it gets really bad, they start moulting and end up with bald patches."

"That's terrible."

Phil's lip was quivering.

"I feel like it's my fault."

"Not at all," I reassured her. "You look after them beautifully. How were you supposed to know? Is there anything the vet can do?"

"No. We have to make sure they don't eat any more buttercups and keep them out of the sun."

"Right."

There was no point in asking how we were supposed to do that when their entire field was filled with buttercups and it was the middle of summer. I knew the donkeys wouldn't be happy if we shut them in their stable all day long.

"It's the Donkey Sanctuary I'm worried about," Phil sniffed. "They stressed how important it is for us to look after Victor and Moses properly. They were really strict about it. They said if there were any problems, they would take them back."

I tried to reassure her.

"I think the best thing is to talk to them."

We were all relieved when Phil came off the phone after a long call and told us the lady from the donkey sanctuary had been helpful.

She admitted she had spotted the buttercups in the field herself when she had delivered the donkeys, but hadn't thought there were enough of them to cause a problem. She had no intention of taking Moses and Victor away and was going to come over the next day and bring some herbal remedies that might help.

"She even suggested the donkeys might like to wear straw hats to keep the sun off their heads," Phil said.

Suddenly I saw the funny side of the situation.

"Seriously? Donkeys in sun hats?" I giggled. "Do you think we should get them sunglasses to go with them?"

*****

At the beginning of August, we celebrated Lucy's second birthday. Her first birthday had passed in a blur of peak-season chaos, and I had comforted myself that she was too young to notice she had missed out. This year, however, I was determined to mark the occasion.

As soon as we closed, I threw a cloth over a table on the tea lawn and laid out pizzas, sausage rolls, crisps and jellies.

The children had been in the ticket box with their grandparents and now Claire and Michael raced up the drive while Lucy trailed behind them holding Mum's hand.

"Where are the presents?" Claire demanded as she reached me.

"Under the desk in the office," I said, and she and Michael ran inside.

By the time Mum and Dad arrived with Lucy, I had finished laying out the delicacies.

I caught Lucy and lifted her high in the air.

"Happy birthday, Lucy-Lu!"

"Cake! Cake!" she giggled down at me, her silky hair flying around her face.

David appeared from the front door with Ossie and Dino bounding behind him. The dogs liked to search the tea lawns in case visitors had left crumbs among the grass and the smell of food drew them to the table.

"Not for you, boys," I warned them.

"Not you," Lucy repeated.

Abbie and Martha joined the family and cups of tea and glasses of orange squash were passed around. Claire and Michael burst out of the house with their arms full of presents and stacked them in a pile in front of Lucy.

"But you can't open them yet," Michael instructed her.

A moment later, Bob emerged from the tea rooms carrying a cake topped by two shining candles and everyone sang a rousing chorus of Happy Birthday to You.

"Cake! Cake!" Lucy squealed again, but she waited patiently while Abbie took a photo before puffing out the candles.

Lucy never showed any sign of shyness. She made friends with everyone she met and loved being the centre of attention just as much as Bob.

When we finished eating and Lucy had torn the wrapping paper from every one of her presents, Abbie and Martha waved goodbye. The rest of us played Musical Statues, Pass the Parcel and Pin-the-Tail-on-the-Donkey in the warm evening sunlight. I couldn't imagine how life could be any better.

*****

Earlier in the year, Zac had suggested to Bob that we should hold a Jugglers' Convention. After the experience of hosting a Clown Convention, I was not convinced we were ready to be overrun by a multitude of jugglers, but Zac assured us it would be a very different event and much less frantic.

"Jugglers are introverts," he told us. "All they want to do is spend time with other jugglers. If you invite them, they'll be happy to stand in groups wherever you put them and perform all day. As long as you feed them, they won't ask for anything else."

It sounded too good to be true. We had shelved the idea at first, but the unexpected dip in our visitor numbers persuaded Bob we should go ahead.

"Anything that gets extra publicity at the end of the season has to be good," he reasoned.

The Jugglers' Convention was booked for the first Sunday in September, and it would be followed by a run of Outdoor Shakespeare. This time the play was to be Julius Caesar.

"How are things going with the jugglers? Do you know how many are coming yet?" I asked Bob as the end of August approached.

"They certainly seem more organised than the clowns," he admitted. "I've had some lovely letters back from them explaining what they do and saying how much they'd like to come. I don't have the exact numbers, but I think it's about forty so far."

"Forty! That's a lot, isn't it?" I gasped.

"Not really. Zac says some conventions have hundreds attending."

"But that's when the convention is only for jugglers. We need space for the public too," I reminded him.

"If September is anything like May, space won't be a problem," Bob reminded me.

Silverlands was still packed each day and it was hard to remember the quiet days of spring.

"I suppose so, but it still seems a lot," I grumbled.

I was grateful we didn't have any functions booked during the school summer holidays. I knew we needed the money, but working seven days a week and tending the gardens in the evenings was taking its toll. Coping with evening events as well would have been unbearable.

As I watered the hanging baskets one evening, I found myself looking ahead to the autumn when we would be able to close the doors and Silverlands would be ours once again.

I rolled up the hosepipe and climbed the stairs to the flat.

"I forgot to tell you. Zac's had a brilliant idea," Bob announced as I walked in.

"Oh?"

"He thinks we should make the convention into a competition. If we offer a prize – it doesn't have to be a big one – we can have knockout rounds all day and a finale at the end of the afternoon. We'll have to find some judges, but I think it will work really well."

"Yes, I suppose so."

"It wouldn't be compulsory. If the jugglers want to turn up and perform without competing that will be fine, but it will add a whole new dimension."

I could see Bob was enthusiastic about the idea.

"I suppose it would be something else to put in the press release."

"Exactly."

"As long as it doesn't make a lot more work," I said as I kicked off my shoes and collapsed on the sofa.

The next day, Bob invited Zac into the office and the two of them made plans. The juggling competition had caught Bob's imagination and he spent hours on the phone or drawing up lists of performers and timetables.

"I hope it all goes smoothly," I said to Dad. "Some of the jugglers do sound pretty amazing. One is even coming over from Germany."

"Really? How did he hear about it?"

"Bob said he read about it in a juggling magazine."

"In Germany? That's incredible. I didn't even know there were magazines for jugglers."

I laughed.

"Neither did I, but I do know Bob has been sending out an awful lot of press releases!"

The jugglers began arriving the evening before the convention, and I soon saw that Zac was right. Jugglers were a completely different breed to clowns. Many of them wore distinctive outfits with latex leggings, striped trousers or bright waistcoats, but they were all quiet and withdrawn.

Most of them turned up on their own, but there were a few groups and some brought their partners. They would all be staying at a campsite nearby, but Bob had arranged to hold a BBQ on the lawn to give them a chance to get to know each other.

I was worried our German visitor would be disappointed. He had sent us one of his leaflets with photos of him performing in large venues with huge audiences, and I wondered if he was expecting a high-powered event. How would he feel performing to a crowd of hundreds on our front lawn?

I needn't have worried. Oskar beamed with delight from the moment he arrived. He spoke perfect English and assured me that Silverlands was enchanting. I guessed he was in his late thirties and he explained that he worked as a speciality act on cruise ships and at holiday resorts across Europe. He loved his work and was very well paid, but he rarely had the chance to mix with others who shared his passion for juggling.

He happened to have a month off between contracts, and when he saw an article about our convention, he decided it was too good an opportunity to miss.

Oskar entertained me with an account of his experiences working as a warm-up act for a well-known rock band. He had a great sense of humour and soon gathered a crowd eager to hear his stories.

As food and drink was served, the jugglers relaxed and a buzz of chatter and laughter filled the air. Fortunately, Zac had warned Bob not to order too many burgers for the BBQ as the majority of the jugglers were vegan, but they feasted on jacket potatoes, charred sweetcorn and vegetable cassoulet. We had expected them to make their way back to the campsite once they had eaten, but it seemed new friendships were being formed. Most of the jugglers had brought balls and clubs with them, and as the light faded, they sat around the lawn chatting and sharing their skills.

As dusk fell, Bob and I decided to leave them in peace, and when I looked out across the lawn from our flat, I could see flaming clubs and fire torches flying through the air and poi and yo-yos being swung by torchlight.

*****

The next morning, the jugglers arrived early and Bob went downstairs to explain the day's agenda to them. After that, I barely saw him until the evening.

The weather was perfect and Bob's press releases must have worked because we had a steady stream of visitors all day. The tearooms and restaurant were busy, but many families brought picnics.

Soon after ten in the morning, there was a knock on the kitchen door and I opened it to find one of the jugglers holding his hands close to his chest. Blood trickled between his fingers.

"Do you have a first aid kit?" he asked hopefully.

"Of course." I stepped back to let him into the kitchen. "What happened?"

The young man looked embarrassed.

"It's silly, really. I caught it by the blade."

"Caught what?"

"My knife."

He looked down at a scabbard hanging from a belt and around his waist. It contained three large silver-bladed knives.

"You juggle with those?"

"Yes. They're lovely to handle."

"But surely they're not supposed to be sharp?"

"No, I usually run a nail file over the edges, but I only got these yesterday and I haven't had time."

I tried to stay calm as crimson drops splattered across the floor. Abbie stared as I pulled the first aid kit from a drawer.

"Has anyone else brought knives?"

The juggler looked surprised by my question.

"Oh yes. They're very popular. Most of the guys here have them."

I cleaned the wound and bandaged it, then hurried through to the shop. David was selling ice-creams to a bunch of children, but I dragged him away.

"We have a problem," I hissed, trying not to be overheard.

"Which is?"

"Knives. Big knives. The jugglers are using them as props. One of them came in asking for a plaster. Luckily it was only a nick, but he could have sliced his finger off."

"Dear God!"

"Shhh!"

But David wasn't going to be shushed.

"What if a kid gets hold of one? This is not OK..."

He was gone in a moment.

"Don't be long. I'm supposed to be in the kitchen..." I called after him.

It was an hour before he came back.

"Sorted?" I asked.

"I hope so. You wouldn't believe what they've got out there. Knives, swords, daggers. There's even one guy with hatchets. I made them bring everything up to Dad's workshop, and we blunted the blades on the emery wheel."

"Thank God for that."

Suddenly David began to laugh.

"I'll say one thing about Silverlands. Life here is never boring!"

Throughout the day, I heard applause drifting up from the lawn so I guessed the juggling competition was going well but it was only after we closed and an evening meal had been served in the restaurant that I was able to sit down with Bob and hear how everything had gone.

He explained that the juggling contest had been made up of challenges that became increasingly difficult as the day went on. Three judges watched each contest and eliminated jugglers at each stage.

The first challenge had been to go through, over or under all the activities and climbing frames on the Pirate Trail while juggling three balls. I couldn't imagine that such a thing was possible, but Bob told me that only a handful had been unable to complete the course.

After that, the jugglers were challenged to throw a diablo as high as possible and still catch it. Then juggle four balls in one hand for the longest, then juggle with their eyes closed, then balance a chair on their chin, use their foot to flip a coin into the air and catch it on their head and many other seemingly impossible challenges.

"Oskar was the outright winner," Bob told me. "He's incredible. Everything he does looks so effortless, but when you stop and think about his skills... well... it left me speechless."

David had made a sculpture of a juggler with three clubs in his hands, and when Bob presented it to Oskar, there was a great roar of approval.

When the jugglers came to say their farewells, I was sorry to see them go.

*****

John, the director responsible for the Shakespearean production we had staged two years before, had been holding rehearsals for Julius Caesar in a local hall, but now they moved to the lawn. It was a long time since I read the play at school and I had forgotten the finer details.

"Did you know it has fifty-one characters?" Bob asked when he finished a phone call with John one afternoon.

"Now you mention it, I did know there are a lot. But is it really that many?"

"Yes. Fifty-one. And they all need costumes."

"Is that going to be a problem?"

"No. John's got everything in hand, but it's going to be a complicated performance. There are eighteen people in the cast and some of them will be playing five or six roles."

"I suppose that's how it would have been done it in Shakespeare's day."

"True, but it means they'll have to get changed in the bushes between scenes. There won't be enough time for them to come up to the house."

I tried not to smile but failed miserably.

"So, we're going to have actors stripping off in the bushes."

Bob frowned at me.

"It's not funny. Do you think David can put up some screens?"

"I'm sure he can. Don't worry. It will be fine."

The following evening, Bob went out to watch the first rehearsal on the lawn. There was no scenery but David had built a raised platform with a sloping ramp on each side which served as the Roman Forum and Capitol as well as a hill overlooking the battleground.

"How did it go?" I asked when Bob returned.

He hesitated, and I knew something was wrong.

"One of the actors has had to pull out."

"You're joking! There's less than a week to go. What's going to happen?"

"John's trying to find a replacement. Fortunately, it's not one of the leads. In fact, the guy only had two speaking lines, but he did play several roles. Third Soldier, Fifth Plebeian, that sort of thing."

My panic faded.

"That doesn't sound too bad. At least there aren't loads of lines to learn."

The substitute actor arrived the following night. I didn't see him as I was upstairs with the girls, but Bob told me he was young and very enthusiastic.

"Will he be all right?" I asked.

"I don't see why not. After all, he really doesn't have much to do."

Bob went down to watch the next rehearsal. When he came back, he was frowning.

"What's the matter?"

"It's Simon. The new guy. He has to die."

"I beg your pardon?"

"In the play. He has to die. Half way through the fifth act there's a fight scene and he gets stabbed with a spear. It's not complicated, but we spent most of the rehearsal going over and over the same thing. I thought John was going to blow his top at one point."

"That doesn't sound good."

Bob made a face.

"It's not that Simon's a bad actor. He can deliver his lines, but he's so awkward. He doesn't know what to do with his body."

I tried to sound reassuring.

"I'm sure he'll improve. Don't worry. There's still a couple of days to go."

*****

The weather on the opening night was perfect. The heat of summer had given way to the pleasant warmth of early autumn, and the still air was heavy with the scent of honeysuckle.

By half past seven, the audience was seated on rows of chairs lining the road around the lawn or sprawled on picnic blankets on the grassy slopes.

The bar had been busy and I could hear a gentle hum of voices as I loaded the last of the glasses into the dishwasher.

I locked the till in the servery and headed out to watch the performance. Julius Caesar was centre stage, being warned about the Ides of March as I found an empty chair and sat down. The scene ended and Caesar and his followers turned and marched down the ramp.

At the back of the group, a young man was wearing a long toga and an intense expression. He marched with great determination and was halfway down the ramp when he fell off the side.

Suppressed laughter rippled through the audience as the young man picked himself up and hurried after the others.

I guessed it must be Simon.

After that, I found myself watching for him each time a group came on stage. I recognised him in a band of conspirators, a crowd of Roman citizens, as a messenger and as a sentry.

I've heard it said that great actors have the ability to steal a scene without saying a word. It would be an exaggeration to say Simon was a great actor, but there was something about him that was fascinating.

He listened more intently than the other conspirators, rebelled more indignantly than the other citizens, and stood to attention more rigidly than any sentry had ever done before him.

The leading actors were excellent, but my eyes were constantly drawn away from them towards Simon. I suspected the rest of the audience had a similar reaction because each time he appeared, there was a murmur of anticipation.

Simon's biggest moment came in the second act when he delivered his two lines. I could tell the character he played was an old man because he leaned heavily on a stick and dragged one leg behind him as he inched across the stage.

His words were delivered in a tremulous voice, and as he limped towards the exit, I found myself looking forward to his death scene.

Half way through the final act, a battle took place. The scene opened with soldiers from the opposing armies rushing onto the stage, fighting fiercely. I spotted Simon at once, as he lunged and parried with his opponent until suddenly, reaching the centre of the platform, he stopped and lifted his left arm. His foe thrust forward, appearing to impale him, and Simon dropped gracefully to the ground with a spear clenched between his arm and his chest.

He writhed and moaned before expiring, but the scene didn't end with his death. It was followed by a lengthy discussion between other characters while Simon's body remained in full view. For several minutes he stayed convincingly still, but then the spear slid slowly to one side.

Simon twitched, and the movement halted, but a few minutes later, the spear began to move again.

I struggled to control my delight when, instead of letting the spear sink to the ground, Simon slid his right hand across his body, grasped the spear and jerked it upright.

The scene went on and the action was repeated. When the corpse adjusted his spear for the third time the giggles from the onlookers were unmistakable.

As the cast lined up to take their applause, it was the actors playing Caesar, Anthony and Cassius who received the loudest cheers, but for me, Simon was the unforgettable star of the evening.

*****

September had been a disappointingly quiet month, but Bob had one last duty to perform before we closed for the winter.

He had been invited to judge a Majorettes' competition.

"But I don't know anything about majorettes," he had protested when he showed me the letter. "Why would they ask me?"

"They probably thought the red coat would look good when you give out the prizes," I laughed.

"You don't think they expect me to wear my ringmaster's outfit, do you?"

"Yes, I'm sure they do. The letter's address to The Ringmaster, isn't it?"

Bob groaned.

"I suppose it will be good publicity," he muttered.

"Keep telling yourself that," I laughed. "Be brave. It will only take a couple of hours."

Bob was still muttering as he drove off, but when he returned from the competition, his mood had changed.

"How did it go?" I asked.

"It was good. It wasn't what I expected at all. There were ten teams, and they were all really impressive."

His enthusiasm surprised me. I had expected him to disappear upstairs to change out of his outfit, but instead he sat on the window seat in the tearooms. We had no customers, so I made some tea and joined him.

"What did the majorettes do?" I asked.

"Marching mainly, but it included lots of complicated manoeuvres and some of the teams had their own bands leading them. They were really good."

He sipped his tea before continuing.

"There was one team in particular. They weren't as well turned out as the others, but they were brilliant. They must spend hours practising because they were all perfectly in time and their musicians were amazing."

"I take it they won?"

"Yes. They were the best by far..."

He hesitated, and I sensed there was more to come.

"I got talking to them when everything had finished. There are three mothers that run the troupe. They're from Tiverton. Not all that far from here..."

He paused again.

"And?" I asked.

"It turns out they've got a bit of a problem. They have to hire a coach to go to competitions and they were sponsored by a local company but last year, when the recession started to bite, the company told them they couldn't afford it anymore."

"That's a shame."

"Exactly." Bob pounced on my words. "It would be a waste if they had to disband, wouldn't it? The kids are so good. The mothers have been trying to raise funds to keep going, but they're struggling. That's why their outfits looked a bit worn."

I started to feel uncomfortable.

"It's a shame, but there must be lots of others in the same position," I reminded him.

"I wish you'd been there. It was too good an opportunity to miss."

"What do you mean?"

"I said we'd sponsor them. Next season we'll have our own team. Silverlands' Majorettes."

"You're joking?" I gasped.

"No. It will be great advertising. They go all over the place. And they're happy to give out leaflets."

"But how much is it going to cost? You can't agree to these things without asking the rest of us!" I burst out.

Bob looked at me in surprise.

"But it's a great opportunity…"

"That's not the point!"

Mum and Dad appeared with the bag from the ticket box and Bob stood up and marched out of the room.

There was an awkward silence.

"Problems?" Mum asked.

My words poured out before I could control them.

"I don't know much about majorettes," Mum said when I finished.

"Neither do I," I admitted, "but I know we can't afford to sponsor a team. We're going to be struggling this winter as it is."

"But Bob thinks they could help with advertising?" Dad asked.

"Yes, but I can't see how. He's talking about paying for their coaches and everything."

"Maybe we should listen to what he has to say," Mum suggested.

I couldn't believe what I was hearing.

"We can't afford it," I repeated, but Mum wasn't looking at me. She was looking at Dad.

"We spent a fortune on advertising this year, and the results haven't been great. Maybe it's time to try something different."

"We don't know anything about these people," I cut across her. "We haven't even met them."

"No, but Bob has. He wouldn't have suggested this unless he thought they were genuine."

I stared at her in disbelief.

"So, you think it's a good idea? Handing out blank cheques without knowing how much it's going to cost or what we're going to get in return?"

"I didn't say that, dear. Be reasonable."

I remembered Martha and Abbie were still in the kitchen and lowered my voice.

"I thought you would support me."

"I always support you," Mum said calmly. "But that doesn't mean you're always right."

Chapter 5

Once the summer season was over, Mum and I sat down to review the year's figures. I had not expected them to be good, but seeing the numbers in black and white was a sobering experience.

Since the country went into recession, I had been paying more attention to the news, and now I understood that John Major, the current Prime Minister, was not the Eurosceptic his predecessor Margaret Thatcher had been.

Major wanted Britain to be at the heart of Europe and was determined to forsake the pound in favour of the Euro despite a large part of the country being against the idea. As a result, the UK had joined the Exchange Rate Mechanism as the first step towards adopting the common currency.

The Exchange Rate Mechanism, or ERM, was a device that managed the pound's exchange rate, but it was also a test. If the UK was to be allowed to join the Euro, the government needed to prove it was capable of maintaining its currency within certain limits.

At the time, it was hoped that following the ERM rules would bring the country's high level of inflation under control, but instead, the whole of the British economy slowed down. By the autumn of nineteen ninety-one, inflation was approaching ten percent and the country had been in recession for more than a year.

In practice, the ERM had become a financial straightjacket that prevented the chancellor from acting to boost the flagging economy.

My relentless optimism convinced me the government would find an answer to the crisis soon, but in the meantime, there was no point in dwelling on things we couldn't control. We needed to concentrate our efforts on our business. It was essential to find a way to meet the targets we had submitted to the bank.

"It's not all gloom," Mum said as she ran a pencil down a column of figures. "The number of visitors during the school holiday period was good. It was the early and late parts of the season that were so poor."

"But even when they were here, people weren't spending as much as they used to do."

"True. The only times we took more than we expected was when we had a big function. It's a shame we didn't have more of them."

"I know, but it took Bob a huge amount of work to arrange the ones we had. Maybe we need to find a new way of advertising."

"Like using majorettes?"

I glared at her.

"Don't bring that up again. I've given in, haven't I?"

I still couldn't believe Mum and Bob had ganged up against me.

"I think we need to be open to new ideas, that's all. The things that worked in the past might not be right any more. Times change."

I nodded.

"David said that a few days ago. He was talking about package holidays. Do you know it's cheaper to fly to Spain for a week than it is to stay in Torquay?"

"Really? Surely that can't be right?"

"It is. It's hard to believe, but it's true. There are so many package holidays available at the moment and the cost of running hotels out there is much cheaper than here."

"And there's guaranteed sun in Spain." Mum sighed. "It's easy to see why people go abroad."

We looked over the figures again, searching for something positive.

"The accounting year ends in April, doesn't it? That means we still have six months to go. Our projections only show a few functions over the winter, but maybe we can attract more."

"I suppose it's possible," Mum agreed, "but I don't know how we'll find them."

"Me neither, but it has to be worth trying."

I was full of hope when I left Mum and went to find Bob. He was tapping away on the computer in our flat while Lucy chased Sammy, the cat. Dino had retreated to the bedroom.

The moment I saw Bob's face, my heart sank.

"Are you OK?"

He tried to smile, but his eyes betrayed him.

"I wasn't going to say anything until I got everyone together, but you might as well know now."

"What's happened?"

"It's Eric. He's given us notice. He's closing the Motor Museum."

The hope died inside me. Without the quarterly payments from the Motor Museum, we had no chance of reaching our targets.

"But why? I don't understand. The last time I saw him, he seemed happy with the way things were going."

"He didn't give me a reason. He said his wife has persuaded him he has to give up. My guess is that he has health problems, but I didn't like to pry too much. He sounded really down. It's a bit of a blow, isn't it?"

I wanted to scream and shout, but I merely nodded.

"Yes, it's not the best timing."

*****

David was less reserved when Bob broke the news to the others.

"He can't do that! He signed a contract, didn't he?"

"Yes, he signed a contract, but there were get-out clauses written into it," Bob explained. "If he, or we, wanted to end the contract, we could do it at specific times. This is one of them..."

But David was too worked up to listen.

"It's not right. It can't be. We need to phone the solicitor."

"If the man's ill. That's an end to it," Dad said simply.

"I don't think he wants to close. He sounded embarrassed when I spoke to him," Bob added.

"But where does it leave us?" David asked.

Dad shrugged.

"We'll have to find another tenant, won't we?"

It sounded simple, but I knew the chances of finding a replacement for Eric were miniscule.

As mum said, times had changed.

*****

After a lot of discussion, we agreed to open for a Christmas season. We had no idea if we would be able to attract enough visitors to make it worthwhile, but we had to do something.

We decided to concentrate on weekends, functions and the final ten days before Christmas. The opening day would be the second Saturday in November, which meant we had a little over a month to prepare.

Without the influx of summer visitors in the area, we planned to target local families and organisations. Bob was convinced there was a lot of potential for Christmas functions and settled down immediately to make out lists of people and businesses to contact.

The craftspeople were delighted by the idea, and Abbie was over the moon with excitement when I phoned her. Martha was happy to come back too. As we had no way of predicting whether our new venture would be a success, we decided not to take on any other staff. Liza agreed to be available if we had bookings from playgroups, but we couldn't commit to paying Zac. Without daily live entertainment, we needed other things to promote.

"If we're going to do this, it has to be really special," David said.

"It will need to be completely different from the summer," Phil agreed. "If the weather's bad, no-one's going to want to walk around the grounds, or the Animal Meadow for that matter."

"We ought to have a grotto so the kids can get a present from Santa," Bob suggested.

"Definitely, and the whole house has to feel magical and Christmassy,"

Mum added.

"With lots of decorations," Phil said. "We could have tinsel up all the staircases and paper streamers everywhere."

"But it's not that sort of house," I protested.

"Isn't it?" David frowned at me. "I think it would look great. We could get cut-out Santas and put them along the corridors."

"We could," I agreed, "but don't you think we should do something different? Something people can only find here?"

"That's easy to say, but what?"

"Do you remember how lovely the house looked when we had the outdoor Shakespeare? At dusk with the lights shining out across the lawn?"

"Of course. It was magical."

"It made me think about what it must have been like living here. The house was built in the nineteenth century, wasn't it? Why don't we have A Dickensian Christmas as our theme?"

David was off at once.

"That's brilliant! We can decorate the place as it would have been in Victorian times! Lots of holly and candles and red ribbons. And we can sell Dickensian specialities in the shop. Old-fashioned wooden toys and things. Doesn't one of our suppliers do a range of Mr Pickwick chutneys? We could make a feature of that and..."

"Slow down a bit," I complained, "I'm trying to take notes."

But it was no good. The family were in a creative mood and the ideas came thick and fast.

"And it's not just the shop. We can serve Dickensian food in the restaurant," Phil suggested. "I'm not sure what, exactly, but they always show big feasts in things like A Christmas Carol, don't they?"

"And we could all wear Dickensian outfits." Bob said.

"What?" I was horrified.

"Brilliant idea! I've got a top hat somewhere," David beamed.

"But it wouldn't be very practical..." I objected.

"Could we wear long dresses?" Phil asked.

"I could do with one in the ticket box. It would keep me warm." Mum joined in.

"I've got some tail coats tucked away somewhere," David said. "They're Victorian. If we wore them with brightly coloured waistcoats, they would look awesome."

"I don't mind making up some waistcoats, if you want me to," Mum offered.

"Do we really have to dress up?" I asked.

"Absolutely!" Bob's eyes were gleaming. "It will be fun."

I was outvoted again.

Lucy was sitting on my lap, looking around with a puzzled expression, trying to work out why the grownups were so excited.

"Do you want a long dress too, darling?" I asked her.

She nodded happily, not wanting to be left out.

"You would look cute in a little pinafore." I told her.

"That's it!" Lucy jumped as David's voice boomed out.

"We should make the theme A Dickensian Family Christmas. If we take a picture of all of us in Victorian outfits, the kids too, we can use it in our publicity. Come and join the family for an authentic Dickensian Christmas at Silverlands."

"It would have to be old-fashioned," Phil said, "like the photos they had in the old days when everyone stood still and posed."

"It should have a great big Christmas tree behind us. We could take it in the entrance hall, maybe? Or at the bottom of the stairs?"

"That's a great idea," Bob grinned. "That would work really well. I could circulate it to the nurseries and playgroups as well. I'm sure some of them must do outings at Christmas."

"But how soon would you need it?" I asked.

"As soon as possible. Can we do it now?"

"No!" I protested. "If you want a decent photo, we'll have to get everything ready. It's not only costumes. We'll need props and our hair put up in buns and everything."

"And a Christmas tree," David reminded us.

Bob nodded.

"All right, but it can't take too long. I need to start sending leaflets out as soon as possible."

*****

It took a week for David to unearth his tail coats, for Mum and me to make waistcoats and dresses, and for Bob to arrange with Elliott, the glass engraver from the craft workshops, to be our photographer.

"But what are we going to do about a Christmas tree?" David asked.

We had decided to take the photos by the fireplace at the bottom of the main stairs. The ceiling in the hallway was very high and there was plenty of room.

"There won't be any trees for sale yet," Phil pointed out.

"And you can't buy any that are more than eight feet tall anyway," Dad said.

"Isn't that enough? How big were you thinking?" I asked.

"It will look a bit silly if you have a little tree in that great big space. It's the first thing people see when they come in through the front door. It needs to be impressive."

I looked around and realised he was right.

"I suppose so, but where can we get a big tree that won't cost a fortune?"

"Leave it with me," Dad said.

The following day I heard the rumble of a tractor chuntering past the house. Phil and I were in the shop finishing an order for Christmas gifts and novelties.

"Do you know why there's a tractor here?" I asked.

"Not exactly, but I heard your Dad ask David if he could phone Alan earlier."

"OK..."

I decided not to ask any more questions.

An hour later, I was in the office when Mum pushed the door open.

"I think you'd better come and see what your father's done."

As I hurried along the corridor, I could hear the throb of the tractor's engine outside. The front door was open, but all I could see was a mass of greenery.

"What on earth's that?"

"It's all right, dear. We can still get out of the fire exit."

I pushed down on the emergency crash bar and Mum and I emerged from the house to see a huge tree laying along the porch completely blocking the entrance.

"My God! It's enormous!" I gasped.

"It's a beaut, isn't it?" Dad grinned. "I knew you'd like it."

I was stunned.

"Where did it come from?"

"Down by the back gate. There's a little glade with oak saplings coming up. They'll be glad of a bit more space. It wasn't the place for a pine tree anyway."

"But it must be twenty feet," I gasped.

"Yes, that's about right. I'll have to trim a bit off the bottom to tidy it up, but it should still be tall enough."

"Tall enough? It's massive. How are we going to get it through the door?"

"Not a problem, love. Leave it with me."

I knew better than to argue when Dad was enjoying himself. He had a coil of rope under his arm and began wrestling with the prickly pine branches, easing them back into a more manageable shape.

Mum chuckled.

"Do you think we should find the others?" she asked.

I nodded.

"We're going to need all the help we can get."

Fortunately, several of the craftspeople were in their units, so we returned with a sizeable team.

Bob, David and Phil looked as shocked as I had been when they saw the fallen giant laying outside the house.

"Won't it touch the ceiling?" Phil asked.

"No. It's just right," Dad reassured her.

I didn't want to doubt him, but I was not convinced.

"How are we going to do this?" David asked.

"We'll carry it in and put it in the pot," Dad replied.

David looked at me, but I could only shrug.

We lined up on either side of the tree and grabbed hold of the ropes.

"Tree in house," Lucy gabbled excitedly as she held Mum's hand.

The number of volunteers made the tree's weight bearable, and we manoeuvred it through the entrance without any disasters. Dad had spread an old blanket over the carpet and we laid our load down and stood gasping until we got our breath back.

"Now what?" Bob asked.

A huge brass coal scuttle was standing at the bottom of the stairs.

"All we have to do is pop the trunk in that and push it upright," Dad said.

It sounded easy.

Everyone took their place, and we heaved on the ropes again. As the tree lifted off the ground those at the stump end lowered the trunk into the coal scuttle while the others pushed the tree upwards. This took much more effort than I had expected. There was a chorus of grunts as everyone pushed and shoved, but finally the tree stood erect, its highest needles barely brushing the ceiling.

"There, it's a perfect fit," Dad beamed. "Hold it still while I get it settled."

We crowded around, balancing the tree, afraid to let go in case it toppled, while Dad scrambled underneath to fill the coal scuttle with rocks and soil. Then he dragged a ladder across and scurried up with a hammer, drill, rawl plugs and a coil of wire in his hand.

A few minutes later, retaining wires secured the tree to the walls and we could stand back and admire the result of our efforts.

Once Dad descended the ladder, he untied the ropes and the branches sprung down to take their natural form.

"Now it smells like Christmas." He beamed. He was right. A rich pine scent filled the hall.

"It looks incredible," Bob said.

Mum nodded. "I can't wait to see it decorated."

Claire and Michael exploded with excitement when they arrived home from school to find the mighty tree waiting for them.

"It's the biggest tree ever!" Claire shrieked and Michael helped Phil carry a jug of water and pour it into the coal scuttle.

Lucy was still talking about the tree when I settled her into bed.

"Mummy like tree, Daddy like tree, Claire like tree, Michael like tree."

"What about Auntie and Uncle?" I smiled.

"Auntie like tree, Uncle like tree."

"Anyone else?"

"Grandma like tree, Granddad like tree, Lady like tree."

"Do you mean Abbie?"

"Not Abbie. Lady like tree."

"Marion?"

Lucy shook her head.

"Lady like tree."

"Then I don't know which Lady you mean."

Lucy yawned widely and snuggled her head into the pillow.

"Night-night sweetie," I said and kissed her goodnight.

*****

There were three rooms on the first floor which had still not been brought into use. I guessed they had once been bedrooms as the walls were covered with wooden panelling, but they were scarred and damaged from years of abuse and had been covered in dark green gloss paint.

The rooms had doors that opened into each other, which made them the perfect place to create a grotto.

Dad and I painted the walls and ceilings of the first two rooms midnight blue, then arranged Christmas trees, branches, and artificial snow to create a miniature winter wonderland. With the addition of toy animals, and a myriad twinkling lights, it looked enchanting.

David, meanwhile, transformed the third room into a cosy cottage for Santa, complete with a magnificent fireplace draped with stockings, an impressive bookcase filled with magical books and a multitude of toys, sacks and beautifully wrapped presents.

Dougal, the woodcarver, had offered to be our Santa, and I was sure his soft voice and gentle manner would be perfect for the job.

Everything was going well.

It was a Saturday morning when we gathered in front of the tree to have our photo taken.

The thick branches blocked the light from the window behind us, but David had found some photographic lights and set them up on stands, and Elliot was fiddling with the camera to bring us into focus.

Bob had put a cassette of Christmas music into the sound system in the shop and the strains of Slade's Merry Christmas Everybody filled the house.

"That's not very Dickensian, is it?" Phil commented as she listened.

"No, but it's very cheerful," Bob grinned.

We had not yet turned on the central heating, and the hall was chilly. The men were comfortable in waistcoats and lined jackets, but the newly finished dresses were made of thin cotton material and did little to keep out the cold of an October morning. Both Mum and Phil found shawls to wrap around themselves, but I resorted to wearing a jumper and jeans under my dress to keep warm.

As usual, the children were oblivious to the cold. While the adults set up lights and positioned the camera on its tripod, they ran up and down the corridors, Michael pretending to be Brum the car, while Claire galloped on an imaginary pony and Lucy trailed behind them trying to keep up.

Dad was in a particularly happy mood. He had been tucked away in his workshop all week, building props for the grotto, but now, as he stood back and watched his family, a wide smile lit his face. For some reason, the idea of sending out leaflets with a photo of us all on the front really amused him.

"Right, I think I'm ready," Elliott said at last. "If you'd like to take your places, please..."

We had known Elliott for years now and were used to his formality. He was a kind and patient man, but he was naturally reserved.

"Claire, Michael, can you come back now?" I called.

The patter of footsteps told me they had heard.

"Where's Lucy?" I asked as they appeared around a corner.

"I don't know," Claire shrugged. "We were having a race."

"You're supposed to wait for her. She's only little," I scolded. "Stay here with Daddy, I'll go and get her."

I found Lucy sitting on the floor staring into space.

"There you are. Come on, it's time to have your photo taken."

I reached down to pick her up, but her face morphed into a frown.

"What's the matter?" I asked, but Lucy only shook her head.

"Are you sad because Claire and Michael left you alone?"

She gazed at me with huge eyes but said nothing.

"Come on, Honey, we have to go back."

Lucy twisted away from me as I picked her up.

"Don't be silly, Lu, you can't stay here. Everyone's waiting for us."

She was still frowning when we reached the others.

"What a pretty little girl." Mum smiled when she saw us. "Do you want to sit on my lap?"

Lucy only pouted, but I handed her over and Mum played Incy-Wincy Spider to keep her amused.

Elliott had placed three chairs in front of the tree and Phil, Mum and I perched on them with David, Dad and Bob standing behind us, while Claire and Michael sat on the floor in front. Lucy stayed on Mum's lap.

"Perhaps you can all move a little closer together," Elliott suggested.

We shuffled obediently as he peered through the viewfinder.

"No, perhaps not."

We changed places, adjusted the lights, tried the camera from different angles and finally returned to our original positions.

"I think that's the best I can get," Elliott said at last. "Now, please remember, if you want this to look authentic, it's important that none of you smile."

We nodded our agreement and stared straight ahead as Elliott pressed his finger and the camera clicked.

"That was good, but I think we'd better take a few more in case. Please remember, no smiling."

There were twenty-four frames on the film in the camera and Elliott took every one. Between each shot he reminded us not to smile and I worried that the children were misbehaving. I could only see the tops of their heads.

"This really is very important," I said at last. "I don't want any messing about. You two are being good, aren't you? I don't want to find you've been making silly faces."

Michael and Claire peered up at me.

"Remember, keep looking serious and we'll be finished very soon," I told them.

Elliott clicked the camera a few more times.

"There, that's the lot. I hope there will be one among them that you can use."

"I'm sure there will be. Thank you so much for helping," Bob said. "I'm taking the film into Newton Abbot this afternoon to get it developed, so it should only be a few days before we get the photos back."

I was putting the finishing touches to the grotto when Bob returned from Newton Abbot with the developed photos.

"Are they any good?" I asked.

He handed over the envelope.

"See what you think."

I took the photos out and inspected the first one. At a glance, it seemed perfect. The children were adorable. Lucy was frowning but Claire and Michael posed prettily and the adults were all formally posed as they should be except... I looked again and saw that Dad was smiling.

I sighed. I put the photo aside and looked at the next. This time, Dad's head was turned to one side, but the smirk was still there.

"I thought the kids were the problem. I should have known."

I flicked through the rest of the photos and saw that Dad was smirking, smiling or grinning in every single one.

"I don't believe it," I groaned. "What are we going to do? Should we try again?"

But Bob was laughing.

"Don't be daft. The photos look great. Pick whichever one you like and I'll drop it over to the printers."

"OK," I agreed reluctantly. "I suppose we should have known Dad wouldn't be able to keep a straight face."

*****

By the time the grotto was finished, Bob had booked the first playgroup.

"There are twelve adults and fifteen children and they've pre-booked their meals so we know what they're going to have."

"Great. That will help in the kitchen. All we need now is a lot more bookings."

We had worked out our menus and ordered our supplies, so now we set about decorating the house. David cut huge amounts of holly, ivy and pine branches and we arranged displays in every room.

I had found a supplier of wide, red ribbon and spent my evenings making enormous bows to brighten up the greenery and add a splash of warmth.

Phil collected fallen tree branches, sprayed them with gold and silver paint, and decorated them with tiny wrapped presents. Propped into the corners of the exhibitions, they looked wonderful.

"I'm not sure they're really Dickensian," she said, "but they do look pretty."

"I think they're perfect," I said. "In fact, I think the whole house looks wonderful."

We had found long dresses for Abbie and Martha with white pinafores and matching mob caps. Martha had looked disapproving when I mentioned the outfits, but she didn't complain once she saw them and I think she secretly liked them.

"They don't get in the way as much as I expected," she said as she floated around behind the counter.

"I never thought I'd say it, but long skirts are more comfortable than jeans." I smiled.

"And they certainly keep the drafts out," Martha agreed.

*****

Abbie arrived early on our opening morning. She finished preparing in the kitchen and had changed into her Dickensian outfit by the time Dad carried Mum's bag down to the ticket box.

"Do you think people wore dresses like this when Fred was alive?"

Her question took me by surprise.

"I've no idea."

It hadn't occurred to me that Fred might have lived in a different era. I had thought of him as my contemporary. Or, to be more accurate, I hadn't been thinking of him at all. Everything had been quiet for months.

"Well, I hope he likes them," Abbie said as she twirled around and watched the skirt of her dress float around her. "Maybe they'll remind him of his own times."

It was nearly midday before the first family arrived in the tearooms. We had decided not to open the restaurant but to serve an extended menu in the tearooms instead. Now I was glad of the decision.

The family ordered jacket potatoes for the adults and fish fingers for the children. As I waited to see if any more customers arrived, I wondered if opening for Christmas was a mistake.

To my relief, more families turned up, mainly grandparents with pre-school children, and, by the end of the day, the trays of cakes and scones in the servery were empty.

"We didn't do too badly," David said when he brought in the day's takings from the shop till. "People were definitely looking for presents, and they liked all the handmade stuff. I'm sure the crafties will have done well."

"That's good to hear. I wonder how things went in the grotto?"

We found out as soon as Phil arrived.

"It was an eye-opener for Dougal," she giggled. "He thought it was going to be easy. We didn't have a lot of children, but two of them were little horrors. One screamed the whole time but wouldn't leave. When his mother tried to take him out, he clung to Santa's trousers and wouldn't let go."

"Poor Dougal," I laughed. "I hope it hasn't put him off too much."

"I don't think so. Most of the other kids were lovely, but they asked him so many questions. He hadn't expected that at all."

I grinned.

"Never mind. By Christmas Eve he'll be an expert."

Bob had booked several functions for the beginning of December and they all went well. The restaurant looked stunning, with greenery and red bows around the arches and centrepieces on every table.

Our guests arrived in a festive mood, ready to enjoy themselves. They spent heavily at the bar and I was relieved that we had no more problems with the gas supply to the beer pumps.

On weekdays we were kept busy with a stream of playgroups and on the weekends families with older children queued to see Santa. The Christmas season was lovely, and it was wonderful to see customers enjoying themselves, but each evening as we added up the daily take, the figures fell far below our targets.

When we closed on Christmas Eve, Mum and I tallied up the final figures.

"We're going to have to tell the others," I said gloomily. "We don't have any choice. We're going to have to go back to the bank, aren't we?"

Mum closed the book with a snap.

"Yes, we are," she said briskly, "but there's no need to talk about it tonight. There's no point in spoiling Christmas."

*****

The following morning dawned bright and frosty. It was perfect Christmas weather. Claire had woken long before our alarm clock went off and burst into our bedroom, dragging a stocking full of presents with Lucy close behind her.

Bob and I struggled to open our eyes as wrapping paper flew everywhere. Sammy disappeared out of the room and Dino barked at the early morning intrusion.

We had decided to keep the central heating switched on for the holiday and it was lovely to run through warm corridors chasing the kids while the aroma of roast turkey and Christmas pudding wafted from the kitchen.

Silverlands was ours once again. It was bright with decorations and alive with laughter. We exchanged presents beneath the tree in the hall, toasted the coming year, and listened to Bob's favourite carols.

I am not a religious person, but I closed my eyes and said a quiet Thank You for all the good things in my life.

"I told you we would have Christmas dinner in the restaurant this year, didn't I?" Bob said as he set a magnificent turkey down on the table. Around it, bowls held a vast selection of vegetables, roast potatoes, stuffings, cranberry sauce and pigs-in-blankets.

We laughed, pulled crackers, shared jokes and ate far more than we should have done.

"That was incredible," David groaned, patting his stomach. "I'm absolutely stuffed. I couldn't eat another thing."

"You won't want any pudding then?" I teased him.

"That's a terrible thing to say. You know I want pudding, but it'll be your fault if I explode."

I carried the pudding to the table as the others cleared the used dishes, and Bob prepared a jug of brandy and a candle.

Once everyone was back, Bob poured a generous quantity of brandy over the steaming pudding and held a spoon over a candle to heat.

"What's Daddy doing?" Claire asked.

"Don't you remember? He does this every year. He's setting light to the pudding."

The brandy in Bob's spoon shimmered briefly as a blue flame licked across the surface.

"Did you see that kids? It's on fire. Now I'm going to pour it over the pudding. Watch."

There was a rapt silence as Bob moved the spoon towards the pudding. He tipped it slowly and the flaming brandy ran across the top and rivulets of fire flowed down the sides.

The children were mesmerised.

I had been so busy watching the flames that I hadn't noticed the brandy form a puddle on the serving plate. Now I saw it, and the puddle was not confined to the plate. It had spread to the tablecloth.

"Bob..." I began, but I was too late.

The flame reached the plate and spread around the pudding like a blazing moat, then it followed the brandy and escaped in every direction across the tablecloth. Grabbing a napkin, Bob tried to smother the conflagration, but the flames licked eagerly around the edges, singeing the cloth and the hairs on the back of his hands as they went.

"Daddy!" Claire squealed as everyone jumped to their feet.

"Quick, the fire extinguisher!"

David ran to the side of the room.

Instead of dying down, the flames on top of the pudding were growing higher every moment, a haze of black smoke floating above them towards the ceiling and the smoke detector.

Bob was still flapping at the flames with the napkin. Dad grabbed a tea towel and joined him as David raced back, releasing the nozzle from the side of the extinguisher as he came.

"No!" I squealed. "Don't squirt my pudding!"

"Here!" Phil pulled a silvery fire blanket from its holder behind the bar and tossed it to me. I threw it across the blaze and the others caught the edges and hauled it across the table.

Without the flames, the room felt dark.

"Are you OK?" I asked Bob, but he was already on his way to the kitchen.

"I'm fine. Just going to put my hands under the cold tap,"

"Let's give it a moment before moving the blanket," Dad suggested.

We stood in silence, assessing the damage. A glass had been upturned and red wine dripped onto the carpet, but nothing was broken.

"At least the alarms didn't go off," Mum said.

A few minutes later, Bob returned, drying his hands on a towel.

"Right," he said brightly. "Who's ready for pudding?"

Chapter 6

The New Year brought a spell of freezing weather. Heavy frost transformed trees and bushes into ice sculptures, and artic winds rattled the windows.

We had several functions booked which passed without incident, and Bob spent most of his time searching for a new tenant to replace Eric and the Motor Museum. So far, he had had no luck.

There was only one more function booked. It was an engagement party, and we had specific instructions about how the restaurant was to be decorated.

We made sure everything was ready to be laid out the night before the function.

I was dressing the girls the following morning when there was an urgent tap on the flat door. Dino exploded, and I heard David's voice above the hullaballoo.

"What's happening?" Bob demanded as he hurried from the bathroom, a towel around his waist.

I opened the door and Dino rushed out onto the landing, but David had already disappeared downstairs.

"Keep an eye on the girls," I called over my shoulder. "I'll find out what's going on."

Dino raced ahead of me, following David's footsteps until we reached the restaurant. I couldn't believe my eyes.

At first glance, it seemed the carpet had been replaced by rippling glass, but then I realised the whole room was flooded. Water was pouring through the ceiling behind the serving counter.

David appeared through the door from the kitchen at the far end of the restaurant.

"I told you to bring wellies," he called across to me.

"I didn't hear. Dino was barking. I'll come around."

I retraced my steps through the corridor until I arrived in the kitchen. My wellies were by the door, so I grabbed them as I passed and pulled them on.

"Where's it coming from?" I asked David as I reached him.

"Burst pipes."

He was scrabbling under the sink but stopped to listen.

"There. It's easing. I wasn't sure if I'd got the right stopcock."

The cascade of water gradually reduced to drips.

"Luckily that pipe only supplies the upstairs loos and the old bathrooms at the back. We can manage without it until we can get a plumber in to fix it."

"But what about the function?" I wailed. "We've got eighty people coming this evening."

David wriggled out from under the sink.

"We'll have to cancel it. We've got no choice."

"We can't! We need the money. I've spent a fortune on decorations."

"Don't be ridiculous. You've seen what it's like in there. There's no way on earth we can go ahead."

"It's only water," I snapped. "Clean water. It's not as if it's dirty. There must be a way to dry it."

But David only snorted.

"The room's inches deep. It'll take weeks to dry."

His certainty infuriated me.

"It will if we leave it as it is! Don't just stand there. We've got to do something!"

He shook his head in disbelief.

"All right. I suppose we're going to have to clear it up anyway, but you're mad if you think it's going to be ready for tonight."

I glared at him, then headed to the storeroom and pulled out a selection of buckets and brooms.

Splashing through the flood, I threw open the French windows, and we began sweeping the water out of the restaurant onto the road.

Fortunately, as the tarmac sloped away from the building, the deluge ran towards the lawn. Bob's car was parked outside, and the water hit the tyres and splashed up over the bonnet.

The exercise kept my body warm, but my hands and feet ached. The temperature was well below freezing and icicles hung from the branches of the trees opposite.

I jumped at the sound of a voice.

"Have you got another broom?"

I hadn't heard Dad behind me.

"Plenty. You can have one in each hand if you like."

Soon the whole family joined in. Claire and Michael loved making waves across the carpet, although I'm not sure how much their efforts helped. They were much more interested in splashing each other than pushing the water over the threshold.

"If you two get any wetter, you're going back upstairs," Phil warned them. "I'm not having you catching pneumonia."

Even Lucy found a bucket and paddled happily in the shallows in her red wellies.

After an hour, the water level had lowered considerably. The carpet was a ribbed variety and the tops of the ribs were already returning to their normal colour.

"It's looking much better," I said.

"But it's still soaking. It squelches when you walk on it." David reminded me.

"Let's have a break, then we can decide what to do next," Dad suggested.

"Good plan," I agreed.

"If we're stopping for a while, can we close the doors?" Mum asked. "It's so cold in here."

She was right. The temperature in the restaurant had dropped dramatically. Even with thick gloves and all the exercise, my fingers were numb.

"I'm going to turn the heaters up full," David said. "It might help dry the place out."

I nodded.

"You might as well collect any other heaters you can find and bring them in too." It wasn't long before we went back to work. As the water level went down between the ridges of the carpet, it became increasingly difficult to sweep.

"I don't think we can move anymore," David said at last, but Dad had other ideas.

"How many rakes have you got?" he asked me.

"There are three or four out in the storeroom that Ian left behind. Why? What are you thinking?"

"Fetch them and I'll show you."

Once we had washed the mud from the rakes, Dad took one and turned it upside down so the tines were pointing upwards and the back of the head was on the floor.

"There. That makes a pretty good scraper. If we go over the floor again, we'll get a lot more out."

He was right. We worked as a team, scraping the rakes across the carpet and new waves of water were squeezed outside.

By mid-morning, we were all exhausted, but the carpet had lost its soggy feel.

"Now all we have to do is dry it," Dad said.

The combined efforts of the radiators and heaters had raised the temperature, but we soon noticed condensation running down the walls.

"We'll have to open the French windows again," Mum sighed.

Luckily, David managed to contact a builder friend who arrived with a couple of industrial sized dehumidifiers. I was amazed at how quickly their tanks filled with water pulled from the air.

Mum brought down a vast pile of towels and blankets and we laid them on the carpet and walked on them to draw out as much moisture as possible.

Finally, every hairdryer in the building was brought into use. For hours, we crept across the room on our hands and knees, drying the carpet as best we could.

As the winter daylight faded, I looked around and felt a twinge of pride.

The carpet looked excellent. In fact, it looked cleaner than it had done since the day it was laid. It was still damp to the touch in places, but there was nothing more we could do.

"Let's bring the tables and chairs back and get everything laid out," I said.

The parents of the happy couple were due to arrive at seven o'clock so I put the outside lights on a little beforehand to welcome them. We used the French windows as an entrance when we held functions, and I noticed Bob's car was still parked outside.

"Don't worry, I'll move it now," he said.

I was checking the cutlery when I heard the squeal of an engine outside. A moment later Bob was back.

"I can't move it."

"Why not?"

"Come and look."

I followed him outside and gasped to see the front wheels of the car were encased in an enormous mound of ice.

"Oh, my God! I didn't think! The water must have frozen where it splashed over them. What do we do now?"

To my surprise, Bob was laughing.

"It's not a problem. I'll meet the guests at the front door and bring them through the house. We can chip the car out in the morning."

He put his arm around me and I laid my head on his shoulder.

"Can we have a sleep-in tomorrow?" I asked.

"Possibly." He grinned. "But you can't rest yet. We've got eighty people to feed first."

*****

In February, Bob attended another DATA meeting. When he returned, he looked glum.

"How was everyone?" I asked.

"To be honest, I wish I hadn't gone. It was all bad news. I thought we were having a difficult time, but some of the others are in real trouble. The Rare

Breeds Farm have already decided to throw the towel in and close."

"Really?" I was shocked. The Farm was often in the news for its conservation work and I knew it had an active band of supporters.

"What's going to happen to the animals?"

"I'm not sure. I think the farm may be going on in some form, but it won't be opening to the public anymore."

"That's such a shame. They must be really upset."

"They are. They've spent years building it up and they've had to let all their staff go."

Every night, the news was full of reports about the rising unemployment figures.

"It's good to know it's not only us," Bob said.

"I suppose so," I agreed, but I didn't think that would be much help when we had to explain our figures to the bank.

*****

To cheer ourselves up, Bob and I booked a few nights at a caravan park in Cornwall during the February half-term week. Claire was seven and had changed from a little girl into a young lady. She was tall for her age and already showed the artistic talent and devotion to fashion that would guide her later in life.

Lucy was two-and-a-half years old, but she couldn't see any reason why she should be treated differently from her big sister. Her only aim in life was to be able to run as fast, talk as much, and stay up as late as Claire.

In regard to talking, Lucy was close to achieving her goal. While Claire had been a peaceful toddler, Lucy never stopped chattering. She talked constantly and was forever asking questions. Her vocabulary was still quite limited, which made it difficult to understand what she was saying at times, but it didn't stop her from expressing her opinions.

At home, Lucy went to bed considerably earlier than Claire, but while we were staying in the caravan, it was agreed that they would both go to bed at the same time.

The camp site had a children's club with a disco which ensured that both girls were tired out by the time we got back to the caravan so I didn't anticipate any problems settling them, but once I had them both changed and curled up in their bunks Lucy became restless.

"What's the matter, Angel?" I asked her.

"Want say goodnight."

"That's OK. You can say goodnight."

"Say goodnight, Lady."

"You mean you want to say goodnight to the lady?" I asked, thinking of the young woman who had looked after the children at the disco.

"Yes."

"I'm afraid she's not here, is she? Don't worry, you'll see her tomorrow."

"Lady home."

"That's right. The lady's gone home. And now it's time for you to go to sleep."

"Lady Lucy's home."

"No more talking now. It's time you were both asleep."

I pulled the curtains across the front of the bunk beds and Bob and I settled down to read. It was only days later that Lucy's words came back to my mind.

Although the weather was miserable, the days at the campsite were filled with activities and when the girls arrived home, they were tired but happy. Every outfit they had worn was covered with mud, so I emptied the bags onto the bedroom floor and began sorting out the washing.

Lucy grabbed a pile of toys from her bed and deposited them on the floor.

"Are your teddies pleased to see you?" I asked.

"Teddy happy," Lucy nodded seriously.

"And your dolly?"

"Dolly happy."

"Good. That's all right then."

"Teddy happy. Dolly happy. Lady happy."

I stopped what I was doing and watched her arrange the toys in a line.

"Which one is Lady?" I asked.

"Lady."

I tried again.

"Which one of your toys is called Lady?"

"Lady not toy. Lady Lady."

"I don't understand. Can you tell me about the lady?"

But Lucy had lost interest. Abandoning the toys, she ran into the lounge to find Claire.

*****

We still only had a small number of functions booked. It seemed corporate entertainment, which had been so popular during the eighties, had fallen out of fashion as quickly as shoulder pads and glam rock.

In a world grappling with soaring unemployment and job insecurity, it was no longer necessary to incentivise workers with extravagant dining or team-building social events.

With hindsight, the projections the bank had considered realistic two years ago now seemed wildly optimistic.

"If we can't get companies to book events for their staff," Bob said, "we can still put on Theme Evenings ourselves and target people directly."

"Do you think that's possible?" I asked.

"I don't see why not. The Medieval Banquet we put on for the double-glazing company last year was brilliant. I'm sure holiday makers would love to go to one."

When Bob put the suggestion to the rest of the family their reactions were mixed.

"It's a brilliant idea," David said at once.

"But it would be a huge amount of work without any guarantee that people would come." Mum frowned.

"But it would be worth the risk," I reminded her. "You saw how much we made from a handful of functions last year. Even the small ones were very profitable."

"We have to try it." David said eagerly. "We can have a separate leaflet with all the dates and what themes we'll be doing. Then, if people enjoy their visit during the day, they can come back again in the evening."

"We'd have to choose themes that appeal to different types of people," Phil said.

"And keep everything family friendly," Dad added.

"The take on the bar would be really useful," I said.

"I suppose so," Mum agreed at last, "after all, what have we got to lose?"

After a lot more debate, we settled on Medieval Banquets, Jazz evenings, Country & Western, and Old Time Music Hall.

Bob suggested we kept Friday and Saturday evenings available for any other bookings that came in, and we decided not to open on Sundays. We didn't question whether working seven days and six evenings a week was a sensible idea. We must have been mad.

As soon as we made our decision, we started work.

Bob booked the performers, I designed the leaflets and Dad and David set about making the props that would create the appropriate atmosphere for each theme.

The tables in the restaurant were circular and only big enough to seat four people, so Dad made wooden covers that could be laid over the top to create a rectangular table big enough for eight people. When these were placed end to end, we could quickly create rows of banquet tables perfect for a medieval feast. Yellow and red fabric made opulent tablecloths, and we replaced glasses and cutlery with clay goblets and finger bowls.

David carved ornate shields to hang on the walls and managed to acquire a multitude of other props from pewter tankards to leather table runners.

In addition to finding ourselves costumes for the various themes, we had to decide on a uniform for our new team of Silverlands Majorettes.

Janice, the team secretary, was responsible for sewing the girl's outfits and she asked us to send over drawings of our suggestions. I was completely out of my depth. I knew nothing about majorettes.

"Draw anything you like," Bob said dismissively. "As long as they look eye-catching, it will be fine."

"That's no help," I protested. "What sort of outfits do they usually wear?

You must know. You went to the competition."

"Well... some had skirts and tops. Others looked more like gymnasts. A few of them were quite glamorous..."

I went to the library and asked the librarian if they had any books with pictures of majorettes. The following week I collected six books and leafed through them with interest. They were mainly about American Culture and one had a two-page spread of a Thanksgiving Parade with college girls wearing leotards and waving fluffy pom-poms.

Bob loved my drawings, but Janice was not impressed. She pointed out that most of their girls were under fourteen and the carnivals they attended took place in the evenings, often in the rain. The skimpy outfits I had drawn were out of the question. Something with long sleeves, high necks, and knee-length skirts would be needed.

I was duly chastened. My next attempt was a military look with a pleated silver skirt, red tunic, silver trimmings and a peaked hat. This time Janice approved. Fortunately, she had a contact in a fabric mill in Tiverton who gave us a large discount on the materials.

*****

Liza Berlin and Roly the Wonderdog were due to perform their first show with the Indian Runner ducks on Easter Sunday.

Phil had been reporting back to us about Liza's progress as her training sessions took place at the edge of the Animal Meadow each day.

"The Indian Runners are really strange," she told us. "They don't waddle like ordinary ducks, they really can run. Roly has to dart around all over the place to get them to behave."

"But what do they do, exactly?" Dad asked.

"It's a bit like sheepdog trials, but with ducks. Liza's made an obstacle course and Roly has to guide them through it and get them into a pen at the other end."

"That sounds a bit odd to me," Mum commented.

"It is unusual," Phil agreed, "but the ducks look very sweet with their bow ties on. I'm sure the audience will love it."

Easter Sunday dawned wet and grey. A chilly wind blew along the valley, and my mood was as dark as the clouds as I prepared lasagnes in the kitchen.

"Never mind," Dad said as he passed through. "At least families won't want to go to the beach today. Anyone who's camping will be looking for somewhere indoors, so we'll probably be packed."

I hoped he was right, but the trickle of people coming through the gate never turned into a flood. By mid-morning the clouds had lifted a little and I decided to head over to the lawn to watch Liza's show. Bob was about to introduce the act and quacking sounds from the bushes told me Liza was waiting in the wings.

"Ladies and Gentlemen, please give a big hand for Liza Berlin and Roly the Wonderdog!" Bob roared.

The audience clapped excitedly and Liza bounced into view, her red wig as vibrant as ever.

"Hello, everyone!" she shouted over her opening music. Pulling a whistle out of her pocket, she blew three short blasts and the train of ducks burst out from behind the bushes. The audience gasped and giggled as Roly followed close behind, his nose low to the ground, ears pricked.

The obstacle course was laid out on the grass, hoops, slalom poles and ramps, as well as a tunnel, a high beam and a see-saw.

Liza blew her whistle again and Roly veered sharply to the right, driving the ducks towards the first ramp. Without hesitating, the sleek white birds raced up the ramp and Roly ran ahead and lay on the ground waiting for them at the other side.

The audience was delighted. As they clapped, the lead duck hesitated and looked around. Roly jumped to his feet, and the bird hurried forward and weaved its way through the slalom poles. The others followed, and the audience clapped again.

The ducks scampered around the course, bobbing theirs heads as they disappeared into the tunnel, then emerging to teeter, one by one, over the see-saw. As they paraded up a steep ramp onto the high beam, the audience clapped loudly. A dog barked and suddenly they froze. The lead duck swivelled its head, searching for the dog, and Roly paced on the grass below, ears back, eyes fixed on his charges.

For a moment, the ducks stayed perfectly still, heads up, eyes peering around them. Then the dog in the audience barked again and they scattered. White wings rose in the air as the ducks fluttered from the beam and ran in every direction. Roly charged after them, barking excitedly, and several other dogs joined in the hullabaloo.

"No! Come back!" Liza shrieked, but it was too late. Families jumped to their feet and toddlers cried as the ducks raced around, their beaks wide-open, giving tiny high-pitched squeaks as they went.

Bob calmed the audience, but the show was over. The last of the ducks wasn't found for hours.

Liza was distraught.

"I'm so sorry. It won't happen again…" she broke off as tears overwhelmed her. "Poor Roly," she sobbed. "He was doing so well."

Liza persuaded Bob to let her try again the following day, but this time the ducks were nervous.

"I think they were stage-struck," Bob told us later. "Roly did his best, but those birds weren't going to do anything. In the end, they stood in a huddle and turned their backs on him. Fortunately, the audience thought it was funny."

"But what are we going to do? The act's on all the leaflets," I groaned.

"Liza says she can go back to the old routine for now. She's cut out a lot of Roly's tricks, but she can do more magic. She hasn't given up on the new act, though. She still thinks she can make it work if she can get Roly and the ducks to bond."

"And how's she going to do that?"

Bob's expression betrayed his doubts.

"She's going to move the ducks into the flat with them."

"Seriously?"

He nodded.

"I know. It sounds a bad idea to me too."

*****

At the end of each day, we compared our takings with the numbers on our projections. It was a depressing experience. We knew the craftspeople were struggling because several asked us if they could have a reduction in their rent and our knitwear designer warned us that if things didn't pick up, she would have no choice but to close her business.

When the children went back to school at the end of the Easter holidays the figures dropped even lower but our costs continued to rise.

Mum and I booked an appointment to see James North at Torrington Bank.

As we waited to be shown into his office, I felt that I had failed. Mr North had put his faith in us and I had let him down. I expected him to shout at me, but instead his manner was one of resigned sadness.

He seemed to have aged since we last met. He asked a few questions but there was a quietness about him that made me uneasy.

"What is it you want?" He asked at last.

I explained that we needed to increase our borrowings, and he nodded.

"We will want an updated valuation but I don't anticipate that being a problem. My secretary will arrange the details. And I would like you to send monthly reports of your income and expenditure for the rest of the summer."

"Certainly," I agreed.

"That was easier than I expected," Mum said as we drove home. She was right, but I didn't feel any better.

The surveyor arrived a few days later.

"I don't see the point," David muttered as we watched him walking around the ground. "It's no time since he was here, but I suppose it will be interesting to see how much the value has gone up now that we've opened the restaurant and the other buildings are finished."

*****

We didn't have any functions booked on Saturdays, so Bob decided to use the evenings another way. There were several large caravan parks near to us and each one hosted a Welcome Party for their new arrivals each week.

The entertainment managers wanted the events to be as exciting as possible and were delighted when Bob offered to make a short appearance and tell them about Silverlands. To add to the excitement, he took Zac with him to perform ten minutes of his most impressive tricks. As soon as the brief show was over, Bob and Zac jumped into a car and hurried on to the next site.

The parks already stocked our leaflets and now they agreed to put up a poster in the reception advertising our Theme Nights.

Bob's tactics worked, and our first medieval banquet drew a good crowd. The evening's entertainment was run by Benedict the Bard, and two minstrels played period music throughout the evening.

I had wondered why Bob placed the two long tables at either side of the room with a large gap in the middle. Now I understood.

Between courses, Benedict told the diners that each table represented a different team and challenged volunteers to join him in the middle of the room for singing contests, drinking contests or jousts where victims charged from one end of the room to the other trying to catch quoits on their heads.

The evening was full of silly fun, and the diners loved it. They even laughed at Benedict's appalling jokes.

Bob had acquired a hog's head from the local butcher which he roasted, dressed with a red apple in its mouth, and paraded around the hall before the main course was served.

The hog's head looked both authentic and macabre and drew gasps from the diners.

At the end of the evening, I loosened the lacings on my bodice and breathed a sigh of relief.

"That went well," I said.

"Yes, they loved it, didn't they," Phil agreed.

Bob came back from locking the door behind the last visitors and surveyed the room.

"I wish they wouldn't throw bread at each other," he tutted.

"At least it wasn't the bones," I laughed.

"What do you want me to do with the hog's head?" Phil asked.

"I thought we could stick it in the freezer," Bob said. "It's only for decoration, so we can freeze it and bring it out again each week."

*****

When the surveyor's report arrived, I tore it open and flicked through the first pages looking for the valuation. When I found it, my heart skipped a beat. Instead of increasing, the value had gone down.

"It's ridiculous! The man's an idiot. Didn't he see all the work we've done?" David was livid. "You'll have to phone him and make him change it."

"It does seem strange," Dad agreed. "Perhaps it's a mistake. In all my years, I've never known the value of property to go down."

It was not a mistake. The surveyor was apologetic, but he assured me the valuation was correct.

"I know it won't be any comfort to you, but property prices are going down all over the country. It's unprecedented. In the last couple of months, they've dropped every day."

Fortunately, Torrington Bank still agreed to extend our borrowing.

*****

As the weeks passed, the numbers attending our Theme Evenings increased.

Medieval Banquets were the most popular, but each theme appealed to a different audience.

Jazz evenings attracted older couples who preferred to sit and be entertained, while the Country & Western sessions were much livelier and drew younger people who wanted to try line dancing.

My favourite theme was Old Time Music Hall which appealed both to families with younger children and more mature couples.

Bob acted as Master of Ceremonies and welcomed guests with authentic Victorian greetings. He had an extensive selection of truly awful jokes which he delivered with such conviction the room was full of laughter all evening.

To my surprise, we often had whole families arrive in Victorian costume. I never knew whether they were local families who kept such things in the back of their wardrobe or if they were holiday makers who had made the effort to hire fancy dress outfits. In either case, it happened so often that Bob began offering a prize for the best period outfit.

We left song sheets on the tables, and the audience joined in with the singing. Our two performers for the evening were very different. Elaine had a magnificent voice and performed family favourites and emotional ballads. Clarissa, however, was a complete contrast. She recreated the comic performances of Old Time stars such as Marie Lloyd with such charisma she brought the audience to their feet.

Clarissa acted every song and performed, not as a trained singer, but as a cockney washerwoman, a landlady or a drunk. She deliberately missed high notes, let her voice crack with emotion, and emitted ear-splitting, cackles of laughter at her own jokes.

The audience loved her and always demanded more. At the end of the evening, it was wonderful to hear people tell us how much they had enjoyed themselves.

Without doubt, the Medieval Banquets were the most profitable evenings. Benedict was an excellent host and by dividing the guests into two teams, his games and banter created an instant camaraderie. This had a measurable impact on the bar takings which were nearly double those of any other evening.

*****

Since moving into Silverlands, the family had developed certain routines. There was always a great deal to do and life was easier if we all followed the same patterns. We didn't discuss the routines. They simply evolved over time as the most sensible way of doing things.

One habit was that whoever was in the shop at the end of the day would tidy up before locking the door. It had become a signal we all understood. If the shop door was locked the room was ready for the next morning.

At night, the last person downstairs turned off the lights and switched on the burglar alarms before going to bed. It was a simple system, but it worked.

It was approaching the middle of May when I unlocked the shop door one morning and was surprised to see three horse brasses lying on the carpet.

The shop contained a beautiful old fireplace which we used as a feature to display brass and copper ware. The mantelpiece and shelves above it held ornaments, plates and jugs and a row of hooks beneath held pokers, toasting forks and horse brasses.

It was not unusual for customers to drop items but I was surprised the brasses had been left on the floor overnight. However, now that we were working most evenings as well as during the day, I knew everyone was getting tired so I replaced the horse brasses and said nothing.

A few days later, I unlocked the door to find a row of small teddies scattered across the floor.

The next morning, I was late dropping Claire and Michael to school and by the time I got back David had already opened the shop. I could tell something was wrong by his expression but I wasn't sure if he was upset or angry.

"What's the matter?" I asked.

"Look at this."

He led me into the shop and pointed at the floor. A display of fridge magnets stood on the counter but now all the magnets had been removed and lay in a neat row across the floor from the counter to the fireplace.

"What do you make of that?" he asked.

"I've no idea. Could the kids have been in here?"

He shook his head.

"No. Everything was tidy when I finished up last night and I didn't open it until after you left."

"Are you sure no one's been in here?"

"Absolutely. And why would anyone lay them out like that, anyway?"

I considered the magnets but I had no explanation to offer.

"Sorry, I've got no idea, but we can't waste time now. It's nearly opening time."

*****

When we closed, David and I searched the house together. He had clearly been thinking about the fridge magnets.

"I don't understand," he began as soon as we were out of earshot of Mum. "The stand hadn't been knocked over. Why would anyone bother laying the magnets out in a line like that?"

I didn't have an answer so I stayed silent.

"It was the ghost, wasn't it?" he said at last.

"But why would he do that?"

"How should I know?" David demanded. "But it's the only logical explanation."

"It's not logical at all," I objected.

"Think about it. The door was locked. There was no one in the house except the family. Who else could it have been?"

"By why would he do it? What's the point?"

"Ghosts don't need reasons. They do things. That's all."

I was about to argue but I bit my tongue.

"Nothing was broken, so it doesn't matter who did it," I muttered

"Of course, it matters! This is evidence. It proves something happened."

"What? A few fridge magnets on the floor?"

"For Christ's sake, Diana! Those magnets moved by themselves. The door was locked and the alarms were on. The motion detector covers the whole room. If someone had gone in there, why didn't it go off?"

"Are you sure you put the alarm on?"

"Yes, I am!" David's voice was rising.

"OK. Calm down. I admit it's all a bit strange, but let's wait and see if anything else happens."

"All right," he agreed, "but you can't go on ignoring this stuff."

It was nearly a week before anything else happened. I had hoped David would be subtle if there were any further incidents, but I heard his voice from our flat upstairs.

"Come and look at this!"

By the time I got downstairs, Phil and Mum were in the shop too. A rotating display stand was in the middle of the room. Usually, the stand contained postcards but now it was empty and every card was lying on the carpet in perfectly spaced lines that radiated from the centre like the rays of the sun.

"How did it happen?" Phil asked.

"I don't know."

"It's as if the stand spun really quickly and all the cards were flung out," Mum said.

"But the alarms were on." David reminded her. "Why didn't they go off?"

I noticed Claire standing in the doorway watching me.

"I've no idea," I said briskly, "but I need to get the kids to school. We can talk about this later."

*****

For the rest of the day, my mind kept returning to the incidents in the shop. David was right. They didn't make sense, but why would they? I had no doubt Fred was responsible. Was he bored? Should I try to talk to him? Would there be any point?

My thoughts were interrupted by a family in the tearooms. I was behind the counter when they marched in, demanding to speak to someone.

"Can I help you?" I offered.

"We want to make an official complaint. About your potter."

My heart sank.

"Perhaps you'd like to come through to the office?" I suggested.

It was crowded with three adults and two children crammed into one small room, but I didn't want the conversation to be overheard. The mother explained tearfully that Tom had insulted them all, refused to take a commission and thrown them out of his studio.

I listened sympathetically to their complaints, apologised, and then, when the blaze of righteous indignation burned down, I promised I would reprimand the potter and handed them all vouchers for free cream teas.

Then I headed to the craft block.

"You can't speak to customers like that," I scolded Tom, but he was as unrepentant as ever.

"I am an artist. My time is valuable. They wanted me to make a named mug."

I knew how much he detested putting names on things.

"But last year, you told me named mugs were your best seller."

"No. I told you they were the most profitable. I wouldn't make the despicable, artisan rubbish for any other reason. They are purely grockle-fodder."

"But if you've got named mugs, why wouldn't you sell them one?"

Tom's eyes glittered dangerously.

"I was perfectly willing to sell them a mug. Their revolting little sprog is called Elizabeth. I offered her a mug with Elizabeth on it, but No, she didn't want that."

He took a deep breath before continuing.

"I searched my whole display for alternatives. I found Lizzie, Liza, Liz, Beth, Betty or Bets. But no. None of them were acceptable. She wanted Lizzy. I said she would have to choose from what I had available. They asked me to make one. I asked them to leave. End of story."

"Surely you could have made one for them?"

I regretted the question at once.

"No, I could not!" Tom roared. "I make pottery in batches. Firing up my kiln is expensive. I only do it when I have a full load...."

"Yes, I know..." I tried to interrupt, but he was in full flow.

"... if I make a single mug, I have to charge extra to cover the firing cost. I tried to explain that, but did they listen? No! They were too busy complaining I had made their wretched offspring cry!"

"Tom!" I shouted. "Calm down!"

"I am perfectly calm!" he bellowed.

"No, you're not! You can't keep behaving like this! No one's forcing you to make mugs if you don't want to, but you have to be civil."

I glared at Tom and he glared back at me

"I think you had better leave," he said.

*****

"Was this you?" Tom demanded as he flung a large card on the servery counter.

The words BEWARE THE POTTER – HE BITES were written in large, even letters.

"Certainly not," I replied. "What is it?"

"Someone taped it to the door of my unit." Tom scowled. "It's outrageous!"

"Is it?" I looked him in the eye. "It seems quite accurate to me."

"I never upset people intentionally," he snapped.

I hesitated. Tom was a nightmare, but I knew his behaviour hurt him more than it did anyone else.

"All right, I'll have a word with the others." I said.

I didn't need to speak to all the craftspeople. As soon as I stepped into Dougal's unit, his face creased into a grin.

"Come to talk about a sign, have you?" he asked.

"It was you, wasn't it?"

"Me? Never. As if I would do anything to upset the miserable old bastard."

I lowered my voice.

"Dougal, if you do anything else to stir things, I will tell Tom it was you that put the padlock on the toilets when he had diarrhoea last year."

"Oh yes. That was a glorious day, wasn't it?" He chuckled gleefully at the memory.

"Did you hear me?"

"Yes, yes. I promise. If you really want me to, I'll leave the old misery-guts in peace."

*****

When I got back to the house Martha was behind the counter.

"David was looking for you," she told me. "He said if you've got a minute can you pop into the shop."

I found him serving ice creams to a group of elderly ladies. As soon as he finished, he turned and pointed at the fireplace.

"Notice anything?"

"Yes, the tray's missing. You don't mean you've sold it?"

The tray was a large flat piece of brass with ornate hammer work and handles at each end. We had bought it years before because it made an eye-catching centre piece to the display and had never expected anyone would actually buy it.

"Don't get excited," David said. "Nobody's bought it. It jumped off the shelf."

He reached under the counter and brought out the tray.

"What do you mean?"

"Just that. It jumped. Look."

I followed him across the room and he pointed to a row of small brass animals standing along the front of the mantelpiece.

"You know where the tray goes."

"Of course, I do," I said as he put it back in position, leaning against the wall.

"Then tell me how it got from there, with all those things in front of it, to lying on the floor."

"Could it have slipped somehow?"

"It could have, but not without knocking all these things off as it came forward."

I looked at the tray and the pieces in front of it. He was right.

"You tell me how it happened," David went on. "There were quite a few people in the shop at the time, but no one was near the fireplace. Suddenly there was an almighty crash and the brass tray was on the floor. I thought it had slipped down, but now that I've looked again, it's not possible. There's no way that tray came down without disturbing anything unless it jumped up first."

I searched for an explanation but found nothing.

"Admit it. This is seriously weird."

"All right. It is," I agreed, "but what are we supposed to do about it?"

"I've no idea, but we can't go on pretending it isn't happening."

*****

It seemed no time until half-term arrived and brought with it the first of the summer carnivals.

To help with our advertising efforts, we had added the Silverlands logo to the side of our company car and entered it as a support vehicle for the majorette troupe. This meant we could drive it along the parade route and use it to carry our supply of leaflets.

We had made clown outfits for Claire and Michael, and they were excited to ride in the car and wave at the crowds. The carnival was only a short drive from Silverlands but it was due to start at seven o'clock which didn't give us much time for the journey.

As soon as Mum closed the ticket box, Bob and I piled the kids into the car and set off. It was years since I had watched a carnival and I had never taken part in one before. I wished I was feeling as excited as the children.

Liza had offered to lend me one of her clown outfits, but I decided to go with something a little less eye-catching. Instead, I found a brightly coloured dress with a bubble hem and arranged my hair into two plaits with wire inside that made them stand straight up in the air. I painted a red nose and a large red mouth on my face and decided I had done enough.

The majorettes were already lined up when we arrived, and I was impressed by their appearance. The girls ranged from four to sixteen years old and each was impeccably turned out with hair drawn back into a ponytail, red tunic neatly buttoned and silver caps gleaming in the evening sunlight.

The troupe leader stood at the front, practising her baton throwing, and the band was having a last-minute rehearsal nearby.

Janice had kept a space ahead of the troupe for our car, and as we slipped into place, the majorettes gave us a rousing cheer. Michael and Claire waved through the windows, and Lucy squirmed in her seat to see what was happening.

"This is going to be fun." Bob smiled.

As the signal was given to move forward, I climbed out of the car with a pile of leaflets in my hand. The carnival had formed up in a car park on the outside of town, but a few people stood at the side of the road watching the floats as they set off.

I knew I was there to give out leaflets, but my stomach tied itself into a knot at the thought. What if no one would take them? I decided to wait until we reached the centre of the town where there would be more families.

I walked beside the car and Bob steered with one hand and waved at passers-by with the other.

"Do you want to swap?" he asked. "You can drive and I'll do the leaflets if you prefer."

"No, it's fine. I'll do them."

I tried to smile, but I longed to climb into the back seat with the kids and hide.

"Look, there's a big family over there." Bob pointed. "They're the sort we need to reach."

I couldn't put it off any longer. Forcing myself to smile, I walked towards them.

"Here you go."

I shoved a leaflet into a child's hand and hurried away before she could give it back.

Soon the crowds grew thicker and the music from the marching bands and carnival floats bounced off the walls of shops and houses, drowning out voices. I relaxed a little. No one could ask me questions.

The carnival progressed in fits and starts. Each time the procession halted, the lead majorette held her baton high and signalled a new formation. Depending on how much space was available, the troupe would split in two or space themselves into a square. They then marched back and forth, weaving between each other or wheeling in complicated formations.

They were far more disciplined and synchronised than I had expected, and I soon saw why they had impressed Bob.

While the troupe was entertaining the crowd, I made my way along the road handing out leaflets. It was easier now. To my surprise, people wanted the leaflets. Children reached out to me and hands pushed through the crowd from families two or three rows behind the barricades.

The music from the floats ahead of us was deafening, but it was full of life and excitement. The majorettes were clearly loving every moment, and the crowds roared with appreciation.

The procession moved on and suddenly I was running to keep up, scattering leaflets between eager hands as I went. The crowd was endless. I had not thought to ask how long the route would be, but as the last glimpse of daylight faded from the sky, I guessed we had been walking for over an hour and the end was nowhere in sight.

"Are you OK?" Bob asked as I leaned through the passenger window for more leaflets.

"Yes, I'm fine." I smiled. "In fact, I'm rather enjoying it."

The kids slept all the way home and Lucy didn't wake up even as I carried her upstairs and laid her on her bed.

"Can Michael and I give out leaflets at the next carnival?"Claire asked as she pulled on her nightclothes.

"Do you want to?"

"Yes, please."

"I'll have to ask Auntie, but I don't see why not."

Claire yawned widely, and I tucked the duvet around her.

"Night-night, Sweetie," I said, but her eyes had already closed.

*****

I was watering the hanging baskets outside the tearooms one evening when Tom appeared.

"Here," he said and plonked a glass jar on one of the tables under the verandah.

"What is it?" I asked.

"Garlic mayonnaise."

"Right.... What's it for?"

"It's for you." He turned away from me. "I shouldn't have shouted."

"I see," I said to his back. "Thank you."

"I made it myself. Free-range eggs."

His shoulders rose slightly as he crossed his arms.

"That's very thoughtful.... Does this mean we can be friends again?"

Tom turned back abruptly.

"We have always been friends. Ever since I arrived. You and Bob. All your family."

"Good."

He picked up the jar of mayonnaise and thrust it into my hands.

"Don't forget to keep it in the fridge with the lid screwed on," he said and walked away.

Chapter 7

Bob and I were flopped on the sofa enjoying a mug of chocolate before bed when a loud hammering on the flat door shattered the peace.

"What the hell's that?" Bob gasped.

"It must be one of the others. Maybe the phone's not working," I said as I rushed into the hall. Turning the yale lock, I pulled open the door.

There was no one there.

As I peered into the dark corridor Bob caught up with me.

"You heard it, didn't you?" I asked.

"Yes, I heard it."

"Should we search the house?"

He hesitated, then turned back into the flat.

"What's the point? The alarms are on. If anyone was there, they would have gone off."

We went back to the sofa, but the peaceful mood was gone.

"Why didn't he bark?" Bob asked, looking at Dino stretched out asleep on the carpet.

"Because ghosts don't smell?" I suggested.

"It wasn't a ghost," Bob said stubbornly. He stretched out beside me, but I could tell he was as unsettled as I was.

"Perhaps it wasn't really a sound," he said. "Perhaps it was a vibration that sounded like a sound."

My mind wrestled with the concept.

"But a sound is a vibration, isn't it?"

"No, not really. Vibrations move through air. They can even move through a vacuum. You can't see them, but that doesn't mean they're not there. One minute, everything is quiet, then... Wham! A vibration hits your eardrum and you hear a sound."

"But where did the vibration come from?"

"I don't know."

"Then what exactly are you saying?"

Bob let out a long sigh.

"I have no idea.... but I know there has to be some sort of explanation."

*****

There were more knocks on the door.

Sometimes they were quiet. Sometimes they were so faint I couldn't be sure I had heard anything at all and began to think I was imagining things. At other times, it sounded as though the door had been hit with a hammer. I examined the surface thoroughly, but never found so much as a scratch to explain how the noise had been made.

And Dino never reacted. Not once.

The first few times it happened, Bob rushed to open the door. I'm sure he was hoping to catch someone running away along the corridor, but eventually, he gave up.

I worried what I would say to Claire and Lucy when they asked who was banging on our door, but the thumps never happened when they were awake and didn't wake them when they were asleep.

"Is it you, Fred? Is there something you want?" I asked when I was alone in the flat, but my questions went unanswered.

The disturbances in the shop also continued. Several days would pass without anything, and then I would find a pile of books scattered across the window seat or a row of slate coasters piled in the middle of the floor.

None of it made sense.

Each morning, David waited for me while I turned the alarms off, then we opened the shop door together. I knew we were hoping for different things. I wanted the room to be undisturbed so I could get on with my morning preparations while David longed to find something that would prove, beyond any doubt, that we were being taunted by a poltergeist.

*****

One morning, there was a thump on the front door, but instead of a disembodied spirit, I found Liza standing on the doorstep.

"I would like to introduce you to Luna," she said formally.

A small black and white collie was standing beside her.

"Wow! She's beautiful," I said.

Bob and I had shared a painful evening with Liza a few nights before when she confided that Roly would be retiring at the end of the season. I knew how difficult it would be for her to replace him.

I knelt to greet the new arrival, but Luna's ears went down and she took a step backwards.

"She's a bit timid, but she's got a lovely nature," Liza told me.

"And how does she get on with Roly?"

"So far, so good."

"I'm glad to hear it."

I held out my hand and the dog sniffed my fingers, but her tail was clenched tightly between her back legs.

"Does she like the ducks?"

Liza hesitated.

"There haven't been any problems, but I'm going to let them get used to each other before I start training," she said. "Luna's still young so I don't want to rush her."

"That makes sense," I agreed. "Do you want to bring her in to meet the others?"

"No, I won't disturb everyone now. I only wanted to say hello."

As Liza walked away, I watched Luna trot behind her and hoped she and the ducks would make a good team.

*****

Lucy loved to have a book read to her at bedtime, but even as a toddler she had strong ideas about which books she wanted. Stories about princesses, fairies, or ballerinas were of no interest to her. Instead, she liked factual books. Claire had a set of children's encyclopaedias and Lucy loved to stab the pictures with her finger and demand, "What's 'at?"

As a result, Bob and I spent hours explaining about trains, washing machines, glaciers and other diverse subjects. I was glad Lucy had an inquisitive mind, but it was sometimes difficult to find answers she could understand.

Before climbing into bed, she always arranged a row of toys across her pillow.

"Lady likes teddy," she told me one night.

"That's nice," I said without thinking. "Which lady is that?"

"White Lady."

A tingle ran through me.

"How do you know the lady?"

"Lady talks."

"The lady talked to you? Where was she?"

Something in my tone must have alerted her because she looked up at me and frowned.

"Please Lucy, where did you see the lady?"

After a moment, she pointed to the corner of the room and my heart skipped a beat.

"Here? In your bedroom?"

Lucy nodded.

"When was this?" I asked, but she turned away and slid down beneath the duvet. I wanted to pull her up again, to demand she answered my questions. Instead, I stroked her silky hair and kissed the top of her head.

"All right, angel. We can talk about it tomorrow."

I decided not to mention the conversation to Bob.

The next morning, I asked Lucy if she had seen the lady again. She smiled at me and asked if she could have porridge for breakfast. I repeated my question later, but she simply turned away. It was clear interrogating her was not going to get me anywhere, so I let the subject drop.

A few days later, I was pulling Lucy's nightdress over her head when she pointed to the bottom of her bed.

"Lady sit there," she said.

Tingles ran down my spine and I struggled to keep my voice level.

"That's nice. Is she a friendly lady?"

Lucy nodded.

"Does she talk to you?"

She nodded again.

"What does she talk about?"

A shrug.

"Do you talk to her?"

Lucy shrugged again and picked up a toy dog.

"Doggy tired," she said and climbed into bed.

"What does the lady look like?" I asked, but Lucy had lost interest.

The next morning, I found Dad in his workshop and told him about Lucy's visitor.

"Was she upset?"

"That's not the point. She told me a lady sits on her bed and talks to her."

"I know, but she's very little. Was she playing a game?"

"I don't think so. She said it as if it was the most natural thing in the world."

"In that case, it might be best not to make a big thing of it."

"But I can't ignore it," I protested.

He put down the hammer he was using and gazed at me.

"Then what are you going to do?"

The stress and confusion inside me bubbled close to the surface.

"I don't know," I sniffed. "That's why I'm asking you."

Dad put an arm around me, and I leaned my head against his shoulder.

"It's not fair. There's enough to worry about at the moment without this as well," I grumbled.

He patted my head as if I was the same age as Lucy.

"I know, love. How does Bob feel about it?"

Suddenly, I felt awkward. Pulling out a tissue, I wiped my eyes.

"I ought to be downstairs by now..."

"You haven't told him, have you?"

I hesitated.

"I wasn't sure how he'd react. He still won't admit Fred exists. If I tell him there's a White Lady in the girl's bedroom, he'll think I've lost it completely."

"Maybe he will and maybe he won't. Either way, he's their Dad, so he needs to know what's going on."

I wanted to argue, but I knew he was right.

That night, I waited until Bob was calm and relaxed before bringing up the subject of Lucy's visitor.

"Have you been telling her ghost stories?" he asked when I finished.

"No, I haven't. She didn't say anything about a ghost. She said it was a lady."

"And does Claire know?"

"I don't think so, at least, she hasn't said anything. Do you think I should ask her about it?"

"No. We've managed to keep this whole ghost thing away from the kids. Let's keep it that way."

"But what are we going to do about Lucy's Lady?"

"Nothing. Forget about it. Lots of kids have imaginary friends."

"Do you think that's all it is?"

"Of course, I do. Kids come out with all sorts of things. It doesn't mean anything. If you stop asking her about it, she'll probably never mention it again."

Bob kissed me and I felt better. I really hoped he was right.

*****

At the beginning of July, we were invited to a parents' evening at Claire's school.

Bob and I left as soon as the ticket box closed and Claire was eager to show us what she had been doing.

The school was a huge, red-brick building full of dark echoing corridors, but the classroom was light and airy with octagonal tables scattered through the middle. The furniture was scaled to suit seven-year-olds, and it amused me to see that parents were expected to sit on the miniature chairs with their legs stuck out at awkward angles because they couldn't fit under the tables.

The teachers sat on the tables and I wondered if there was a subtle form of psychological warfare going on.

When we arrived, Claire's teacher was deep in conversation with another couple. From their worried expressions, I guessed their child was struggling.

I recognised some of the other parents and nodded at them as they were dragged past by children eager to show them displays of wonky clay animals and volcanoes made out of toilet rolls and cotton wool.

We had been allocated a specific time slot to speak to the teacher and were free to wander around the various classrooms and admire displays of work until then.

"What do you want to look at?" Claire asked.

"You decide, Honey. We'll follow," Bob replied.

Every fifteen minutes, a bell rang. At once, the parents seated in the tiny chairs struggled to escape, stretching themselves to regain feeling in their cramped limbs while the teacher sipped a glass of water before the next parents arrived.

The bell rang again, and it was our turn.

"Good afternoon, Mr and Mrs Townsend," the teacher trilled. "I'm so pleased to see you."

We listened as she ran through the various subjects and listed Claire's achievements. It was clear she was doing well.

It seemed only a few moments before the bell rang again and we struggled to our feet.

"And make sure to look at Claire's artwork before you go. She really is very talented. Have you seen the folder in her drawer?"

We assured her Claire had shown us everything.

"Then don't forget the display in the corridor on your way out. We've been talking about diaries this week and asked the children to write an entry about something exciting that happened to them. Claire's effort was extraordinary. Wonderful imagination."

I was delighted Claire's work had made such an impression.

On the way out, I stopped and searched the sheets of paper pinned to the wall. I recognised Claire's effort at once. The drawing was unmistakable. It showed our gift shop and included the counters, the window seat, the fireplace and a variety of toys and postcards scattered across the floor.

Underneath it, Claire had written in large, even letters. 'The ghost made a mess in the shop today, but Mummy cleared it up before the people came.'

*****

"What have you been telling the kids?" I demanded as soon as I saw David.

"Me? Nothing."

"You've been telling them about Fred, haven't you?"

"Why? What have they said?"

"I knew it!" I gasped. "You had no right. How are they supposed to understand? It's not fair. It's not..."

"Calm down!" he cut across me. "I haven't told them anything. They're not stupid, you know. Did you really think they wouldn't work out what's going on?"

He was right, but my maternal instincts were in overdrive. I could deal with Fred, but how were children supposed to cope with the idea that a ghost was floating around their home watching them?

And what would the other schoolchildren think? Would Claire get teased? Would she be bullied?

"What brought this up, anyway?" David demanded.

I explained about the drawing.

"I thought I'd been so careful," I said. "We never open the shop until I've taken them to school."

"Except on weekends," he reminded me.

I sighed. I was a terrible mother.

"You're looking at it the wrong way," David said. "If Claire's happy to write about the ghost, that means she's not worried about it. She doesn't think it's weird. She thinks it's part of life."

"I suppose so."

"Hiding things from children never works. It's much better to be open."

I nodded. I knew there was truth in what he said. I knew it was better to be open. But I also knew that I was not going to tell Claire, or anyone else, about Lucy's conversations with the White Lady if I could possibly avoid it.

*****

As our financial situation became more difficult, I found talking about it almost as difficult as discussing the White Lady.

We were approaching the height of the summer season and should have been banking a reserve of money to see us through the winter. Instead, we were struggling to pay our bills.

The rest of the family needed to know what was happening, but I hated sharing bad news.

I felt responsible. I felt I should have found a way to avoid the situation. Crowds of visitors were still arriving every day, and we were constantly busy, especially as we had cut back on our staff, but the amount we were taking was far below our targets while our expenses went up by the day.

Mum showed me a letter from the bank informing us that the rate of interest on our loan had gone up yet again.

"That's ridiculous! How can they expect us to keep paying more?" I protested.

"Something has to change," Mum said quietly. "The quarterly payment to the bank is due in a few days. We can pay it, but if we do, we won't have enough to cover the rest of the bills."

"It's ridiculous," I moaned. "The interest rate is so high now our repayments have nearly doubled. What are we supposed to do? Double our prices?"

"No, but we have to do something. We need to talk to the others and then we're going to have to talk to the bank."

I knew the others suspected we were running into problems, but they all looked shocked when I told them how serious the situation had become.

"But I don't understand. We're still so busy," Phil said, "surely it's not that much different from last year?"

Mum shook her head.

"I know we're busy, but we not making as much profit as we were. There are lots of people in the restaurant, but they're buying snacks, not full meals. It's the same in the shop."

"It's true. I haven't sold anything but pocket money toys all week," David agreed.

This time I waited by myself in the reception area of Torrington Bank. Mum was needed in the ticket box. I wore the same grey skirt as when I first met Mr North. I had barely had time to visit a shop since.

I felt a complete failure.

Mr North smiled as he held out his hand to greet me, but there was a tiredness in his eyes.

"How is everything going?" he asked as his secretary placed a china teapot and cups and saucers on the polished wooden desk.

I took a deep breath and rattled off the reasons why our figures were so far from those we had anticipated.

"I'm not surprised. This is proving a difficult period for many businesses," Mr North said when I finished. He asked me questions about our visitor numbers, opening times, staff costs and many other subjects.

"And do you think you are likely to find a replacement for the Motor Museum?"

"I hope so. But, if I'm going to be honest, it will probably take a while. Bob's been searching and putting out adverts, but we haven't had any interest yet."

I felt I should say something positive, but I couldn't think of anything.

"I thought it was best to tell you what's happening," I said.

"Yes, you're right. It's never a good policy to ignore problems."

He drummed his fingers on the polished wood as he considered.

"Unfortunately, although Torrington is an independent bank, we are still bound by the Bank of England rates," he said at last. "This means the level of interest you pay is beyond our control. However, there is one way in which I can assist you. Your current payments are made up of two parts. One element is interest and the second element is repayment of the original borrowing. In the short term, I can suspend the repayments."

He studied me as if satisfying himself that I understood.

"That would reduce the amount you have to pay each quarter, but it would extend the term of your borrowing. It could only be a temporary arrangement. Do you think your family would find that acceptable?"

I jumped at the suggestion.

"I'm sure they would. Can it start straight away?"

"When is your next payment due?"

"Next week."

"I will ask my secretary to delay the invoice. I'm afraid I will have to send you some more paperwork to sign."

"That's not a problem."

As I left the office, I felt I could walk on water. We had been reprieved. The busiest part of the summer was still ahead of us. Surely things would pick up? If we had a good peak season and Bob could find a new tenant, anything was possible. I stopped for petrol on the way back and treated myself to a bar of chocolate to celebrate.

But Mum was not as excited by my news as I had expected.

"It's good that we have a bit longer to pay," she agreed, "but it won't help us in the long run."

"Why not?"

"Because we're not paying off the debt. If we only pay the interest, we'll have to go on paying forever."

"It was that or nothing. I thought you'd be pleased," I said defensively.

"I am pleased. It gives us a breathing space," she said, but I could tell that she was still worried.

From then on, we made economies wherever we could.

Abbie and I managed on our own in the kitchen except for peak times and Beryl's hours in the shop were halved.

Mum had always paid invoices as soon as she received them, but now she waited for as long as possible. Cashflow became a constant struggle.

*****

Fortunately, the atmosphere at Silverlands stopped us getting depressed. Our visitors may not have been spending very much, but they still filled the house with chatter, and laughter floated up from the lawn whenever Liza or Zac were performing.

And our guests never failed to surprise us.

One day a family arrived with a wicker cat basket. I presumed they had brought their family pet with them and watched as they sat down on the tea lawn and undid the straps on the basket.

I expected to see a kitten emerge, but instead it was a tortoise that plodded out and blinked in the sunlight.

When I told Abbie, she insisted on taking out a pile of lettuce which the tortoise munched and dragged around the lawn, much to everyone's amusement.

At the beginning of August, Lucy's birthday came round again. She was three years old, and I felt guilty that we couldn't take time off to take her to the beach or invite her friends around to play. I couldn't even find time to bake her a cake.

I knew she would enjoy the cake from the bakery, but I couldn't shake the feeling I was letting her down.

Abbie was due to finish work at five o'clock and asked if she could look after all three of the children for an hour. They were delighted. Abbie had brought a present for Lucy and as soon as she finished in the kitchen, she took the children to play on the lawn. Lucy tore the paper from her present and squealed with delight as she revealed a frisbee.

The four of them raced around the lawn throwing and catching the frisbee, then Abbie shepherded Claire and Michael through the Pirate Trail, helping Lucy to balance on the beams and clamber over the obstacles.

By the time we closed, the children were exhausted and Abbie was red-faced and beaming.

"That was brilliant!" she giggled. "I've always wanted to do that."

Bob invited her to stay for Lucy's birthday tea and the whole family gathered on the lawn once the visitors had gone. It was a beautiful evening, and for once we sat and talked and played with the children until long after sunset.

As darkness fell, I ushered Claire and Lucy upstairs to bed.

"It's too late for a story now," I told them. "Straight off to sleep."

Claire yawned widely and climbed into bed, but Lucy was still high on ice cream and jelly.

"Not go bed yet. Want play."

I pulled back the duvet and patted the sheet.

"Not now, Honeybun, you can play tomorrow."

"Story! Want a story!"

"Please, Lucy, it's very late. Do you want your teddy?"

She shook her head.

"Lady got."

I pretended not to hear.

"He must be here somewhere."

I looked around the room, but there was no sign of the teddy.

"Teddy gone," Lucy said calmly.

"Maybe he's downstairs." I suggested. "Here, you can cuddle Pony tonight."

Lucy smiled at me.

"Night-night, Mummy. Night-night Claire, Night-night Lady."

This time I couldn't stop a shiver running down my spine.

I glanced behind me, but Claire was already asleep. I searched the shadows with my eyes but saw nothing. Turning back to Lucy, I gave her an enormous hug.

"Night, night, Sweetie," I said.

I didn't want to leave, but I knew I couldn't stay all night. I looked around one more time, but everything was as it should be.

I crossed the room and tucked the duvet tight around Claire. Then, reluctantly, I went out and closed the door behind me.

*****

In the middle of August, Bob had a phone call from one of our clown friends.

Bumble told him he was in Devon on holiday and asked if he could visit us and perform his act for our visitors while he was here. Bob agreed at once. He invited Bumble to bring his family with him and be our guests for the day.

When he arrived, Bumble brought not just his two children, but their partners and three grandchildren. I was surprised, I hadn't guessed that beneath his painted motley, Bumble was old enough to be a grandfather. They were a lovely, friendly family and when they arrived Bob went out to welcome them.

A while later, David phoned me from the shop.

"What is it?" I asked, sensing he was worried.

"Do you know anything about Bumble's act?"

"Not really. Why?"

"His wife's just told me he's going to do a high-dive into a bath-tub."

"Pardon?"

"He's got a metal bath-tub and a massive ladder, and he's going to do a somersault from the top of the ladder and land in the bath-tub."

"You're kidding. Is that safe? Is he insured?"

"I've no idea."

"Does Bob know about it?"

"He's introducing him."

"When?"

"Now."

My stomach knotted as I imagined the headlines - Elderly Clown Paralyzed Performing Dangerous Bathtub Stunt at Tourist Attraction.

"You'll have to manage for a bit," I called to Abbie. "I'll be back as soon as I can."

Hurrying across the lawn, I saw a crowd of people. In the centre, a tall pair of ladders were set up next to an old-fashioned bathtub. It was not a full-length bath but rather a short Victorian-style tub only big enough to sit in.

"And now, let's have a big hand for Bumble!" Bob's voice boomed over the loudspeakers.

The crowd roared and beside the ladders, Bumble took a deep bow. He wore an Edwardian striped swimming costume with a spiky orange wig on his head and outsized boots on his feet. Beside him, his son, Stevie was also dressed as a clown.

As I pushed through the crowd, Bumble began climbing the ladder.

"Ladies and Gentlemen, this death-defying feat has never before been attempted…." Bob paused before finishing his sentence, "at four-thirty in the afternoon."

The audience laughed and Bumble slipped dramatically, flicking his feet in the air and holding tightly to the ladder with both hands. He scrambled to regain his footing as gasps and giggles echoed around the lawn.

"Be careful, Bumble! We don't want any accidents!" Bob reminded him.

I signalled to Bob, but his eyes were fixed on Bumble and he was laughing as much as the audience. I tried to guess the height of the ladder. Two metres? No, it was more than that. Three metres? I shuddered. Surely, Bumble wasn't really going to dive?

Reaching the front of the crowd, I saw a thin layer of foam plastic had been placed in the bottom of the tub.

Bumble was standing on the top of the ladder. He waved his arms in the air and made little bows to the people below. A small child began to cry.

I wanted to shout at Bob, to ask him if this was really a good idea, but I didn't. I stood and watched and prayed that Bumble knew what he was doing. At the bottom of the ladder, Stevie began clapping and walked around the circle, urging the crowd to join in.

Suddenly, he stopped and looked at the tub in alarm. Waving his arms, he ran towards Bob.

"What's the matter? Is something wrong?" Bob asked over the loudspeaker.

The audience held their breath as Stevie pointed to the tub, pointed to Bumble, mimed diving and shook his head vigorously.

"Are you saying it's not safe?"

Stevie nodded dramatically, and I relaxed. Maybe the whole act was just a charade to wind up the audience.

"Then what should we do?" Bob asked.

I watched in disbelief as Stevie pulled a small bottle of water from his pocket.

"Of course! The tub should be full, shouldn't it?"

With a dramatic flourish, Stevie poured a trickle of water into the bathtub.

"That's better. Are we ready now?"

Stevie nodded and pointed both hands up to Bumble.

"In that case, Ladies and Gentleman, let's do this properly. Ten, nine, eight..."

The audience joined in with the countdown. Bumble bent down and kicked his legs up in the air until he was balanced in a handstand high on top of the ladder.

"...four, three, two, one..."

Bumble flexed his arms and launched himself up off the ladder. He coiled into a ball, twisted, flipped, and landed squarely on his shoulders in the centre of the tub with his arms and legs pointing up at the sky. Gasps of amazement rippled through the crowd, followed by cheers and thunderous applause.

I felt sick.

For several moments, Bumble stayed motionless until Stevie took his hand and hauled him out of the bathtub.

The audience cheered wildly as the two clowns bowed and curtsied in every direction.

"Are you all right?" I asked Bumble as soon as we were away from the crowd. He was walking stiffly, and I guessed he was in pain.

"Not bad," he winced. "I'll have a hot bath later."

"Do you do that often?"

Bumble didn't answer, but Stevie grinned at me.

"He hasn't done it for nearly three years. The last time he hit the edge of the bath and it took him six months off work to get over it."

*****

When we closed, David usually waited at the bottom of the stairs to start the search of the house, but one afternoon I found him standing in the shop staring at the fireplace.

"Are you all right?" I asked him.

"No. Not really."

"Why what's happened?"

He held out his hand.

"This," he said, and gave me a small brass lion.

I turned it over, wondering what I was supposed to do with it.

"That was on the mantlepiece this morning. I'm sure it was."

"So?"

"At about four o'clock we had a few families in here. It wasn't crowded, but it was busy enough. I was by the till and suddenly there was a sound like a gun being fired. The next moment the earring stand blew up."

I knew David enjoyed drama, but for once his voice was quiet and he sounded confused.

"What do you mean by blew up?"

"It flew off the counter. Earrings everywhere. The stand ended up on the floor. To be honest, it scared the hell out of me. Everyone in the shop was staring."

"What did you do?"

"I pretended I'd done it. I said I must have caught it with my elbow, but I wasn't even close to it."

"And what's it got to do with this?" I asked, looking at the lion.

"When I was clearing up, I found it under the stand. Like I said, it was on the fireplace this morning. That's what the noise was, I'm sure. That thing flew across the room and knocked the stand right off the counter."

"In the middle of the day with people in here?"

"Yes. And there was something else too."

"What?"

"It was warm. The brass lion. It felt warm when I picked it up."

"Did anyone actually see it happen?"

"No, but I know that's what it was."

I ran my fingers over the lion.

"I believe you," I said, "but I don't think anyone else would."

Later that evening, I slipped downstairs, turned off the alarms and let myself into the shop.

"Are you trying to tell us something, Fred?" I said quietly.

I waited, but there was nothing but empty silence. I had brought a packet of felt-tip pens and one of Claire's drawing pads with me. I laid the pad on the floor, then took the lids off the pens and laid them neatly beside it.

"If you want to tell us anything, feel free."

I was locking the shop door when the absurdity of the situation struck me. Had I really left pens and paper for a ghost to write me a message? For a moment, I was tempted to go back and the remove the stationery, but I reset the alarms and went up to bed.

*****

The next morning, David was beside me when I opened the shop.

"It looks like Fred's been busy again," he said when he saw the pad and pens laying on the carpet.

"No, that was me."

He looked at me in surprise.

"I thought he might have wanted to write us a message, but obviously not. It's all exactly where I left it."

"Did you do these?" David asked.

He picked up the pad and held it out to me. Faint lines, finer than a human hair, covered the surface of the paper.

"No. It was blank when I left it."

We stared at the marks. There were curves, lines and squiggles, but nothing that resembled letters.

"What do you make of it?" David asked.

"I have no idea what to make of any of it," I said honestly. "I suppose I was hoping we could have a conversation, but I guess that would have been too easy."

"It was worth trying."

David picked up a pen and drew a cartoon ghost at the bottom of the sheet.

"Be careful. Fred might think you're teasing him." I smiled.

David drew a human figure beside the ghost. "Leave the stuff again tonight. If he doesn't want to write he might have a go at drawing."

After that, I left pens and a pad of paper in the shop every night, but there were never any more marks.

*****

"This morning was the third day in a row that things have been moved in the shop," I told Bob the next day. I felt he ought to know what was happening.

"And there was something weird yesterday," I went on when he didn't answer me. "David said that an old lady picked up one of the brass candlesticks from the mantlepiece and dropped it. She apologised, but she said it had made her jump because it was hot."

Bob looked at me and raised an eyebrow.

"David said he went straight across and picked it up and she was right. It was definitely warm."

"Did you speak to the woman?" Bob asked.

"No. I wasn't there."

"Then how do you know David's not exaggerating?"

"I don't, but so many odd things have happened recently it doesn't even seem that strange anymore."

"Are you sure it's not David that's behind this whole thing? Could he be sneaking down early in the morning and messing things about?"

"Why would he?"

"Because he likes the excitement. You know he's desperate to prove there really is a ghost here. It wouldn't be difficult. He's got a key to the shop."

I thought about it for a moment. It was true that David wanted to tell the world about Fred, but I didn't believe he would lie to me. As we were getting ready for bed, I dropped three silver keys on Bob's pillow.

"There, that's all the keys to the shop. I checked before we came up and everything was tidy. Will you come down with me first thing in the morning when I open it?"

"No, you can tell me what's there."

"But I want you to see for yourself. There probably won't be anything, but I want you to see what's going on. Please?"

For a moment, I thought he was going to refuse, but then he shrugged.

"If you insist."

The next morning, I turned off the alarms and waited while Bob unlocked the shop door. I felt sure that Fred would choose today to leave everything untouched. As he pushed the door open, I saw Bob flinch. The floor was covered with brightly coloured balls and the basket they belonged in was tipped upside down. I wanted to say Told You So, but I didn't.

Bob looked slowly around at the chaos.

"There. I see it. Are you happy now?"

I don't know what I had expected, but if I had believed that seeing the mess on the floor would change Bob's attitude, I was wrong.

"Do you want me to help clear it up?" he asked.

"No. I can manage. I just wanted you to see it."

"Well, I have. Now I'd better get on."

"It wasn't me, you know," I said.

"I know that."

He turned and walked away.

I wanted Bob to understand how I felt about Fred, but now it seemed as though a wall had gone up between us. Picking up one of the balls, I threw it across the room as hard as I could.

Chapter 8

One morning Mum rang me from the ticket box.

"There is a person here to see you," she said formally. I could tell from her tone that she was not happy.

"Who is it?"

"He says he's from Torrington Bank."

"Really? I wasn't expecting anyone."

"No. He doesn't have an appointment, but he says he was passing through and thought he would call in."

"I see. I guess you'd better send him up."

A few minutes later, John Forrester arrived in the tearooms. He was short with a neatly trimmed beard and a nervous expression. His dark suit and brief case made him conspicuous among the holidaymakers but I pretended not to notice as he joined the queue at the servery.

When he reached the till, I smiled sweetly at him.

"Can I help you?"

"Yes, please. I'm here to see Mrs Townsend."

I asked Martha to take over from me and ushered the banker through into the office.

"Abbie, can you bring in two mugs of tea, please?" I asked as we passed through the kitchen.

"Okey-dokey," Abbie called after us.

As soon as I closed the office door, John Forrester launched into a prepared speech explaining why James North had asked him to call.

"He wants you to know that he has made this decision with great regret, but he is stepping back from Torrington Bank. He has been contending with a serious health issue recently, and it is no longer possible for him to lead the bank in the way he would wish. As a result, Torrington will not continue as an independent institution. It is going to merge with Parkways Bank."

My face must have shown my shock.

"Are you alright?" he asked.

"Yes, I'm fine. It's come out of the blue, that's all. I hope it's not anything serious? Mr North, I mean."

His hesitation gave me my answer.

"I'm sorry," I said. "This must be a blow to you too."

The tension in his face eased a little.

"Yes, it is. I've been with Torrington since I left school. Mr North has been my mentor."

"He's been good to us too," I said. "He isn't like any of the other bankers I've met."

The door crashed open, and Abbie backed into the room with a mug in each hand.

"D'you want sugar?" she asked. "And we've got some of yesterday's scones left if you want one."

"No, thanks, Abbie, this will be fine."

I waved at a chair.

"Please, sit down, Mr Forrester."

"Thank you, but I'd rather you called me John."

"Of course. I'm Diana... So, what's going to happen?"

"To be honest with you, I don't know yet. It's all happened rather quickly. There will be changes, I'm sure of that, but I can't tell you any more at the moment. We have an executive from Parkways coming to see us on Thursday, so I should find out more then. I'll let you know...."

I nodded and waited for him to continue.

"Mr North was very insistent we keep everyone informed. In fact, it was the last thing he said before he left."

We sipped our tea in silence and my mind went back to the first time I had met Mr North. I hadn't realised it at the time but now I understood that he was the last of his species, a banker who controlled his own bank and took a personal interest in his customers. I knew we would never have had the opportunity to create Silverlands without him.

*****

When the tea rooms were quiet that afternoon, I walked down to the ticket box. Dad had taken Claire and Michael to play on the Pirate Trail, but Lucy was playing with her toys on the carpet.

As I let myself in, she stood up and held out her arms to me.

"Mummy! Mummy!"

I picked her up and gave her a hug.

"How's my little angel? Are you being a good girl?" I asked.

"Good," she said seriously.

Mum was handing out golf clubs, but as soon as she finished, she slid the glass window closed and sat down at her counter.

"I have to talk to Grandma for a while. You can play with your toys, can't you?" I asked Lucy as I lowered her back to the floor. Her bottom lip quivered, but she nodded.

"What did that man want?" Mum asked.

I told her about my conversation with John, and her expression darkened.

"Whichever way you look at it, this is bad news. Parkways didn't want our business when we were setting Silverlands up. I can't see why they would want it now."

"But we were just starting out then. All we had was a lot of dreams and hopes. Now, we've got a business that's up and running."

Mum tried to smile, but her eyes were heavy with worry.

"No, darling. Let's be honest, what we have is a business that's up and struggling."

****

I was in the ticket box with Mum a few days later when John phoned to tell me he had been given the task of transitioning the Torrington Bank accounts to Parkways.

"What does that mean?"

"The short answer is that I have to make sure everything complies with Parkways' policies. It shouldn't make too much difference to you, but it does mean adhering to the original terms."

Alarm bells rang in my head.

"In what way?"

"I'm afraid you won't be able to defer the loan repayments any longer."

It felt as though a bucket of icy water had been dumped on me.

"But why not? We signed all the papers. It's a legal agreement. They can't go back on it now."

"I'm sorry." I could hear the embarrassment in his voice. "It was only a temporary agreement. There's a clause stating it can be ended by either party."

"And Parkways are ending it?" I fought to keep my voice level.

"Yes."

"But why would they do that? Mr North only suggested it because he knew we can't pay the full amount this year. Not with the interest rates as high as they are."

"I'm sorry. I really am..."

I wanted to scream at him, but I knew it wasn't his fault. Instead, I slammed down the phone. It was the politest thing I could manage.

Mum listened in silence while I explained what John had said.

"It's impossible," I wailed. "If we have to make the loan repayments now, we won't have enough left to get through the winter."

"Shh!" Mum hushed me as a family arrived to buy tickets. She smiled brightly until they disappeared through the gate, then turned back to me.

"All we can do is stall for time. If we can get a meeting with someone from Parkways, perhaps we can persuade them to change their mind. Or maybe we'll find a new tenant for the Motor Museum."

"And if we don't?"

"Let's take it a day at a time. It's important we try to stay positive."

I nodded.

"Yes, you're right."

I didn't have anything better to suggest.

*****

As soon as the school holidays ended, our evening functions began again. We were already tired after months with barely a day off, and now we faced even longer hours. I thought back to the spring when we had been full of hope and thought working seven days and four evenings a week was a good idea. We must have been mad.

Despite the long hours, I was glad to be back doing Old Time Music Hall and Medieval Banquets. It was impossible to fret about the future while listening to Clarissa sing or Benedict tell silly stories.

The audiences were always happy, and the laughter spilled over into the kitchen. Our friends Kate and Duncan had enjoyed working in the kitchen earlier in the year, and now they volunteered to help us again.

Even Fred decided to put in an appearance. Well, not an appearance as such, but on the evening of the first Medieval Banquet the connection to the gas supply mysteriously unscrewed itself as Bob tried to serve the first pint.

Fortunately, David was at hand with a spanner to reconnect it.

"I take it Fred's still here then?" Kate giggled.

David told her about the constant disruption in the shop and her eyes opened wide.

"That's awesome! You're so lucky. It must be so much fun to have a ghost!"

That wasn't the way I would have described it.

*****

"I explained the circumstances but I couldn't get them to budge." John's voice was crackly on the line. "I told them you wanted to meet directly but they insisted everything has to be channelled through me. And I'm afraid there's more."

"Such as?"

"They want you to submit weekly breakdowns showing all your incomings and expenditure."

I groaned inwardly.

Our company books were handwritten in paper ledgers. Typing up accounts to send by post each week would be a lot of extra work, but I was too tired to argue.

It was nine o'clock in the morning and the Medieval Banquet the night before had been particularly rowdy. I was sitting in the office and held the receiver away as I stifled a yawn.

"And they asked me to remind you that this quarter's payment is due next week."

We had never been late with a payment, and the reminder irritated me.

"I'm afraid that's not convenient. We're going to pay the baker and the greengrocer this time. Maybe it will be Parkways' turn next quarter," I said.

"Do you want me to tell them that?"

"Please do. You can use more colourful language if you like. Let them know how I really feel."

John laughed, and I felt better.

"I really am sorry," he said again.

I waited until we closed that afternoon to tell Mum about the extra paperwork. When she arrived in the servery, I poured two cups of tea and sat down beside her.

"I'm afraid I've got a bit of bad news," I said.

"Have you? That's funny. So have I."

"Go on. You first."

She sighed and patted my arm as she used to do when I was little.

"Some of the kids playing crazy golf had a radio with them. I caught the news headlines before they turned it off."

"What was it?" I asked.

"The bank rate. They're putting it up again. Now, what were you going to say?"

CHAPTER 8

*****

The thump was loud enough to make me jump.

We had finished clearing up after a Jazz Night and I had gone upstairs to relieve Mum who was babysitting the girls. Bob was still downstairs letting Dino out for his last run.

"What on earth was that?" Mum asked.

I shook my head.

"No idea."

The sound had come from directly beneath us, which meant it must have been in the shop.

"Stay here, I'll go and see," I said, but Mum grabbed my hand.

"Get Bob to go with you. That sounded like something heavy."

We listened for a moment, but there was no other sound. Neither of us used the word Burglar, but it hung in the air between us.

"Don't worry, I'll be careful," I said and dropped the latch on the flat door as I went out.

Bob and Dino were coming along the corridor as I got to the bottom of the stairs.

"Did you hear anything?" I asked.

"No. Why?"

"There was a big crash a few minutes ago. It came from the shop."

"Really? We'd better take a look."

I always carried my set of keys with me. It was a single ring with at least twenty different keys that I wore on a long leather cord. Usually I kept it tied to my belt and tucked into a pocket, but now it was hanging around my neck. There were so many doors, cupboards and switches that needed to be locked and unlocked every day I felt lost without it.

Slipping the cord over my head, I unlocked the shop door and opened it a fraction. Bob and I exchanged glances as we listened, but all was silent inside.

"Stay here," Bob said and pushed the door open. I peered into the gloom, my heart thumping, but as he switched the lights on everything appeared normal.

Dino nosed around the room, and I realised I was holding my breath. I let it out in a rush.

"What do you think it was?" I asked.

"No idea. Has anything fallen over?"

We searched the floor, looking for anything that might have caused the thump, but there was nothing.

"Everything's fine," Bob said at last. "Let's go to bed."

As I turned towards the door my eyes fixed on the mantlepiece. There was an empty space on the shelf.

"The jug, the big one… it's not there."

Bob frowned.

"Could David have sold it?"

"No. He would have said. We've had that jug since we were in the Barn in Torquay. If he'd sold it, he would definitely have told me."

"Then maybe someone stole it."

"No. It was there earlier, when we locked up. I'm sure it was."

"Let's not worry now. We can think about it in the morning," Bob said, but I was in no mood to let it go.

"It has to be here somewhere," I insisted.

"But we've searched the floor already. If it fell off the shelf, we would have found it."

"I heard the crash. I know it's here."

I stood by the fireplace and looked around me, imagining the heavy brass jug flying across the room. If it had moved outwards, it would have hit the counter and knocked the displays over, but nothing had been disturbed. There was only one other possibility.

"What are you doing?" Bob asked as I dragged a stool from beside the till.

The whole of the counter was covered by a wooden canopy. Climbing onto the stool, I balanced on tiptoe to peer over the top.

"Don't be ridiculous, it can't be up there," Bob said, but as I peered, I saw a dark shape against the dust. Reaching out, my fingertips touched smooth metal.

"Got it!"

Bob stared up in disbelief.

"What are you suggesting?" he demanded. "That a brass jug flew up there by itself?"

"I'm not suggesting anything. The room was locked. I heard a crash and the jug is up here. Fact."

"But it's not possible."

"I know. I know it's not possible, and I know you don't like this stuff, but it's happening."

"No. There has to be a sensible explanation."

I lifted the jug down and dusted it off with my sleeve.

"If there is an explanation, I'd love to hear it. This jug got up there somehow, and it didn't have any help from a human being."

"No," Bob said stubbornly. "It can't have."

Bob's absolute refusal to believe what was happening baffled me. I didn't have any explanation that made sense, but I didn't see the point in denying things that I could see with my own eyes.

"It must have been David," Bob said as he got dressed the next morning. "He was still in the kitchen when I took Dino down."

"But why would he do it?"

"I've no idea, but it must have been him."

"You can't accuse someone without any..."

"I'm not accusing him. It's a simple deduction. Everyone else was upstairs. He's the only possibility."

"Are you going to ask him about it?"

"What good would that do? He'd only deny it."

I wanted to argue, but I knew there was no point.

*****

A few days later David and I opened the shop as usual.

"Bloody hell!" David gasped.

The shelves above the mantelpiece were almost empty. Candlesticks, horse brasses, pots and ornaments lay scattered across the carpet. Baskets of soft toys had been overturned and books were dumped in piles everywhere.

We tiptoed around in silence. I had become accustomed to Fred's antics, but the scale of the activity took my breath away.

David bent down and picked something up from the floor.

"Oh my God! Look at this!"

He was holding a poker. At least, it had been a poker. Now it was bent into a twisted corkscrew.

I ran a finger around the curves. The main shaft was about a centimetre in diameter. I tried to straighten one of the kinks, but I couldn't even flex it.

"Here, let me."

David grasped the poker in both hands and strained until his face went red.

"That's incredible," he gasped. "How much force did it take to bend it like that?"

I turned around and saw Bob standing in the doorway.

"Come and look," I said, but he didn't move.

"Please. You have to see this."

Reluctantly, Bob picked a way through the chaos.

"Try and bend it," David said excitedly as he handed him the poker.

Bob surveyed the object from every angle before grasping the ends and giving it a sharp twist.

"Wow. That really is solid," he admitted.

"What's going on?" Dad asked as he joined us. I grabbed the poker from Bob and held it out to him.

"Look at this. It's weird, isn't it?"

"Oh my God! There's another one!" David pulled another poker from under a pile of toys. "Look. This one's broken."

The pokers consisted of a decorative head fixed to a brass shaft. The one in David's hand had no head.

"Where's the rest of it?" I asked.

David burrowed beneath the fluffy toys and pulled out a head in the shape of a fox.

"Here."

Dad was still trying out the first poker.

"I don't understand what's happened to it," he said. "Is there another one of these?"

"Yes, I think so. There should still be a few under the counter."

David rummaged through a box and handed Dad an untouched poker.

"Thanks. I want to test something. I'll be in my workshop if you need me."

As Dad left, David held his arms wide.

"Seriously, how much more evidence do we need? This place is trashed. Look at it. We should be calling the papers."

I glared at him.

"We've already talked about this."

"No, we haven't! Not properly. Think of the publicity. This could get us into the nationals. How many visitors would it attract?"

The thought of photographers flashing cameras everywhere and reporters grilling us made me queasy.

"But they'd be the wrong people," I protested. "Our visitors are families. They don't want to see this."

"Right now, we need every penny we can get. If we can use this to bring in more people, we'd be mad not to do it."

"No!" My voice sounded panicky, even to me. "It wouldn't work. No one would believe us."

But David wasn't giving in.

"You don't know that!" He snapped. "We've got nothing to hide. They could set up vigils. Have testing equipment. Do it properly..."

"This isn't ghostbusters!" I yelled. "You can't measure this stuff! What if Fred doesn't like it? What would happen then?"

"You're nuts, do you know that?" David yelled back.

Bob looked at his watch.

"I hate to interrupt," he said calmly, "but do you realise we're opening in less than ten minutes?"

*****

I tried to smile at the customers, but I was in a foul mood for the rest of the morning. Life was spiralling out of my control. After all the work of the last years, our future was being shaped by outside forces. It didn't matter how hard we worked, we couldn't change the bank rate or the rate of inflation. And I certainly couldn't stop Fred attracting attention to himself.

For a control freak like me, it was a hard pill to swallow.

At lunchtime, Dad brought Lucy into the kitchen and made her sandwiches.

I grabbed my daughter and hugged her tight. Her smile and infectious giggles always made me feel better.

"Here you are, Lucy." Dad put a plate of food on the table and pulled out a stool. "Can you sit up here like a big girl?"

Lucy nodded and shrieked with delight as Dad swung her high into the air before sitting her on the stool.

As she bit into the sandwich, Dad turned to me.

"Here, what do you make of this?" he asked, holding out the poker he had taken from the shop. It was no longer straight but had been bent into a right angle.

"Notice anything?"

"It's heavy," I said blankly.

"Yes, but that's not the point."

He mimed bending it.

"I've had a lot of practice with metal rods over the years, but this one is too heavy to bend with my hands. The only way I could make an impression on it was by putting it in the vice and taking a swing at it with a hammer."

He pointed to marks on the brass.

"You see these? That's where it was held in the vice. And these? They were made by the hammer. And what do you notice about the shape?"

"It's very square. It's only one angle, not a lot of curves and twists like the other poker."

"Exactly! All I could do was bend it where it was held in the vice. I tried twisting it with a pair of pliers but that just cut grooves into the surface."

"So, what does it mean?"

"I wish I knew. Maybe, if the poker was heated in a furnace, it might be possible to twist it like that, but I can't see any way that it could have happened in the middle of the shop."

That evening, I repeated the conversation to Bob.

"Do you still think it was David?" I asked.

"I never said he bent the poker."

"Then you do admit there's something going on?"

"Of course, I do," Bob rounded on me. "I'm not an idiot! Things have been happening ever since we arrived. There's no denying that. What I can't accept is that there is any sort of intelligence behind them. Things happen. That doesn't mean something is making them happen."

I didn't answer him. There wasn't any point.

*****

Our visitor numbers had tumbled since the beginning of September and as I wasn't needed in the kitchen except at lunchtimes, I spent more time in the office working on our accounts and the weekly reports for Parkways.

There was no hiding the fact that the figures were poor. Our income for the year was lower than we had anticipated, and our expenses had gone through the roof since inflation and the bank rate soared.

My hopes rested on John. He had agreed to speak to Parkways on our behalf. If he could persuade them to honour the agreement we had made with Mr North, and we had a reasonable Christmas season, we should be able to cover our expenses until the next spring.

But if not...

I didn't want to think about it. None of us had come up with a Plan B. The loss of the Motor Museum had left a huge hole in our finances and, despite all our efforts, our future hung in the balance.

I was finding it extremely difficult to go on as normal while waiting to hear back from John. Every time the phone rang, my heart pounded, but when he called, I didn't need to hear his words to know the answer.

"Good morning, Silverlands. How can I help you?" I recited.

There was a tiny pause.

"John, is that you?"

"Yes..."

His voice was expressionless, and my hopes died.

"They said no, didn't they?"

"I'm sorry...."

*****

Mum had been complaining of toothache for some time, but had hoped to leave it until the end of September before visiting a dentist. Now, as her symptoms worsened, she decided she couldn't wait any longer. Luckily, when she phoned the surgery, she was offered an emergency appointment.

It was a Tuesday morning, and we assured Mum that we could manage without her. As I took her place in the ticket box, I hoped it was true. Phil was going to help Martha and Abbie in the kitchen, and it seemed unlikely we would have to deal with a crowd of customers.

As Dad drove Mum to Exeter, I decided to enjoy the novelty of being in the ticket box. Scruffy was curled up asleep at my feet and Lucy sat at the counter behind me, drawing. I had nothing to do but watch the first golden leaves of the season fluttering to the ground outside.

By eleven o'clock, I had sold tickets to a selection of senior citizens and a young family with twin toddlers. I was reading a book to Lucy when I heard voices approaching.

A row of cars had driven up to the car park a few minutes earlier, and I was delighted to see a group of people heading back down the hill. I put on a welcoming smile and waited for them to arrive at the ticket box.

A large black-haired man took control.

"Stand here, Sara. Keep hold of the kids. No one's going in until I've got the tickets." His voice was loud and harsh.

Another trio ambled down the hill, and the man lined them up behind the first arrivals.

"Stay where you are, won't be long now. We're just waiting for Mandy and Joe. Is that right?"

There was a murmur of agreement and a pair of lanky teenagers wandered across.

"Hurry up, you two, or you'll have to pay for yourselves."

The man turned to me and pulled a roll of notes out of his pocket.

"Right then. That will be ten adults and nine children. What time does the restaurant open?"

"It will be open from one o'clock but the tearooms are open all day." I smiled.

"Right. We'll start there. I'll need a receipt."

"Yes, no problem," I said and felt under the counter for the book. I filled in a page and tore it off.

"There you go, sir."

The man took the receipt without looking at me.

"Right you lot, off you go," he said as he held the gate open.

Once they had gone, I relaxed. A blackbird sang nearby, and I spotted a bunch of autumn crocuses flowering on the grass verge opposite. I could see why Mum liked it here.

At lunchtime Bob came down so I could have a quick break.

"How's it going?" I asked him as he picked Lucy up and cuddled her.

"Not bad. There's one big, rowdy family in, but no problems. You won't be long, will you?"

I promised I would be back soon and hurried up to the house. Phil and Abbie were rushing around in the kitchen preparing a row of steak pies and lasagnes.

"Are they all for one big family?" I asked.

"Yes. How did you know?"

"Just a guess," I smiled as I made a sandwich for Lucy and grabbed a packet of crisps and some flapjack for myself before heading back to the ticket box.

"Are you sure you'll be OK?" Bob asked as I settled myself back on the stool. "I'd stay longer, but I need to get back for Zac's last show."

"Don't worry about me. This is the most relaxing day I've had in months."

I watched Bob stroll back to the house and was still admiring the view ten minutes later when I saw him emerge with Zac and introduced the show on the lawn. The crowd was small, but I could make out a smattering of applause. Even at this distance, I recognised the harsh laugh of the black-haired man.

Dad returned with Mum halfway through the afternoon. I could see she was pale as I opened the gate and let the car through.

"I'm glad I took her up," Dad told me. "It was an abscess. The dentist had to drain it."

"That's horrible," I grimaced. "How are you feeling?"

"I'll be fine by tomorrow," Mum whispered.

"Good. Why don't you go and put your feet up?"

"That's what I suggested," Dad said. "You're all right there, aren't you?"

"Yes, no problem. See you later."

As the afternoon went on, I handed out golf sticks, giant draughts pieces and sold a few ice creams. Then I sat back and waved at smiling families as they left.

"Granddad!" Lucy squealed as Dad appeared at the window.

"Mum's having a sleep," he told me as I let him into the ticket box. "I thought my little friend here might be getting bored. Shall I take her out for a bit?"

"Do you want to go with Granddad?" I asked Lucy.

"Can we see the piggies?" She asked excitedly.

"Go on then, as you've been such a good girl."

It was nearly closing time when I saw the black-haired man and his family approaching. I was ready to wave, but instead of walking past, the group stopped in front of me.

"Can I help you?" I asked.

"Yes." The man put his hands on the counter and leaned forward until his breath steamed the glass. "You can give us our money back."

For a moment I thought he was joking, then I saw the sneer on the face of the woman behind him.

"Why would I do that?" I asked.

"Because it's crap. It's a ripoff. There's nothing here worth paying for, is there?"

The rest of the family jeered at me as he slapped his receipt on the counter. Then he pulled out a second receipt, and I recognised Phil's handwriting.

"And we'll have that back too. The food was shit. You should be ashamed of yourself."

He lowered his head again.

"Go on then. Where's my money?"

"No."

The man's eyes bored into mine, but I remembered Bob repeating a warning he had been given at a DATA meeting earlier in the year. A warning about a group of families that spent whole days at attractions then demanded their money back when it was time to leave.

I hadn't paid much attention at the time. I hadn't thought it would ever happen to us.

"It's not worth getting into a fight with an unhappy customer," Bob had said. "Give them their money back and let them go. Concentrate on the happy ones."

But the happy customers had all gone home. And I was damned if I was going to give this man his money back.

"What did you say?" he demanded.

"I said no. If you'd come back at lunchtime and said you didn't like it here, I would have been happy to reimburse you, but you've been here for nearly six hours. You must have found something to entertain you."

The man's vocabulary was limited, but his volume was impressive. I braced myself as a torrent of obscenities and spittle hit the glass partition.

Scruffy jumped to his feet. I put a hand on his head, but he growled loudly.

I waited until the man drew breath.

"Have you finished?"

He had not. A fresh outburst followed.

"Are you going to give me my money back or not?" The man roared, his face scarlet.

"No."

I jerked backwards as he slammed his fist down on the counter.

Scruffy was up in a moment, his paws on the edge of the counter, his barks rasping through my ear.

The man swung around as if remembering his family were still behind him.

"What the fuck are you lot looking at?" he screamed. "Get the cars down here!"

The adults gathered the children and hurried away until only the man and a lanky teenager remained.

"You're going to regret this!" He kicked the front of the ticket box.

At once, Scruffy exploded against the window, barking frantically. I pulled at his collar but he was enraged, his eyes wide, teeth bared.

"I'm going to hurt you, little girl!" The man yelled above the racket. "And who's going to stop me? That stinking mutt? Pay up, or I'll smash the door down, and take everything you've got!"

Sweat slid down my back.

"If you don't leave now, I'm calling the police."

"And how long will they take to get here?" he sneered. "Ten minutes? Fifteen? What do you think I can do by then?"

Scruffy was howling now. I picked up the phone and dialled.

"This is your last chance," the man thundered.

Suddenly, he turned to the teenager hovering behind him.

"Have you got any petrol with you?"

"Sure..."

"Bring it here. Now!"

As the youth ran off towards the car park, a voice answered my call.

"I need the police. A man's threatening me."

Fear fogged my brain, and I struggled to hear the operator's questions.

"My address? Yes..."

Sensing my distress, the man's face twisted into a sneer.

"Hot and bothered, are you? I'll bet you've wet yourself already!"

Suddenly my fear gave way to anger.

"He's standing right in front of me," I said into the phone. "About six feet tall, overweight, shoulder-length, greasy black hair..."

"Give me the money!" the man bellowed.

Scruffy erupted again, and I had to quieten him before I could go on.

"Yes, he's wearing a signet ring on his left hand and there's a small tattoo of a blue rose on his right hand."

I lowered the phone and leaned forward.

"Why don't you make it easy for them and give me your name?"

The man's eyes glittered, and he smashed his fist straight into the glass inches from my face. Instinctively, I screwed my eyes shut, expecting to be covered by flying fragments, but the glass held.

The man leaped back clutching his fist and Scruffy's teeth flashed as he threw himself against the window.

"What's happening? Are you still there…?" I picked up the receiver. I hadn't realised I'd dropped it.

"Hello?"

"A car's on the way. Our officers will be with you very soon."

Suddenly, I heard more barking. Dino and Ossie were charging along the road from the house, their tongues lolling, their tails flying out behind them.

A horn tooted as the teenager pulled up by the gate. The man glanced at the dogs racing towards him, then turned and ran to the car.

"I'll be back! I know where you live!" he shouted over his shoulder as he pulled open the door and climbed in.

Dino and Ossie reached the gate and bounced their paws on to the top bar, barking frantically as the car roared off.

I buried my head in my hands.

I was still sitting there, weeping, when Bob opened the door.

"Are you all right?" he asked. "I thought you'd be up by now."

"I'm fine," I sniffed. "Nothing to worry about. I'm just waiting for the police."

It took an hour to answer all the questions and make my statement. I didn't think I had much to say, but the police went over and over every detail.

"They said the descriptions matched a family they're looking for already," I told Bob later.

"I still don't understand why you didn't call me," he grumbled. "We had no idea what was happening. What's the point of having a phone if you don't use it?"

"I know. I'm sorry."

I lay in bed that night listening to the wind in the trees. I knew the chances of the man coming back were negligible. I kept reminding myself that we had burglar alarms and fire detectors all over the house. Bob was beside me and I knew I was safe, but it was hours before I finally closed my eyes and slept.

*****

Since Parkways had terminated the agreement we had signed with James North, the future looked bleak.

Even with the most optimistic projections for the Christmas opening, it was going to be touch and go whether we could make enough to cover the bank repayments until the following spring.

We booked radio adverts to boost the rest of our functions and Bob redoubled his efforts visiting caravan parks. We needed every penny we could get.

Mum and I joked that we were squirrels trying to stock up enough nuts for the coming winter. We tried to be cheerful, but it was hard to remain positive.

Wednesday, Sixteenth of September, began in the same way as every other day. I drove Claire and Michael to school, cleaned the house, checked the exhibitions and started work in the kitchen.

Recently I had taken to keeping a radio by the sink and turned it on to catch the news. I told myself I was waiting to hear the economy had turned a corner and things were about to improve.

I hadn't been paying much attention to world events, but I knew there was disquiet about the French referendum on ratifying the Maastricht Treaty while the British would not be allowed to vote.

Even in the early nineties, there was growing opposition to John Major's

European dream. Joining the ERM was supposed to have reduced inflation and brought about financial stability. In practice, it had caused an economic slowdown and left the pound vulnerable to City speculators.

What I didn't know was that the speculators, led by George Soros, were about to make their move.

At lunchtime, the headlines announced that the chancellor, Norman Lamont, had increased the bank interest rate from ten to twelve percent. I was horrified. It was a massive increase and an equally massive blow to our hopes.

At the end of the afternoon, Mum looked depressed as she flopped down on the window seat.

"You've heard about the increase, then," I said.

"Yes, both of them," she sighed.

"Both?"

"Didn't you know? The rate's gone up again. It's fifteen percent now."

I was stunned. If the bank rate had really risen that much it meant our repayments would go up by nearly fifty percent.

Surely it couldn't be true?

It was years before I read a full account of what happened that day. When I did, I discovered that Soros had found a loophole in the financial regulations that allowed him to make vast profits by selling sterling he didn't own.

By the time the stock market closed, Soros had racked up a personal fortune of over a billion pounds and earned himself the nickname "The man who broke the Bank of England."

That evening, John Major threw in the towel, and Britain crashed out of the ERM.

Later, when the significance of the day was understood, it became known as Black Wednesday. At the time, all I knew was that our dreams were over.

*****

With interest rates at fifteen percent, there was no hope of reaching our goals. Even if the Christmas season went well and we had functions every night, we would not have enough money to cover our repayments until the spring. Without support from the bank, we could not go on.

The others joined Mum and me in the tearooms, and we explained the significance of what had happened. There were no tears. We were all too tired for dramatics. Instead, we took comfort from being together.

We had worked so hard for so long, and now it seemed everything had been in vain. My mind drifted back to the many obstacles we had faced and the battles we had fought.

It was Mum who dragged us back to the present.

"It's no good feeling sorry for ourselves," she said. "We knew from the beginning this was a gamble. We can't change what's happened."

She looked around, and we all nodded our agreement, but no one was thinking clearly. It felt as though the floor had collapsed beneath our feet.

All I wanted to do was sit and stare into space. My mind was numb and my heart thumped like a hammer. I longed to be still and silent and alone.... but that was not possible.

Instead, I cleared the kitchen, fed the children and prepared for a medieval banquet.

Chapter 9

Silverlands closed at the end of September.

Despite everything that was stacked against us, we weren't ready to give in without a fight. We had overcome so many obstacles to get this far and we clung to the hope there might yet be a way to survive the winter and open again the following spring.

Our first thought was to raise a mortgage on the property but we soon discovered we couldn't do so without Parkways' permission, which they refused to give.

To my surprise, John became our unofficial adviser. He passed Silverlands on the dual carriageway each day and often called in for a chat on his way home. I trusted him to keep our secrets, and he began starting his sentences with - "Technically, as I work for the bank, I shouldn't be telling you this, but..."

It was good to have him as an ally.

One evening, after the children were settled in bed, the family gathered together.

Mum spoke first.

"We have some serious decisions to make. As far as I can see, our only real chance is to bring in a partner to help finance the business. If not, we're going to have to make a clean break and sell up. It won't be easy, whatever we decide, but if we want to make the decision ourselves, we need to do it soon, and not let the bank take the choice away from us."

We all nodded.

"John told me Parkways wants to liquify some of its assets," I said.

"And what does that mean in English?" David asked.

"I think he was talking about us. They see us as a bad risk. They want to get their money back so they can invest in something more profitable."

"Then why did they take us on in the first place?" Phil asked.

"Because they're asset-strippers," Dad said bluntly. "They never intended to keep the business running."

"You don't know that," David protested.

"But it's obvious, isn't it? How difficult was it to find a bank that would lend to us in the first place? I can't imagine Parkways offered Torrington much for our account. I'm guessing they got it for a pittance, but now, if they can get the debt repaid in full by forcing us to sell up, they'll make a healthy profit."

"But that's immoral!" David burst out. "It shouldn't be allowed!"

"Calm down." Mum frowned at him. "Getting upset isn't going to change anything. We have to concentrate on what we can do."

Bob leaned forward. "Your Mum's right. We need to find a partner," he said earnestly.

"But is that even possible?" I asked.

"I don't see why not. There must be someone with enough vision to see the possibilities of what we have here. All we have to do is find them."

*****

Liza finally abandoned her attempts to train Luna to work with the Indian Runner ducks.

"I've tried, I really have," she told me. "It's frustrating, because Luna can do it. She can drive the ducks right around the course and make them go wherever I want them to go. The problem is, she's not a performer."

We were standing on the tea lawn and Luna peered at me from behind Liza's legs.

"I've tried so hard to encourage her. I give her lots of praise and treats. I've done everything I can to build her confidence, but it's no use. She just stands there looking as though she's been beaten. It's a shame, but either a dog has star quality or it doesn't."

"What are you going to do?" I asked.

"She's got a lovely nature. She's very sweet, very gentle, so I'm giving her to Penny. They're already good friends and I know Penny will spoil her and take her for lots of walks."

I smiled.

"That's a good plan, they suit each other, but what about you?"

Liza wiped away a tear.

"That's what I wanted to talk to you about. I'm afraid Roly can't manage another season. It wouldn't be fair on him. It's been wonderful being here. Silverlands has been our home, but it's time for us to leave."

I felt a lump in my throat and pretended to cough.

"I'm sorry to hear that. Where will you go?"

"Back to Southampton. Roly has given me so much. There'll never be another dog like him. Now, I have to put him first. I can do children's parties to pay for his retirement and we can still enjoy a few more years together."

We invited Liza and Roly over for a last meal before they left. Bob brought out a bottle of his favourite wine and Liza told us about her early life as a dancer.

"Do you know I used to dance for the Prince of Bahrain?" she asked.

"Really?"

"Yes. There were three of us, we had our own dance troupe. The Prince saw us dance in London once and he was so impressed he invited us out to his palace to dance for him on his birthday."

"All the way to Bahrain?" Bob asked.

"Yes. It was amazing. He sent one of his planes for us. It wasn't very big, but it was really swanky and the palace was incredible."

"That must have been an experience."

"Yes. It was surreal. The Prince said I was his favourite."

"I'm sure you were."

Liza leaned forward and began swaying her shoulders from side to side.

"Do you know why I was his favourite?"

"No."

"Because I could do something for him that none of the others could manage..."

Bob's eyes opened wide.

"And what was that?" he asked.

Liza smiled dreamily as she remembered.

"I could make my nipple tassels go round in different directions."

A few days later, we waved goodbye as Liza and Roly drove off. We were sorry to see them go.

*****

Bob and I devoted ourselves to the search for an investor. We contacted anyone we could think of that might be able to put us in touch with a financier or an eccentric sponsor, but every lead ended in disappointment.

At last we resigned ourselves to the inevitable.

"This isn't going to work, is it?" David asked as yet another potential investor turned us down. "We might as well admit it. We should be looking for a buyer."

"There's no reason why we can't do both. We can put the place up for sale and still keep looking for an investor," Dad said.

"I guess so," I agreed, "after all, nothing's definite until it's actually signed, is it?"

One afternoon, John called in. I could tell he was uncomfortable.

"What is it?" I asked as I poured him a cup of tea.

"I've been asked to have a word with you about your account."

"Why? What's wrong?"

"I believe you've been withdrawing money."

For a moment I couldn't think what he was referring to. Then I remembered.

"I sent some cheques out to pay our suppliers, if that's what you mean."

"I'm supposed to remind you that the bank has first priority over money being taken from your account."

"What do you mean? How are we supposed to operate if we can't pay our suppliers?"

John didn't meet my eyes. Instead, he stared out of the window as he spoke.

"Parkways are under the impression that you've ceased trading."

"Only for the summer," I protested. "This is a seasonal business. We'll be opening again for Christmas."

"I'm afraid the bank feels that in the current circumstances you may not be able to trade profitably. They feel they can't take the risk."

"That's ridiculous! They can't stop us opening!"

"No, they can't stop you opening, but they can freeze your account."

"You're joking!"

"I'm sorry. It's not my decision."

I wanted to scream, but I knew it wasn't his fault.

"There's nothing we can do to stop them, is there?"

"No, I'm afraid not," he said.

*****

"We'd already decided to put Silverlands up for sale, so I don't suppose it makes that much difference," David said sadly.

"Yes, it does," I objected. "We wanted to sell the business as a going concern. That's very different to selling it as something that's already failed. It's so..."

"Let's wait and see what the estate agents say, shall we?" Bob interrupted me.

We had already spoken to several agencies, and they all agreed that marketing the business openly would be a bad move.

"The truth is, there will only be a few potential buyers for a business of this sort. I would advise you to allow us to approach interested parties directly," one agent told us.

Each agency carried out a separate valuation and sent us a letter explaining how they would handle marketing Silverlands. The experience was immensely depressing, especially the fact the valuations were considerably less than the surveyor's report of three months ago.

"How can the value have dropped so much?" I asked. "I know inflation's high, but surely it can't have had that much effect."

"Don't forget we're in the middle of a housing slump and it's getting worse every day," David muttered.

"Thank you. That's just what I needed to hear," I muttered back.

Eventually, we chose an estate agent and provided them with a wealth of information and ground plans.

"Do you have any idea how long it will take to find a buyer?" I asked when the agent called in with the papers for us to sign.

"Not really," the man replied cheerfully. "That's what I love about this business. It's completely unpredictable. We may find the perfect buyer for you on day one, or it may take years."

"Wonderful," I sighed.

*****

"What are we going to do about the functions we've got booked?" I asked Mum. "We could really use the money and I don't want to let people down."

"We go ahead, of course. There's no reason not to."

"But the bank's frozen our account."

"Then we'll have to use our personal accounts, won't we? The bank doesn't own us, you know."

She was right. I have always been an extremely law-abiding person, but suddenly I wanted to rebel. The bank had proved it had no loyalty to us. It was time to fight for ourselves.

I waited until lunchtime when we were all together.

"I've been thinking. If we're going ahead with the functions, is there any reason why we can't still open for Christmas? There's plenty of stock left in the shop. If it starts to look empty, we can take out a few display stands."

"But we'll have to pay the baker and greengrocer what we owe them," David pointed out.

I nodded.

"I've been feeling guilty about them anyway. I'm sure they're having as difficult a time as we are."

"I'm sure a lot of local businesses are struggling," Bob agreed. "It's always the small traders that get hit first."

"I've been thinking, there must be lots of things tucked away that we don't need any more. Things we collected but never used in any of the exhibitions."

"Loads," David agreed. "There are boxes full of stuff in the attic and in the rooms at the end of the dormitory wing. Some of them have been there since we moved in."

"Do you think there's anything we could sell?"

"Possibly. Are you thinking of Christmas?"

"Yes, and the functions. If we raise enough to pay the bills ourselves the bank can't stop us going ahead, can they?"

"Good point. I'll see what I can find."

David knew every auction house in Devon, and we began entering items into every sale. It was hard to part with things we had owned for years, but I told myself there was no point in leaving them tucked away in boxes. Far better they go to new homes.

Within weeks, we had raised enough to pay the bills of most of our local suppliers and placed orders for the first function.

We decided we would only open from Thursday to Sunday each week from the beginning of December until Christmas Eve.

"What are we going to do if the bank finds out?" David asked.

"Let's not think about that unless it happens," I said.

"OK. Well, if we're going to open again, I've got another suggestion. I have a friend who runs discos. He's got all the equipment and a great personality, but he's fed up of working through to the early hours every morning. Especially now his wife's expecting."

"Go on."

"He's offered to set up an under 18's disco here once a week. It would only run until ten o'clock and we would split the entrance money fifty-fifty."

"But do you think any kids would come?" I asked.

"Dale seems to think so. He lives in Chudleigh and he says there's nothing for kids to do in the evenings. It wouldn't cost us anything. We'd just have to be around to make sure it all ran smoothly and we could sell drinks and sweets if we wanted to."

I thought about it for a moment.

"Why not? What have we got to lose?"

*****

Dale arrived the following Friday. He parked his van outside the restaurant and started unloading huge black speakers and crates of equipment.

"Are you sure he knows what he's doing?" I asked, but David only laughed.

"I told you. He's a professional."

I watched as Dale struggled through the French windows carrying a massive lighting bar. I guessed he was in his thirties, but he already sported a pot-belly and sweat ran down his face.

"Do you really think any kids are going to turn up?" I asked.

"Yes, they'll all want to belong to the Silverlands Club."

"The what?"

"Didn't I tell you? I thought it would be best to make it a club. That way, the parents have to sign the children in when they arrive and leave a phone number so we can contact them if there's a problem."

"That's a good plan," I admitted. "You'll need a notebook to write it all down."

"I'm ahead of you. Look."

A leather bag hung from his shoulder. Pulling it open, he showed me a large notebook and an ink pad and stamp.

"When the kids arrive, you take the money and sign them up as club members. I'll stamp their hands. That way we'll know who's paid."

"You really have thought this out, haven't you?" I grinned.

The first child arrived on the dot of seven thirty. While his mother filled in the membership form, a car pulled up outside and four more children climbed out. I started to feel hopeful.

It was thirty minutes before my optimism faded.

"That's the lot, isn't it?" I asked as we watched the five children running around in circles chasing the lights the glitter ball threw across the carpet.

"Looks like it," David sighed. "Dale said it might take a couple of weeks to build up."

I bit my tongue.

"At least it's not costing us anything," I reminded myself.

"They're younger than I expected," David said. "I thought they'd be sixteen and seventeen-year-olds."

I looked at the children and guessed they were all about eleven.

"They are quite little, aren't they?"

"Mummy!"

I was surprised to find Claire behind me.

"What are you doing here?"

"Daddy said we could come to the disco."

"There's plenty of room." Bob smiled as he arrived with Michael and Lucy. "I thought they might as well join in."

The children loved having their own private disco. Even Lucy stayed on the dancefloor all evening, bobbing and twisting to the music. And David was right about Dale. He was extremely good with kids, chatting and telling jokes as well as demonstrating dance moves.

The music was suitably deafening and the flashing lights were hypnotic as they drove all thought of our problems from my mind.

"It's the Birdie Song!" Claire shouted above the music.

"You can join in, Auntie Di." Michael grabbed my hand and dragged me to the middle of the floor. Lucy had already tucked her hands under her armpits and was waving her elbows around like chicken wings.

Claire held up her hands, snapping her fingers.

"With a little bit of this and a little bit of that..." she sang.

"...and shake your bum," I joined in.

Looking up, I caught Bob's eye, and we both burst out laughing.

At the end of the evening, I split the proceeds with Dale.

"Is that going to cover your petrol for driving here?" I asked him.

"Probably not," he admitted, "but the kids loved it. You saw how much fun they had. If they all go to school on Monday and tell their friends how great it was, we could be in business."

I admired his optimism.

The following week three new members turned up for the disco.

"Is this really worth the effort?" I asked Bob as we cleared the sweet counter afterwards.

"Not really, but you have to admit it's fun," he smiled.

To my surprise, Dale was right. Word spread about the disco and within weeks the Silverlands Club had over one hundred members.

As the number of children increased, the average age went up and we found teenagers needed a lot more supervision than the youngsters. We were grateful when Kate and Duncan volunteered to come along and help each week.

One evening I was surprised to find a uniformed police constable standing at the door watching the crowd of dancing children.

"Can I help you?" I asked.

"You already have," he replied. "I thought I'd come over and introduce myself. I've been wondering why Friday nights have been so quiet lately. I'm PC Ed McGinty, by the way."

A few of the teenagers stared across, and the policeman raised a hand and waved at them.

"You know the kids?"

"I certainly do. You've got most of my best customers in here."

"Really? What does that mean?"

"It means I'm a happy man. There's a lot less graffiti and broken windows in Chudleigh on the nights when they're all here with you."

"I see."

He squinted across the room, past the flashing lights.

"Have you had many problems so far?"

"No. Nothing yet. Some of them are a bit loud and we've had to confiscate a few bottles of cider, but that's been all."

He handed me a card.

"Excellent. I'll pop in every so often, to keep an eye on things, but right now, I'm going back to the station for a cuppa while it's quiet. That's my direct line. Give me a ring if you need me."

*****

In the middle of November, I was cleaning the throne for Santa's Grotto when Bob appeared.

"I've just had the strangest phone call," he said.

"Really? Who was it?"

"Duncan Matthews."

My stomach tensed.

"What did he want?"

"He asked me up to Norbrook for a drink."

"You're not going, are you?"

"I don't see why not."

"Because he's vile. That's why not!"

"Don't be so dramatic. I know you don't like the man, but he was polite enough. I'm curious to know what he has to say."

I dropped the cloth I was using and grabbed Bob's arm.

"No. Please… I don't trust him."

But Bob only laughed.

"Calm down. You're being ridiculous." He took my hand and squeezed my fingers. "I said I'll meet him at seven o'clock. I won't be long."

When he came back, Bob's expression was inscrutable. I had finished putting the girls to bed and was sitting waiting for him.

"Well? What did he have to say?" I demanded as soon as he walked in the flat.

Bob sat down beside me before answering.

"He wants to buy Silverlands."

"No!" I was horrified.

"He's heard a rumour we're in trouble. He's guessed we're going to sell, and he wants to make an offer."

The thought of losing Silverlands was bad enough. Losing it to Matthews was unbearable.

"Don't listen to him. It's a trick. It must be..."

"No, I think he's serious. He offered to have an independent survey done to agree a price."

My heart was racing. I detested Matthews, but there was more at stake than my feelings.

"It makes sense, after all," Bob went on. "He owns the land all around us and he wants to integrate everything with the caravan park."

Frustration swept away my self-control.

"I don't care what he wants! I don't want to hear!"

"Please, Diana, we have to face this."

I jumped to my feet and ran out of the room. My hands itched to slam the door behind me, but I didn't want to wake the girls. Instead, I tiptoed along the dark corridor in silence.

I knew we would have to tell the rest of the family about Matthews' offer, but for now I needed to be alone. I wandered through the house and the shadows wrapped around me.

"Is this how you feel, Fred?" I whispered. "Helpless? Watching things happen?"

I let the tears wash away the worst of the pain.

"It's horrible, isn't it?" I whispered again when the sobs subsided. "Not being able to stop things. Not being able to make things the way you want them. It must be tough, watching people mess up your beautiful home year after year, without being able to do anything about it."

I pulled out a tissue and wiped my eyes.

"I'm sorry if you didn't like what we did with the place."

The silence was loud in my ears and as rich as velvet. For a long time, I sat and watched the moonlight filtering through the branches of the trees outside until the coldness of the night crept over me and I shivered.

Blowing my nose, I walked back and let myself into the flat.

"All right," I said to Bob. "You'd better tell the others in the morning."

*****

The rest of the family were as surprised by the news as I had been.

"If he makes a serious offer, tell the solicitor to double-check everything. I wouldn't trust that man until the money's cleared and in the bank account," Mum said.

"Don't worry, none of us trust him," Bob said.

A few days later, I watched as yet another surveyor arrived. His valuation was even lower than the previous one.

"I suppose we're going to have to accept it, aren't we?" David said grudgingly.

I nodded.

"We haven't got much choice, have we?"

"Look on the bright side," Bob said, "once this is all agreed we can start planning ahead. We can look for a new house."

I tried to feel excited, but I failed. Silverlands was so much more than a house. It was our family business and the focus of all our dreams. Letting go was incredibly painful.

*****

"You're not going to believe this!" Bob's face was beaming. "The estate agent wants to show someone around."

"A buyer?"

"Hopefully. The odd thing is he can't tell us who it is."

"Why not?" I demanded.

"It's a celebrity. He has a TV show based around an imaginary character, and he's looking to open a theme park. Apparently Silverlands ticks all his boxes."

"And this mysterious celebrity is coming to look around?"

"No, not him, but his business partner is coming to take a video. And he had a question."

"Which is?"

"Do we have somewhere they can land a helicopter?"

I laughed.

"Seriously?"

"Yes. The partner's flying down from somewhere in the midlands this afternoon."

"Are you sure it's not a joke?"

"No, it's serious. You wait and see."

Later that day the helicopter landed on the car park exactly as Bob had described and a team of five, including a cameraman, spent the afternoon walking around the site, asking questions and recording everything.

When they left, we watched the helicopter rise into the sky and whirr away into the distance.

"Now what?" David asked.

"Now we wait," Bob replied.

*****

Luckily, we didn't have to wait long. It was less than a week before the estate agent phoned to say he had received an offer. It was only a fraction higher than Matthews' offer, but those few pounds made me very happy.

I rushed to find Dad and tell him the news.

"Do you know what the best thing is?" I asked.

"No."

"It means I can tell Matthews to go to hell!"

He laughed.

"Not yet. It's only an offer. Once everything's signed and sealed, then you can tell him to go to hell."

I gave Dad an enormous hug, and for the first time in months, the tension inside me eased.

*****

At the beginning of December, Silverlands reopened for Christmas. We found another enormous tree, prepared Santa's Grotto, put up decorations, and hung garlands of holly and ivy, but it was hard to feel festive.

Bob had told Matthews we were not going to accept his offer, but we had not yet exchanged contracts with our new buyer.

My biggest concern was the craftspeople. I felt terrible that we hadn't told them about the sale. The estate agent had sworn us to secrecy, warning us that our celebrity buyer was notoriously protective of his privacy.

"If rumours get out about a sale, it could ruin everything. It's essential you carry on as normal."

"But we can't keep it up indefinitely," I protested.

"It won't be long," he assured me. "I'm expecting to hear back any day now."

*****

"At least it's not only us," Bob said the next morning as he put the phone down.

"Why? What have you heard?"

"I've been talking to Simeon from DATA. Two of the other attractions are closing. They won't admit it's anything to do with the recession. They've just announced they're retiring."

"I'll bet I know which two it is," I said, but I was wrong. Nothing was predicable any more. It felt as though the whole world was changing, and I was not surprised when John told me he was looking for another job.

"I've had enough of banking," he confided. "I loved working for Torrington, but there's no room for small, privately run banks any more. The future belongs to the multinationals. The problem is, I don't want to be a tiny cog in a huge machine where all the decisions are made by computers."

"What are you going to do?"

He shrugged.

"I haven't decided yet. My uncle lives in Canada. I'm thinking of visiting him for a few months. See if it changes my perspectives."

"Does that mean you'll be leaving soon?"

"No. I promised Mr North I'd stay until all the Torrington issues have been resolved and that's going to take a while yet."

"Is that what we are? A Torrington issue?"

He laughed.

"No, not after all these months, I prefer to think of you as friends."

*****

It was good to have people in the house again. We couldn't risk spending a lot of money on advertising, so our visitor numbers were even lower than the previous year, but our guests were as happy as ever. It was good to hear David chatting to old ladies in the shop and Abbie cooing over babies in the tearooms.

We had several small functions in the evenings, but the bar takings were not as high as we had hoped.

The only large function was a Christmas party for a local car sales firm. The owner had visited a few weeks before and booked a Medieval Banquet as a treat for his staff. I had seen him standing in the middle of the restaurant with Bob, waving his arms and demanding discounts.

I recognised him when he arrived on the night of the function. It was more than an hour before we were expecting guests and I was still laying out the tables.

"Hello darling," he grinned, eyeing me up and down.

"Can I help you?" I asked.

"I'm looking for Bob Townsend. Is he about?"

There was something about the man's leering expression that made me uncomfortable.

"No, I'm afraid he's not here at the moment."

"Never mind. Give him this." He held out a plastic carrier bag. "I've been to one of these things before, so I know the routine. Tell him I'm going to be the King and they're to use this. Not the cardboard rubbish they had last time."

I took the bag, and the man winked at me.

"I'm Ben, by the way. Ben Newman."

As he disappeared out of the door, I peered into the bag and saw an ornate golden crown encrusted with glass jewels.

"Does he really want to wear that?" Phil asked when she saw the crown.

"That's what he said."

"But the whole thing about crowning the King is a joke, isn't it?"

I shrugged.

"If he's paying for the evening, I guess he can wear his own crown if he wants to."

"I suppose so," Phil agreed, "but I don't think Benedict's going to like it."

I suspected she was right. Benedict hosted all our banquets. He played the part of a jester and had a dry sense of humour and a gift for creating a happy, welcoming atmosphere. He liked to make everything feel spontaneous, but he worked to a strict format. He was the one who appointed the King for the night and I had noticed he always chose a quiet, inoffensive man who went along with the fun.

As the first guests arrived, Benedict stood at the door and greeted them while I handed out glasses of mead.

The room was already half-full and alive with laughter when I noticed Ben. He was wearing an expensive suit and his arm was draped around a young woman in a low-cut evening dress.

"Hello, hello, I'll bet you remember me," he boomed, and I noticed Benedict falter.

"Indeed, I do, my liege. Methinks you did drink all our ale last time you visited us."

"Did I? Probably. I can't remember much past the pig's head. I hope you've got an extra barrel in tonight."

Benedict made a sweeping gesture with his arm and bowed his head.

"Yes, my lord, I'm sure we have more than enough to pickle your wits."

As soon as everyone was seated, Kate, Phil and I served the starters. I carried plates in from the kitchen and noticed the guests were more boisterous than usual. They were mainly in their twenties and many had wine bottles standing next to their glasses.

"The bar takings should be good," I whispered to Bob as I passed him.

"Get on with it, Benedict! We want the games!" Ben shouted.

The minstrels were playing at the far end of the room as Benedict paced between the tables.

"Before we can start our merriment, I have an important duty to perform," he announced in a loud voice.

"It is my honour to crown a King for this Merry Eve." He drew the golden crown from behind his back. "Who is worthy to wear this mighty coronet?"

Benedict looked around the crowd.

"Is any man here courageous enough to rise and declare himself as King?"

He stopped in front of a nervous young man with ginger hair.

"Will you rise to this challenge, Sire?"

He held the crown out enticingly, but the young man shook his head.

"Or you, Sire?" Benedict turned to the man next to him.

As I headed back to the kitchen, I saw Ben climb to his feet.

"Me. It's going to be me."

Benedict's reply was drowned by the whir of the dishwasher as the double doors swung shut behind me.

I grabbed another round of plates and hurried back to the banquet. As I emerged from the kitchen, Benedict was standing behind Ben with the crown held high in the air.

"All hail King Benny," he exclaimed.

"It's Ben, not Benny. Get on with it you fool."

Benedict let go of the crown, and it dropped heavily on the royal head.

"Ouch!"

"Forgive my clumsiness, My Liege. Here, let me assist you."

Benedict nudged the crown, and it slid down over Ben's eyes, until it came to rest on his ears.

Nervous giggles rippled around the room.

"Alas, King Benny, methought your head was plenty big enough for such a garland."

Ben pushed the crown back into place and glowered at Benedict.

"I told you. It's Ben."

Ignoring him, Benedict turned and signalled to the musicians at the end of the room.

"Come hither, good minstrels. We'll start the evening with a contest. Do we have any volunteers to sing for our Good King?"

I was on my way back to the kitchen when Ben's voice rang out.

"No need for volunteers. I chose Tom and Sajid. The useless buggers can sing for their supper."

Kate was already preparing the fish course, laying fillets of pickled mackerel on plates covered with watercress.

"That Ben's a nasty piece of work, isn't he?" she muttered. "There's something about him that makes my flesh crawl."

As the evening went on, we compared notes each time we returned to the kitchen.

"Did you hear what he said to the girl in the green dress?" Phil asked. "She got up to go to the loo, and he told her to sit down again."

"Seriously?"

"Yes. He told her no one can leave without the King's permission. He was laughing his head off because she was so embarrassed, but it wasn't funny. It was creepy."

"And were you there when he made that young guy walk like a duck?"

"No..."

"I'm not going to repeat what he said, but it was gross. And he's his boss."

"I've got some laxatives in my bag, I could crush them into his mead if you like," Kate offered.

"No. Don't do that," I said quickly.

We were dividing vegetables between the serving dishes when Benedict put his head around the door.

"Can someone come and clear up, please?"

He was gone before I could ask what had happened.

"I'll go," Phil offered and grabbed a brush and pan.

The main course was ready to be served by the time she returned. Her face was scarlet.

"Are you OK?" I asked.

"Yes, but I hope that tacky crown slips and strangles him."

"What happened?"

"One of them had thrown up, so I had to scrape it all off the carpet."

"I'm sorry, you shouldn't have to do that," I said.

"That wasn't the problem. I was crouching down and that idiot, Ben, started throwing bread at me. Not little bits. He threw half a roll, and it was covered in butter."

"I'm not having that..." Phil grabbed my arm as I turned to the door.

"It's OK, Benedict stopped him. Then, instead of throwing things at me, he started lobbing bones at the guys on the other table."

"I saw them," Kate joined in. "They chucked them back and when they ran out of bones, they started throwing carrots. It's disgusting. You should see the state of the carpet."

"How's Bob doing?" I asked.

"He's kept his patience so far, but I'm sure he'd like to throw them all out," Kate replied.

Indignation churned my stomach. I didn't understand why people behaved so disrespectfully. I wanted to march out and confront them, but I knew it would only make the situation more difficult.

With an effort, I kept my voice steady.

"Look, we've got to keep moving. You serve the puddings, I'll fetch the clotted cream."

I crossed to the back of the kitchen and let myself into the corridor. Usually, I enjoyed medieval banquets, but this one was turning into a nightmare. As I passed the toilets, someone stepped out. Lost in my thoughts, I stopped and unlocked the door to the walk-in fridge.

Suddenly, I sensed someone behind me. There was a reek of beer and strong arms wrapped around me, holding me tight. For a moment, I froze, then hot breath touched my neck, and a hand slid down inside my blouse, clutching my breast.

Swinging around, I clenched my hand as I punched. The man jerked backwards and my fist grazed past his cheek.

It was Ben.

"Get away from me!" I screamed and shoved him back against the wall.

He lurched unsteadily and his eyes blinked as he tried to focus.

"Oh, it's you. Sorry, I thought it was just a waitress."

"What the hell does that mean?" I demanded, but he only smirked.

"Never mind. No harm done, eh?"

"What's going on? Are you alright?"

Kate stood at the end of the corridor, staring.

"I'm fine, thanks," I scowled. "Him, he's an arsehole."

*****

"You have to tell Bob," Kate said once we were safely back in the kitchen.

"I know. I will..."

I was still fuming. I wished my aim had been better, but I doubted Ben would have paid his bill if I had given him a black eye.

To my surprise, my legs felt shaky.

"Go up to the flat. We can manage here," Kate offered, but I had no intention of leaving.

"No, I'm fine, thanks. I'll see if Bob needs any help."

The drinks were still flowing freely and King Benny had returned to his throne as I slipped behind the bar.

Bob gave me a questioning look, but I said nothing. I would tell him what had happened later when everyone had gone. For the time being, I leaned against the bar and counted the minutes until last orders.

Two teams of young men were charging around the room, jousting with wooden lances under Benedict's watchful eye. I noticed him push back his hood and mop his forehead with a handkerchief. It was the first time I had seen him look stressed.

As the contest finished, the teams returned to their seats, laughing and gasping for breath.

"That was crap!" Ben shouted as a man sat down near him. "You're pathetic, all of you. Nothing but losers."

Suddenly, Benedict stepped forward.

"Of course, my Liege. As King, you too must have an opportunity to prove yourself."

Ben looked at him in surprise.

"Is that not right, my Lords and Ladies?" Benedict held out his hands and turned around slowly. "Is it not time for our King to show his mettle?"

A voice slurred, "Go on, King Benny!"

Others joined in, and Benedict lifted his hands in encouragement as the chant grew.

"Benny! Benny! Benny!"

Ben frowned uncertainly. "I'm King Ben," he muttered.

"Indeed. And a mighty monarch you are," Benedict reassured him. "Come forward and acknowledge your subjects."

Ben stumbled to the centre of the room and Benedict turned and looked in our direction.

"Good Sir Robert, do you have in your possession a Yard of Ale?" he asked.

Suddenly, Bob began to smile.

"Indeed, I do. I'll prepare it at once."

"Are you sure?" I whispered. We used the Yard of Ale as part of the decorations for the banquet, but we had stopped inviting guests to drink from it during banquets because of the problems it had caused.

"Oh yes. This I want to see," Bob assured me.

The Yard of Ale wouldn't fit under the beer pump, so we had to fill it with jugs. It consisted of a glass tube nearly a metre in length which flared out into a wide cone at one end and had a round glass bowl at the other end.

I held the glass upright while Bob filled it to the brim. It held nearly four pints.

"Here, I'll take it," Bob said.

While we were pouring, Benedict dragged the throne to the centre of the room and persuaded Ben to climb on to it. He stood unsteadily with his crown balanced on his head.

"Now Sire, would you like a royal cape to protect your finery?" Benedict held up a clear plastic raincoat, but Benedict waved him away.

"I don't need that. I'm not wasting a drop."

The room fell silent, and every eye watched as Bob handed the Yard of Ale up to Ben.

"Some support for your King, please!" Benedict cried.

At once, the chant began again.

"Benny! Benny! Benny!"

"Remember Sire, the Yard must be emptied in one draft."

"No problem. I've got this." Ben said as he lifted the Yard of Ale to his lips. "Jesus Christ! It weighs a ton."

The crowd began a new refrain.

"Drink... drink... drink."

Taking a deep breath, Ben drank, swaying from side to side, the upraised bulb tracing a figure of eight in the air.

"Don't stop," Benedict ordered.

Ben kept drinking, but the level of the beer barely moved.

"One draft, Sire, you must finish it in one draft," Benedict reminded him.

Ben gulped down more beer, but as he slid his hand further along the glass, a wash of froth splashed across his face and he gasped.

"Keep going, you're nearly halfway..."

Bob glanced at me, and we winced, waiting for the inevitable. Ben lifted the glass higher and the level of the beer crept down towards the bowl at the end.

"Don't stop now, Sire, you're almost there..."

Ben raised the glass a fraction higher and a bubble of air forced its way into the bowl. At once, the seal was broken and the contents of the bowl flooded down the glass towards Ben's face.

Eyes wide, he stretched his lips in a desperate attempt to contain the torrent, but a brown tidal wave overwhelmed him. Beer filled his mouth, choking him, foam cascaded down his front, soaking his arms, splashing down his legs, forming frothy puddles on the carpet.

Fighting to breathe, Ben snorted and choked, beer shooting out of his nose and dribbling from his mouth.

The roar of laughter was deafening. Everyone in the room was convulsed, holding their sides, laughing until their sides ached.

Benedict reached up and took the Yard of Ale from Ben's shaking hand.

"Never mind, Sire. You did your best. Would you like a towel?"

But Ben didn't answer. He couldn't. His chest was heaving. His hands flew to his mouth, but there was nothing he could do to stop the geyser of vomit that erupted from deep inside him.

"Eew! Gross!" a girl squealed as the outpouring hit the carpet and splashed over her legs.

"Down you come, Sire."

Benedict offered the King his hand and helped him clamber down from the throne. Ben's face was white, and he was shaking visibly. He looked around the room, but no one met his eye. They were all helpless with laughter.

For a moment, I almost felt sorry for him.

Almost.

I was relieved he paid his bill before he left.

*****

The rest of the Christmas season went smoothly. I was determined we would still enjoy our own family Christmas, and Bob and I went for a shopping trip one Monday while the girls were at school.

We had all agreed that we would only buy each other inexpensive presents this year, but we wanted to find novelties that would make people smile.

Walking through Exeter, we found ourselves in the Guildhall Shopping Centre. A handwritten sign proclaimed Santa's Grotto, and an arrow pointed to a small, pre-fabricated shed with a string of Christmas tree lights strung around it.

A small boy and his mother were walking towards us.

"Go on then. See what Santa's given you," the woman said.

I glanced down as we passed and saw the boy tear open a small parcel. His face fell when he saw a packet of six wax crayons.

"Is that it? Oh dear, never mind," his mother comforted him.

"Did you see that present?" I asked Bob as we emerged from the shopping centre onto the High Street. "I'd be ashamed to give away gifts like that. Especially when they're charging so much to visit the grotto."

"And I'd be ashamed to call that shed a grotto," Bob agreed. "Never mind.

What have we still got to get?"

When the final visitors left on Christmas Eve, we locked the doors and breathed a sigh of relief. At last we had nothing to do but relax and play with the children. We ate more than was good for us, toasted the future, and watched Christmas films.

On Boxing Day, Claire and Michael announced they were going to put on a show. They pushed back the tables in the tearooms, arranged the chairs into a row, and instructed the grownups to sit down. We all sat obediently.

Michael and Claire left the room, but a moment later Michael reappeared. Lucy was sitting on my lap eating a packet of jelly beans and Michael grabbed her hand.

"Come on, it's time to get ready for your act," he said as he pushed her out of the room.

Minutes ticked by.

"What happens now?" Dad asked.

"I'm sure they'll come back eventually," Mum replied.

We sat patiently until the door burst open and Michael and Claire dragged an enormous cardboard box to the middle of the room. Claire was wearing a lime green mini dress that I kept for hot summer holidays. It reached to her knees and was held in at the waist by one of my scarves.

Michael was sporting black trousers, a red jumper and had Bob's top hat on his head. He had stuffed it with scrunched up newspaper but it still sat on his ears and wobbled every time he moved his head.

"Good evening, Ladies and Gentlemen," Michael began, and we erupted with laughter at his impression of his uncle. "First of all, I will amaze you with my juggling tricks."

He produced three balls and threw them into the air, retrieving them from the floor at intervals.

"Wonderful!" Mum cheered. "More, more!"

Michael took off his hat and bowed.

"And now, for your delectation, Miss Clarissa is going to sing some songs."

Claire had a tape cassette ready. She pressed a button and Christmas carols rang out.

"You can join in if you like," she said, and we all did.

"And now, for our final act, we have Miss Clarissa and Lucy, the Wonderdog," Michael announced.

Claire lifted the top of the cardboard box, and Lucy climbed out on all fours. She had a piece of tinsel around her neck in place of Roly's ruff, and she let her tongue loll out of her mouth.

"Woof, woof," she barked and sat on her haunches next to Claire.

As Michael commentated, Claire and Lucy worked through Liza's entire act. By the time the children finished, we were all hoarse with laughing and gave them a massive round of applause.

"That was incredible," Bob exclaimed. "You deserve a reward. How about some hot chocolate and Christmas cake?"

*****

We decided to take the rest of the week off. For once, there was nothing for us to do. It was not until the second of January that Bob went back to the office.

I was upstairs getting the girls dressed when he handed me the letter to me.

I read it slowly, not wanting to believe the words. Our celebrity buyer had pulled out. I dropped the letter on the table. I didn't need to know the rest.

The joy and happiness of Christmas was gone.

*****

The others were as shocked as us.

"He can't back out now, can he?" David asked.

"He's not backing out. He's decided not to go ahead. It's different," Dad said.

"Is there any point in going back to Mr Matthews?" Mum asked.

I grunted, but she tutted me.

"I'm sorry, dear, but we can't afford to be choosy anymore."

"I can try, but I don't know what sort of reaction I'll get," Bob frowned.

"You won't get any reaction at all," David said. "Haven't you heard? He's disappeared. Everyone's been gossiping about it."

"What do you mean disappeared?"

"He's vanished. No one knows where he's gone. There's a rumour his business partner's suing him. Or he might have killed someone. Or at least been involved in a fight that got out of control…"

"Do you know anything definite?" Bob demanded.

"No, not really," David admitted. "Only that he's gone."

"I've got his phone number and an address. I'll try to contact him." Bob phoned repeatedly and wrote to both Matthews and his solicitor, but he never got a reply. The rumours and gossip flourished, and the explanations for the sudden disappearance became more outlandish by the day. We never heard the truth, but it didn't really matter. A few weeks ago, there had been two potential purchasers for Silverlands. Now there were none.

It was a disaster for us, but a tiny part of me still rejoiced that Matthews wouldn't be buying the old house after all.

Chapter 10

Telling the craftspeople Silverlands had been put up for sale was horrible. They were not just our tenants. They had become our friends and had formed a solid community of their own.

I knew they had guessed what was coming, and they understood it was not our decision, but I still felt we had let them down.

Normally, once New Year was over, I would be straight back to work, designing and planning for the new season. Now, for the first time that I could remember, I had nothing to do.

I packed away the Christmas decorations and took the children to school, but I had nothing to plan, nothing to design.

Phil kept busy looking after the animals and Dad and David checked the roofs for leaks and did minor maintenance jobs, but none of us had a sense of purpose.

I found myself sitting in the tearooms watching the rain lash against the windows. Everything seemed bleak.

We spoke to the estate agent, and he assured us he was doing all he could to find a purchaser, but my hopes of a quick sale had faded.

"What will happen if we can't find a buyer?" I asked Bob.

There was a long pause before he answered.

"I suppose, eventually, the bank will put the place up for auction."

"And, if they do, and it sells for next to nothing, the bank will take whatever money it raises, and we will be left with a huge debt?"

"Yes, I suppose so…"

There was nothing else to say.

*****

Bob bumped into Martha in Exeter one day and took the opportunity to tell her we wouldn't be opening again. I was left to break the news to Abbie. I arranged to meet her for a coffee in a little café in Chudleigh.

She was already sitting at a table when I arrived.

"You're closing Silverlands, aren't you?" she asked before I could say anything.

I nodded. I felt I should apologise, but I didn't trust myself to speak. Tears were pricking my eyes, and I needed to blow my nose.

"It's all right. I've heard the rumours, so it's not a surprise."

I sniffed. "I wanted to tell you myself... I wish we could keep going, but it's not possible."

I sat down opposite her and pulled a tissue from my pocket.

"Do you want a doughnut?" she asked. "Or an Eccles cake? My treat."

"I was going to get you something..."

"No, it's OK. I'll get it. I want to say thank you."

"What for?"

"For taking a chance on me. I know I haven't always been the best. Martha's told me how useless I am often enough."

"No, Abbie, she didn't mean it. Martha has a soft spot for you, you must know that. She'll miss you."

Abbie nodded seriously.

"I'm going to miss her too. She taught me loads. I didn't even know how to work a microwave before she showed me."

"Yes, I remember that," I smiled.

We chatted about the things that had happened over the years and, to my surprise, we ended up laughing so loudly the other customers stared at us.

"Do you remember when Fred took Bob's pie?" Abbie giggled.

"How could I forget it?" I gasped.

"The look on his face!"

"It was priceless, wasn't it?"

"Is Fred behaving himself?"

"Mostly. He's still throwing things around in the shop sometimes."

"Say goodbye to him for me, won't you?"

"Of course, I will."

Finally, Abbie paid the bill and gave me a huge hug.

"Bye, then," she called as I walked away.

*****

As days went past, the house grew colder.

There was no point in turning on the heating, except in our flats, and the corridors and empty rooms felt chilled. In the past, I had hurried from one exhibition to another, always in a rush, too busy to notice the temperature. Now, I wrapped myself in a coat and scarf whenever I walked through the corridors.

Dampness hung in the air, and a faint mustiness crept through the house. Bob insisted on opening windows, but it didn't help. When he wasn't looking, I closed the windows and shivered in the empty rooms.

One by one, the crafts people left.

Penny found a job in Exeter and Marion and Elliott, the glass engravers, left for a new start in Ireland. Elliott had formed an unlikely friendship with Nelson, one of the geese in the Animal Meadow.

"I'll miss him," Elliott told us, "and I think he'll miss me."

"It's true," Phil told us, "Nelson seems to have adopted him. He trails around after him and even goes and sits in his workshop with him. He's more like a puppy than a goose."

We didn't want Nelson to be unhappy, so we agreed that Marion and Elliott could take him with them. They sent us a lovely photo of the goose in his new home.

Victor and Moses returned to the donkey sanctuary, and we found new homes for the rest of the animals.

Tom was the last to leave the craft block.

"First in, last out. I suppose that's fitting," he said as his kiln was loaded onto a trailer.

"Where exactly is it you're going?" I asked.

"No idea. Somewhere in France. I'm going to be an artisan. I shall get on a train and see where it takes me. I'm leaving the kiln with a friend of mine and when I'm settled, he's going to send it on to me."

"That sounds very adventurous," I said.

"What is life without an adventure?"

"Boring?" I suggested.

"Exactly. And we creative types must never be bored. I've left a few pieces in the unit for you. I'm sure you'll find a use for them."

When he had gone, I went back to the empty unit. It felt desolate. I gazed at the familiar view across the fields, then pulled open the door of the storeroom.

I gasped.

The shelves were stacked full of pots, vases, plates, mugs and ornaments.

"What on earth are we going to do with all these?" Bob asked when I showed him.

"I've no idea," I said, "but we'll never need to buy a plate again. Ever."

*****

The under eighteen discos went on. Every Friday, Dale arrived with his van full of equipment and parents delivered children to enjoy an evening of loud music and silly games.

Over the months, we had got to know our regular members and PC McGinty attended most weeks.

I sensed that Fred enjoyed the discos too. There was little sign of him during the week, but each Friday something moved in the shop. David and I made a point of taking a look as soon as the children had gone home to see what had been disturbed.

One Friday I found him showing Kate and Duncan a scattering of postcards spread across the carpet.

"What are you doing?" I asked.

"They already know about Fred," David said defensively. "What's the point in trying to hide it?"

He was right. Fred was a secret I had carried for too long, and it was a relief to share what was happening. After that, opening the shop after the disco became a ritual and Fred rarely failed to provide some new excitement.

The children had taken to riding their push cars through the house, and one Friday Michael left his in the shop. By the time the disco finished, a heavy copper coal scuttle had been upturned and dropped over the steering wheel.

On another occasion, books had been piled against the inside of the door, so we had to push them out of the way to get in.

Our share of the profits from the discos was useful, but it was not enough to pay the rates and all the other bills that were mounting up.

"There has to be something else we can do," I said to Bob one evening. "I hate feeling that we're sitting around wasting time."

"I know," he agreed. "But until we find a buyer, I don't see how we can move on."

*****

Fortunately, the children seemed oblivious to the changes around them. Claire and Michael had been given parts in a school production and their attention was focused on learning their lines and raiding their parent's wardrobes for costumes.

Claire was now eight years old, with the poise and self-confidence of a teenager. Michael was seven with a permanent grin and his father's easy manner. We were hugely proud of both of them, and all the family promised they would be in the audience to watch their performances.

On the day of the show, Phil took Claire and Michael to school and promised we would all be there to watch them in the afternoon.

David and Phil were taking Mum and Dad in their car while Bob and I would bring Lucy in ours. There was no particular pressure as we had nothing else planned for the day and I checked the car seat was ready and packed a few small toys into my bag to make sure I had something to distract

Lucy if she became bored.

As we would all be leaving at the same time, we agreed to have lunch together and leave at two o'clock.

Not wanting to be rushed at the last minute, I sorted Lucy's clothes and laid out a clean dress, tights and shoes on the bed.

"There. You like that dress, don't you?"

Lucy nodded, and I smiled at her.

"Good. Let's go downstairs and have your sandwiches, then I'll get you changed."

As soon as we had eaten, I took Lucy back to her bedroom. She wasn't interested in getting dressed and wanted to play instead.

"Come on, Lucy. It's time to put your dress on."

With a squeal of delight, she dropped to the floor and wriggled under the bed.

"No! We can't play now." I put on my stern voice. "We promised Claire and Michael we would go and watch them. Remember? We mustn't be late."

Scrabbling sounds came from under the bed and Lucy's head appeared.

"Good girl. Up you come."

Reluctantly, she climbed to her feet and let me take off her clothes.

"We will play later, I promise."

Lucy wriggled her toes into her tights and stood still while I pulled the dress over her head. Then she winced dramatically as I brushed her hair.

"There. You look lovely. Let's put your shoes on and we'll be ready to go."

I reached behind me on the bed, but the shoes were not there.

"Have you moved your shoes, Honey?"

Lucy shook her head.

"Are you sure? They were here a minute ago."

There was no answer, so I stood up and looked around the room. The shoes couldn't have gone far. I looked under the duvet, then stooped and looked under the bed. Nothing.

"Did you put them somewhere, Lucy? I'm not cross, but I need to know."

"No shoes," Lucy said.

"But they were here, weren't they?"

"Yes."

"So, they must still be here somewhere."

I glanced at my watch. The others would be downstairs by now, waiting for us.

"Are you sure you don't know where they are?"

Lucy reached for a toy pony.

"No shoes," she said calmly.

I reminded myself that Lucy was still only three. She couldn't be expected to understand adult concepts like time. Or keeping promises.

"Never mind. You'll have to wear your black shoes," I said, but Lucy shook her head.

"No shoes," she repeated.

I remembered that I had not been able to find the black shoes the previous day.

"What about your slippers? You were wearing them when we came upstairs."

"No shoes."

"Why not? Where are they?"

She looked at me with innocent eyes.

"Lady took."

The hairs on the back of my neck bristled.

Bob's voice floated up from the hall. "Are you coming, Di? We should be leaving."

I took a deep breath and started again.

"Listen, Lucy, we have to go. Now. But first, we have to find your shoes. Any shoes. Where are they?"

"Lady took shoes."

I swallowed hard. I was out of my depth and starting to panic. I knew the shoes had been on the bed behind me. And now they weren't. There was no point in denying they had vanished.

"OK, Lucy. Where did the Lady put them? Do you know?"

To my surprise, she nodded.

"Wonderful. Can you show me where she put them?"

Lucy nodded again.

"Great. As quickly as you can, please."

I followed Lucy out of the bedroom, through the flat and down the main stairs. At the bottom, she turned left and walked towards the kitchen.

"Where are you going?" David asked. "We should have left by now."

"I know. You'd better go on. We'll be there as soon as we can."

"But what's..."

"I'll explain later. You go. Save us some seats."

I hurried after Lucy and saw her pass the kitchen door and turn the corner. When I caught up with her, she was standing staring at a blank wall. My heart missed a beat as I realised it was the section of wall that blocked the bottom of the old staircase.

"Is the lady there?"

Lucy nodded.

"And she's got your shoes?"

I couldn't believe what I was saying.

Another nod.

It felt as if all the logic and certainty had been sucked from my world.

"What's going on?" Bob demanded as he walked along the corridor behind me. "We're going to be late."

"We can't go yet."

"Why not?"

I turned to face him.

"Lucy doesn't have any shoes. She says the Lady took them."

"That's ridiculous!" Bob exploded.

"The shoes were in her bedroom earlier, but they're not there now."

"Jesus Christ! You can't have looked properly. I'll bet they're under something."

He stomped off and Lucy watched him go. I didn't know whether to be indignant or tearful. The thought of disappointing Claire and Michael made me feel wretched, but I couldn't take Lucy in her tights.

Desperation makes us do strange things.

Taking a deep breath, I turned around and addressed the wall.

"Hello. I'm Lucy's mum and she says you've got her shoes. I really need them back now because I can't take her to see her sister without them. Please let her have them back. Please..."

Lucy looked up at me.

Nothing happened.

I waited a little longer.

Lucy turned around in circles, then sat on the floor.

Still nothing happened.

Finally, I reached down and stroked Lucy's hair.

"Come on, darling. Let's go and find Daddy."

She climbed to her feet, and we walked back along the corridor.

Bob was at the bottom of the stairs, looking pale.

"Are you all right?" I asked.

He said nothing but held out the red shoes.

"Thank goodness! Well done."

I helped Lucy pull on the shoes and fastened the buckles. It was only when I finished that I realised Bob hadn't moved.

"Are you all right?" I asked again.

"No, not really."

"Why? What happened?"

He swallowed hard.

"I went up to the flat. The others had gone. There's no one in the house except us, is there?"

"No..."

"I couldn't find the shoes," he went on. "I searched the girls' bedroom, our bedroom, everywhere. I came back downstairs and there they were. Lined up neatly on a step half-way up the stairs."

I turned and looked back along the corridor.

"Thank you."

Bob frowned at me, but there was no time left.

"Let's go. I'll explain later," I said.

The play had started by the time we reached the school, but we crept to our seats and watched Claire and Michael give their performances. We clapped enthusiastically and treated the kids to pizzas on the way home.

It was only when Claire and Lucy were tucked up in bed that Bob and I were able to talk about what had happened. Bob listened while I described my one-sided conversation with the White Lady, and for once, he didn't tell me that I was being ridiculous.

"Do you believe me?" I asked.

He took my hand and interweaved his fingers with mine.

"Yes… I still don't understand, but I do believe you. There was no way anyone could have put those shoes on the stairs. They weren't there when I went up. I would have fallen over them… And they were lined up so neatly. It was as if they had been put in the most obvious place to make sure I saw them."

He put his arm around me, and I nuzzled my cheek against his shoulder.

"I'm glad you don't think I'm mad anymore."

"I didn't say that," he smiled. "You may have convinced me we're living with a ghost, but I still think you're crazy."

I grabbed a cushion and hit him with it. Holding up an arm to defend himself, Bob laughed uproariously and nothing else mattered. The wall between us had crumbled, and I was happy again.

*****

After the incident with the shoes, Lucy stopped talking about the White Lady. Sometimes, I tried to bring the subject up when she was playing in her bedroom, but she would only look at me reproachfully and turn away.

One night, while I was reading her a bedtime story and Claire was still watching television with Bob, I began talking about people's faces and how everyone had different shaped eyes, noses, ears and so on.

We discussed all the members of the family and then I asked her what the White Lady looked like.

"Lady not got face," she told me.

"Then what has she got?"

"Lots of sparkles. Floaty lights like little sparkles." She wiggled her fingers in the air to explain what she meant.

"I don't understand. What do you mean by sparkles?"

I was desperate to know more, but Lucy only frowned at me. She turned over, buried her face in her pillow and never mentioned the White Lady again.

*****

As winter gave way to spring, the first snowdrops and primroses appeared in the grounds. Bob phoned the estate agent regularly, asking for updates, but no one came to view the property. John still called in to see us occasionally, but he had no news.

One morning, Bob went up to Exeter and while he was away, I wandered through the exhibition rooms. A fine layer of dust shrouded everything. My instincts told me I should start cleaning, but something held me back. What was the point?

Outside, the lawn had grown long and weeds sprouted along the sides of the path. In the kitchen, I opened one of the ovens and found it full of cobwebs. Wandering up the back staircase, I visited the model circus and saw the fingerprints of our last visitors still clouded the windows that protected it.

A stale smell hung in the air, faint and sickly, like bad breath. I wrinkled my nose and made my way back downstairs. Passing through the Enchanted Forest, I slipped out of the fire exit and walked across to the craft block. As I stepped into the courtyard, my footsteps echoed on the concrete path and a solitary rook lifted from the grass, cawing at my intrusion.

Following the path, I peered through a dirty window at the empty space that had been Tom's unit. Memories flooded back, but I pushed them away. There was no point in dwelling on the past.

When Bob got back, I was sitting on the floor in our flat brushing Dino. His ears were flat against his head and he growled each time I pulled a knot.

"I don't think he's enjoying that," Bob commented.

"I'm trying to be gentle, but I have to do something. I can't just sit around all the time."

"True, but you don't have to take it out on the dog."

"Then what am I supposed to do?"

"If you put the kettle on and call the others, I'll tell you."

He refused to say anything else until we were all together, but once everyone was settled, Bob leaned forward.

"How would you feel about making an Easter display for the Guildhall Shopping Centre?" he asked.

"What sort of display?" "How big?" "Where would it go?" Everyone spoke at once.

"Slow down," Bob laughed. "Let me explain. While I was in Exeter this morning, I remembered how awful the centre's Christmas Grotto had been, so I decided to call in to see the manager and tell him."

"You didn't?" I gasped.

"Not exactly. I asked if he'd like us to give him a quote for next year's grotto. Anyway, one thing led to another, and he told me they wanted a display in the centre at Easter. So, I offered to quote for that."

"You mean you walked in without an appointment or anything?" I asked in amazement.

"Yes, it was a spur-of-the moment thing."

"That's brilliant. Well done!" David beamed.

"It's only a quote," Bob reminded him. "It's not anything definite."

"When would they want it installed?" Dad asked.

"Before the kids break up for Easter."

"But that's only five weeks," David gasped. "We couldn't possibly do it by then."

"Why couldn't we?" Dad challenged him. "What else have we got to do?"

After more discussions, David drew some illustrations, Mum and I worked out a price, and Bob submitted a quote the following day. To our amazement, it was accepted immediately.

The design was a Hill-Billy house set in a garden with a collection of animated figures including an old lady in a rocking chair, workmen repairing the roof and a dog playing with a child. Each figure needed a separate mechanism and they would all be in a much bigger scale than we had used before.

"Are you sure we can do this?" I asked Dad when we finished celebrating.

"We have to do it," he said simply. "In fact, I think we should start a new company to do it."

"Really?"

"Yes, we should keep this completely separate from Silverlands."

"That makes sense. What would we call a new company?"

"I've no idea. I suppose we should ask for suggestions."

Everyone agreed that it would be sensible to form a new company, but reaching agreement on a name was far more difficult. We spent hours considering a range of different ideas, but every suggestion was rejected for one reason or another.

"We're never going to agree, are we?" I said at last. "Why don't we choose some initials like BT or KFC? That way we don't have to have a name that means anything."

"Perhaps, but what initials would we use?" David asked.

"How about FHC?" Dad suggested.

There was a general shrugging of shoulders.

"I don't see why not," Bob said.

"But why FHC?" Mum asked. "What does it stand for?"

"Faith, Hope, and Charity," Dad grinned. "By the time Silverlands has gone, that's all we'll have left."

His comment resonated with all of us. If we were really going to lose our homes and our business, we could at least keep our sense of humour.

"OK," I agreed. "I vote for FHC, but only if we never tell anyone what it stands for. It can be our own private joke."

The next day Mum and I contacted our accountants and FHC Enterprises Ltd came into existence.

It was wonderful to be back in the confusion of making things. The scale of the models meant we had to research motors, transformers, electrical control units and many other things we had not used before. The display was too big to be laid out in Dad's workshop, so we pushed back the tables and chairs in the tearooms and transformed the servery counters into work benches.

Bob ordered a book on basic electronics, and he and I spent hours learning how to solder components into micro-circuits to create timing boards.

Mum set up her sewing machine on a table and created miniature outfits for all the animated figures, and Dad and David moulded the characters' hands and faces while Phil painted the scenery and helped create the props.

The days flew by, but progress was slow because we had so many things to learn as we went along. Inevitably, we worked into the evenings and by the last week we were working late into the nights.

Despite the long hours, the work gave us a new focus and made it easier to cope with our situation.

As spring approached, dandelions and thistles flourished alongside the daffodils and anemones on the lawn.

I went through the house opening windows, but a stale smell lingered everywhere. It was faintly sweet and musty and was most noticeable on the staircases.

"Have you noticed the fusty smell on the stairs?" I asked Dad.

"Mmm." He nodded without looking up from his work.

"What is it?"

"Damp. Neglect. A little bit of rot. It's what happens to old buildings when they're left empty."

"It's so sad."

"I know, love, but it's inevitable. The house is waiting for a new chapter as much as we are. We can't help it any more. We have to look ahead."

"I am, that's the whole point of FHC, isn't it?"

"Yes. That's what we have to concentrate on now."

I sighed.

"You're right. I know you are.... But it does feel as if we're building a life raft on a sinking ship."

*****

Installing the display in the Guildhall Centre was a nerve-wracking experience. I was used to working at home or in our own workshops. Having a team of security guards and the Centre Manager watching our every move made me nervous.

"Look confident. You're a professional," Bob reminded me.

"A professional what?" I asked.

"A professional animated display installation expert."

"Thanks for letting me know. You don't think they'll ask to see our qualifications, will they?"

"I hope not." He grinned.

We put the display pieces in place, assembled the animations, wired everything to the control units and added the dressing.

"What do we do now?" I asked David.

"Turn it on, I guess."

"Go on then."

I crossed my fingers behind my back. David clicked the switch and there was a moment's pause as the timers clicked through their sequence. My heart pounded and my eyes flicked to the manager's face as he waited for something to happen.

The first figure to move was the dog. Its tail wagged abruptly, and the manager laughed. He stepped forward and watched as the other figures came to life. The security men joined him and I breathed a sigh of relief as they pointed to the various features and grinned.

"That was a success, wasn't it?" Bob said as we drove home.

"Yes, it was," I agreed, "and as it's Sunday tomorrow, I vote we sleep in until lunchtime."

*****

Bob soon found another opportunity for FHC Enterprises Ltd.

"Have you heard of Brewers' Quay in Weymouth?" he asked me.

"No, what is it?"

"It's a tourist attraction. They have lots of exhibits and I've persuaded them to hire the model circus for the summer."

"Seriously? That's incredible! How far is it to Weymouth?"

I was surprised to learn it was a two-hour drive in each direction from Chudleigh.

"We can't plug the circus in and leave it like the display in the Guildhall. It needs to have the belts adjusted all the time."

"I know that," Bob said. "We'll have to commute each day."

"How long do they want the circus there?"

"Twelve weeks, but I thought when it gets to the school holidays, we could hire a caravan and take it in turns to stay in Weymouth. David and Phil could do a couple of weeks with Michael, then we could take the girls."

"That sounds good. What's Weymouth like?"

"It's fabulous. Wonderful sandy beaches and a real old-fashioned seaside resort."

"OK. You've convinced me."

The first weeks of commuting were hard as we had not allowed for holiday traffic in our calculations. We had to leave Silverlands before seven in the morning and often didn't get back until eight or nine in the evening.

But it was good to see people still loved the circus.

Once the children finished school and we settled into the caravan, my spirits lifted.

It dawned on me that we had never been able to take a break during the summer since we got married. Now, when it was Bob's turn to look after the circus, I took the girls to the beach and spent days building sandcastles and paddling. In the evenings, we barbequed sausages and played outside with a football. Simple pleasures, but a whole new experience.

I phoned home every few days to catch up with the others, and one evening I could tell from David's tone that something had happened.

"There was a bit of excitement after the disco," he told me. "Fred's been quiet for a while, but he stepped things up a notch last night. It was the teapot stands this time. They were everywhere."

"Was anything damaged?"

"No. One of them had a few scratches, but they might have been there already."

I tried to ignore the fluttering in my stomach.

"OK. Let's hope he's got it out of his system. We'll see you soon."

*****

John arrived one morning with the inevitable news. He waited while I poured the tea before making his announcement.

"I'm sorry, but the bank is not prepared to wait any longer. They intend to take possession of the property and auction it," he told me.

I had known it would happen but the words still came as a shock.

"When will it be?" I asked.

"I don't have the date yet, but it will probably be at the end of September."

*****

When the school holidays finished, we brought the circus back and had another meeting.

Until the auction took place, we did not know what our financial situation was going to be. Less than a year ago, we had anticipated a sale that would leave us with enough capital to pay our debts to the bank and leave us with enough to buy ourselves a new home.

Since then, everything had changed. Property prices had continued to drop and the amount we owed the bank in unpaid interest had increased every month. There was no point in guessing what the outcome of the auction would be. Only time would tell.

We were delighted when the Guildhall accepted our quote. Designing a grotto and a range of Christmas animations kept us busy, and the weekly discos provided a regular distraction.

The membership was now over one hundred and fifty and, in addition to Kate and Duncan, David's friends Finley and Viv turned up to help us keep order each week.

The highlight of every Friday evening was still opening the shop and seeing what Fred had done. David looked forward to it immensely, and the others saw it as a harmless amusement. But, as the scale of the activity increased, I grew uncomfortable.

"Do you think this is a good idea?" I asked David. "Do you think we're encouraging him? That we're giving him an audience?"

He looked at me blankly.

"What do you mean? We're only seeing what happens."

"But you don't think Fred's playing up to it? That he likes the attention?"

"Don't be ridiculous. Our friends turn out to help each week. The least we can do is let them share a bit of excitement."

*****

"It's getting boring now. I've seen it all before, Fred," I grumbled as I cleared away the mess one Saturday morning.

"What was that?" David asked as he joined me.

"Nothing. I was wondering if we ought to move the stock out of the shop. I'm worried about things getting broken."

"What's the point? Fred's not limited to the shop, is he? If we move it all somewhere else, he'll either throw it around wherever we put it or find something else to play with."

"Maybe, but he's never been as active as this anywhere else. It might slow him down a bit."

"True. Or it might antagonise him. Do you want to take the risk?"

In the end, we agreed to move the breakable items out of the shop and leave the soft toys and games for Fred to play with.

*****

A few nights later, I was woken in the middle of the night by a gasp next to me.

"What was that for?" Bob demanded.

"What was what?"

"You punched me."

"No, I didn't..."

"Yes, you did! It's still smarting. You punched me in the face."

Bob was sitting up, his hand to his cheek.

"You must have been dreaming..."

"No, I wasn't. I know when I've been punched."

"All right. I'm sorry. Maybe I was dreaming... I don't remember..."

My eyes scanned the corners of the room, dark and impenetrable, lit only by the faint glow of moonlight outside. Reaching out, I clicked the bedside light on.

"Turn it off!" Bob complained.

I checked the room again before clicking off the light.

"Let's get back to sleep, shall we?" I said, but it was a long time before I closed my eyes.

"Did you really think I hit you?" I asked Bob the following morning.

"I did at the time, but I guess it must have been a dream. You know how real things can seem sometimes."

I nodded, but I wasn't convinced. Our bedroom was immediately above the shop, and I wondered if Fred was finding new ways to amuse himself. I hadn't thought of him being in our bedroom before. It was silly because Lucy had told me often enough that her Lady sat on her bed. Why wouldn't Fred visit us in ours?

It was not a pleasant thought. It was bad enough being tormented in the kitchen or the shop, but the thought of being watched in my own bedroom took things to a whole new level. I decided not to share my concern with Bob.

After that, I found it difficult to sleep. Dino had his basket beneath the window, and each time he stirred I woke and peered into the darkness. Owls in the trees outside had never bothered me before, but now I jumped at every call. Soon I was overtired and edgy.

"Mummy! Mummy!" Lucy's cry cut through my torpor. I was out of bed in an instant, bare feet running along the corridor.

"What is it, Honey?"

She was sitting up in bed, sobbing. Wrapping my arms around her, I felt wet tears on my shoulder.

"It's all right, Lucy, don't cry. It was just a dream."

But she shook her head violently.

"Claire hit me!"

I looked across to the bed on the other side of the room. By the glow of the nightlight, I could see Claire's sleeping face and the gentle rhythm of her breathing.

Adrenaline flooded through me. This was too much. I wanted to scream at Fred. To tell him he had gone too far, but what could I do if he didn't listen? How could I stop him?

Lucy clung to me and I hugged her tight. I was her Mother. It was my job to keep her safe. At that moment, I would have faced an axe-man or walked into an inferno to save her, but how could I protect her from something I couldn't see?

Punching Bob had been bad enough, but hurting a child was unforgiveable. If Fred didn't understand that, what else might he do? What else was he capable of doing?

My heart hammered against my ribs, and I felt a terror greater than anything I had ever experienced.

I rocked Lucy until she fell asleep and spent the rest of the night sitting on the floor beside her bed.

*****

"There you are. I wondered what had happened to you," Bob said as he popped his head around the door. His expression changed when he saw my face.

"What's wrong?"

The girls were both asleep and daylight gleamed through a chink in the curtains. I tucked the duvet around Lucy and followed Bob back to our bedroom.

He listened silently while I told him what had happened.

"What do we do now?" he asked.

"I haven't a clue," I wailed, "but we have to do something."

"Maybe the others can help."

"No!"

"Why not? Why do you want to keep it a secret?"

I couldn't tell him. I didn't know myself.

"What about the church?" Bob asked. "Do you think a priest might know what to do?"

"Possibly..." I was not a religious person, but I was desperate.

"There's a church in Chudleigh. Perhaps there's someone there you can talk to."

"I guess so, but what I would say?"

"Just tell them what happened."

It took several phone calls before I reached the local vicar. He sounded friendly when he answered, but as soon as I mentioned a ghost his tone changed.

"I hope you don't mind me asking, but are you under a lot of stress at the moment?"

I hesitated.

"This isn't about me. It's about the ghost."

"Yes, I understand that," he said in a patronising tone, "but sometimes, when people are stressed, their minds can play tricks on them."

"I'm not imagining this..."

"I'm not suggesting you are, my dear. I want to help you. I really do."

"Then can you come and talk to him?"

"Talk to the ghost?"

"Yes..."

"Oh dear. Are you thinking of an exorcism? I'm sorry. I'm afraid we don't do things like that anymore. In fact, we haven't done them for a long, long time."

"Then what can you do?"

"Well... we can talk about what's bothering you." The vicar's voice was soothing. "That can be very helpful. Or I could say a prayer with you if it would make you feel better?"

"No, thank you. I don't think that would help."

I put the phone down with a heavy heart.

"Any luck?"

"No. He thought I was a head case."

Bob wrapped his arms around me and my frustration escaped in a flood of tears.

I spent the next night in the girl's room waiting for something to happen.

But all was quiet.

The following night Bob persuaded me to return to our room, but I couldn't get rid of the knot of fear in my stomach.

A few nights later, I was lying awake when Lucy cried out again. I comforted her, berated Fred, and felt utterly helpless.

The next under-eighteen disco was as popular as ever. When the children had gone everyone hurried to the shop.

David unlocked the door, and there was a collective gasp.

The shop had been trashed. Toys and books lay everywhere. A pile of leaflets had been shredded into tiny pieces and yo-yos dangled from the mantlepiece.

"Wow! That's awesome!" Finley grinned. "I've never seen anything like it!"

"It's not awesome. He shouldn't be doing it." I snapped.

The others stared at me.

"I'm sorry, but it's not right. It's getting out of hand..."

"What do you mean?"

I struggled to contain my tears as I explained about Lucy. When I finished, David looked stricken.

"Why didn't you tell me?"

"What's the point? There's nothing you can do."

"You really ought to try..." Viv began, but David cut across her.

"Let's call it a night, shall we? I'll clear this lot up tomorrow."

*****

At eleven o'clock the next morning, the phone rang.

"I hope you don't mind me calling, but I have been told you need my help." The man's voice was calm and reassuring. "My name is Don Shackleton. I'm from the Spiritualist Church."

"Really? How did you get my number?" I asked.

"One of your friends contacted me. I understand you've been having some disturbances. Is that correct?"

"Yes. Well, sort of..."

"Do you mind if I come over?"

"No, I suppose not..."

"Good. I will be with you in twenty minutes."

"Who was that?" Bob asked when I put the phone down.

"It was a spiritualist. He's coming over to see us."

"When?"

"Now. In twenty minutes."

"Did you ask him to come?"

"No, not really. He phoned me. I think he's heard about Fred."

"Did he ask for money?"

"No. He didn't say much at all. Only that a friend gave him our number."

"Did he say which friend?"

"No. He just asked if he could come over."

"I bet it's a scam," Bob said. "Don't let him in. If you do, he'll sprinkle some holy water and charge you a fortune."

"I don't know... He sounded genuine."

"Well, he wouldn't be much of a con man if he didn't, would he?"

I waited on the doorstep until the car pulled up. To my surprise, it contained four people. An elderly man was driving, and he was accompanied by three round, middle-aged ladies.

The man climbed out and nodded politely.

"Pleased to meet you," he said and held out his hand. "I'm Don Shackleton. We spoke earlier."

"Yes, but I'm afraid there's been a misunderstanding. I don't think we need any..."

I broke off as I realised the three women had walked past me and were already in the house.

"Excuse me," I called after them.

"Don't worry, my dear, we won't disturb you," the man said.

"How much is this going to cost?" I asked.

"Cost? Oh no, dear, we don't charge anything."

"But where have they gone? What are they doing?" I demanded as I pulled my fingers from his grasp.

"The ladies are here to support me, that's all. I can assure you we won't be in your way for long."

He followed me as I went after the women. I found them in the shop, standing huddled in a group by the window.

"Is this the place?" he asked.

"Yes, I think so," one of the women answered.

I felt like an intruder.

"Do you want me to tell you what's been going on?" I offered.

"No, thank you. We will let you know if we need anything," the man assured me.

"Perhaps you can make sure we're not disturbed?" one of the women suggested.

I didn't know what to do, so I backed out of the room and shut the door behind me.

I found Bob in the office and told him what had happened.

"Are you telling me that four people you've never seen before walked into the house without being asked and you've left them alone in the shop?"

"Yes, that sums it up."

"Really, Diana! I'll bet they're loading the stock into the car this minute."

"I don't think so. They're all middle-aged. I can't imagine them stealing a load of toys and jig-saw puzzles."

Bob tutted at me.

"You're too trusting. You don't understand how these things work. Before they go, they'll ask for a donation. You wait and see. Don't give them a penny!"

I agreed not to part with any cash, took a notebook and sat on the bottom of the stairs so I could watch the shop door. I was part-way through designing a mechanism for an animated reindeer, but my mind refused to think about anything except what might be happening in the shop.

For a long time, everything was silent. Then I heard a scuffle and a murmur of voices. The door opened and the tallest of the women appeared. She looked relieved when she saw me.

"Ah, good. There you are. Can we have a glass of water, please?"

"Yes, I'll get one," I said, and the woman disappeared back into the shop.

I returned, moments later, and knocked on the door. There was no answer. A babbling sound was coming from inside, so I eased the door open and peered around.

Don Shackleton was sitting on the floor in the far corner, his knees pulled up against his chest, his arms wrapped around them as he rocked back and forth. His eyes were closed and he let out strange, gasping sobs.

The three women were standing around him, their arms held out as if to form a protective shield.

The tall woman saw me and scurried across.

"Thank you so much," she said, taking the glass of water and closing the door in my face.

I sat on the bottom stair for another hour.

Finally, the door opened and two women came out.

"What's happening?" I asked.

"It's all over. We won't disturb you any longer."

I watched as they headed along the corridor to the front door. I waited again, but there was no other movement. Crossing to the door, I opened it gently and peered around.

Don Shackleton was still on the floor, but now his legs were stretched out in front of him. He looked exhausted. The tall woman was kneeling beside him.

"Is everything all right?" I asked.

Seeing me, they struggled to their feet and the man ran a hand through his dishevelled hair.

"I'm sorry," he said. "We've been a long time."

"That's all right. What happened?" I asked, as I walked across to them.

"There was a spirit here. I made contact, but he's gone now."

"What do you mean? Who was he? Where's he gone?"

"I can't tell you very much, I'm afraid. He was a man, certainly, but I think his mind was more that of a child."

"You mean he was simple?"

He nodded.

"That sounds right, but what happened?" I asked.

"I told him he must move on. He didn't want to go. He told me he was waiting for his mother, but in the end, I persuaded him that she was waiting for him on the other side and that it was time for him to leave."

"And what happens now?"

"Nothing. I have done what I can. You shouldn't have any more difficulties."

"But who was he? Did he tell you his name?"

"I'm sorry," the woman interrupted me, "Don is very tired. I really must get him home to rest."

"Of course. Thank you." I hesitated. "Do we owe you anything?"

She smiled.

"No, my dear. We're always happy to help if we can."

*****

I watched the little car disappear down the drive, then walked slowly through the house. It had never felt so empty.

I felt empty too. The spiritualists had been polite and helpful, but I didn't understand what they had done. I couldn't help envying them. It seemed they had been able to communicate with Fred in a way I could not.

Were they right? Had Fred really gone? They had seemed convinced he had 'moved on' but I didn't know what that meant any more than I understood anything else that had happened.

A sudden wave of guilt washed over me. Had these people driven Fred away? Was it my fault? Was his mother really waiting for him? I hoped so.

I tried to reassure myself that Fred would be happier if he had been reunited with his mother, but I had never thought of him as being miserable. I always felt he was having a lovely time messing about and laughing at us.

After a row of silent days and undisturbed nights, I realised I missed Fred. With hindsight, I didn't believe he had meant any harm. Had I over reacted? Possibly. But it was too late now. I never heard or felt anything of Fred again.

I hope he is at peace.

*****

We didn't go to the auction.

Ironically, Silverlands sold for exactly the same amount we had paid for it, which left us with a huge debt to the bank. They kindly offered us an agreement that meant they would take all the profits our new company earned for the next three years. We had no choice but to accept.

Fortunately, Bob had already found several new customers who wanted to hire our animations, so we knew we would be kept busy.

We found a house in Dawlish large enough for the whole family and took out a lease on a workshop and a warehouse. It was a difficult time, but our friends volunteered to help us move and by the middle of October we were ready to leave.

It took several journeys, but as the afternoon light faded, we packed the last boxes into the vans. David, Dad and Bob drove off to unload at the warehouse while Phil took the kids to the new house to give them their tea and get them ready for bed. She managed to fit Dino, Ossie and Sammy's cat basket into the back but there was not enough room for Scruffy.

My car was already filled to the roof with household items, leaving the front seats for Mum and me, but I packed things even more tightly to make enough room for him.

Once everyone was gone, I walked around the building with a heavy heart, checking the doors were locked for the final time.

The last rays of daylight played through the windows in exactly the same way they had done the first time I saw the house. I felt unbearably sad.

When I got back to the car, Mum was bending down stroking Scruffy. He seemed agitated and was panting. He had barked frantically when Dino and Ossie left in the back of Phil's car, and when Dad drove off in the van, he had howled.

"It's OK," Mum reassured him. "It won't be long and you'll see your new home."

As I opened the door, Scruffy barged past me and scrambled into the driver's seat.

"That's not your place. You're going in the back," I told him.

To my surprise, he lowered his head and growled at me.

"Don't be silly!" Mum scolded him. "Come here."

But Scruffy pressed himself against the seat. His ears were flat back against his skull and he was shaking.

"What's the matter with him?" I asked.

"He thinks we're leaving him behind," Mum said.

I remembered how he had howled after Dad and realised she was right.

"It's OK, boy. We wouldn't do that."

I put out a hand to pat him, but his lips curled, baring his teeth.

"It's going to be all right, Scruffy," Mum said quietly, "but you have to get out now."

The dog hesitated and his eyes held Mum's for a long moment, then with a whine of utter desolation, he slid from the car and collapsed in a heap on the tarmac. His body shook and for a moment I thought he was having a fit.

Mum bent over him and stroked his ears, but he turned his head away from her.

"Honestly, we're not going to leave you," I said, but it was only when I clicked the rear door open that he understood. With a sudden rush, he climbed to his feet and tottered to the back of the car. His legs were shaking too much to jump, but he scrambled his front paws onto the bumper bar and looked at me with beseeching eyes.

"But you weigh a ton," I protested.

"Here, I'll help you. He's never going to get up there on his own in this state."

Mum and I hoisted him into the back of the car, and he lay gasping with relief.

"You daft old thing," Mum whispered as she patted him. "Don't you realise you're one of the family now?"

The old dog licked her hand, but he didn't stop shaking until we reached Dawlish.

*****

The following spring, David passed through Chudleigh and called into the baker's shop for cakes and a chat. When he got home, he was bursting with excitement.

"You're going to love this," he beamed.

"If it's news about what's happening at Silverlands, I don't want to know," I said.

"Yes, you do. You definitely want to hear this."

"Really?"

"You remember the developer who bought the place was going to divide it up into units and convert them to houses?"

"Yes."

"Well, the plan was to get the first house finished before starting any other work, so that a site manager could move in and live there while he supervised the rest of the development."

"OK."

"They started with the rooms nearest to the front door. That means our old shop together with your flat upstairs."

"And?"

"As soon as it was ready, the site manager moved in with his wife and their little daughter, who was about four. Her bedroom was at the front of the house, so it must have been the same one that Claire and Lucy had."

A sudden tingle of anticipation ran through me.

"Go on, what happened?"

"They left within weeks. The daughter started talking about a White Lady that came and sat on her bed in the middle of the night, and the mother freaked out completely. She packed her bags and walked out. Apparently, the thought of a ghost talking to her daughter was more than she could cope with."

"It's just as well she never had to deal with Fred then, isn't it?" I laughed.

David was right. I was delighted with his news. I often thought about Fred and the White Lady and missed Silverlands terribly.

I hoped Fred was happy, wherever he was, but it was good to know that at least one of our ghosts remained.

Epilogue

FHC Enterprises Ltd flourished and supported the family for the next twenty-five years, during which time we supplied animated displays, Christmas decorations and Santa's Grottoes to shopping centres and tourist attractions all over the United Kingdom.

We spent most of the year designing and building our exhibits then, for a few hectic weeks, we travelled around the country installing them. It was a crazy, eccentric lifestyle which suited us rather well.

Dad refused to retire. He continued to design and build beautiful models until he was well into his eighties, but sadly, he suffered from dementia during his last years. Luckily, he was able to stay at home with us right up until the end.

Naturally, Mum missed him terribly, but she often told me that she felt he was watching over her.

Each winter, we hung rotating Christmas decorations from the ceiling of the Guildhall Centre in Exeter, and one of the most time-consuming jobs was installing the turntables from which they were suspended.

Once the holiday season was over, we returned to collect the displays and had to go through the long process of removing the turntables.

In 2002, the whole of the United Kingdom celebrated Queen Elizabeth's Golden Jubilee and the Guildhall Centre commissioned us to provide a special display. As the decorations would be hung from the same turntables we used for the Christmas decorations, the manager agreed we could leave them in place rather than remove them as usual.

At the beginning of January, we left Mum at home and worked through the night dismantling the Christmas displays and returning everything except the turntables to our warehouse. The following morning, Mum told me that she had had a vivid dream. She said that Dad had visited her.

"It was lovely," she said. "He sat on the bed and we chatted away like we used to. I told him about you all and what you've been up to, and he laughed, just like he always did. Then, after a long time, he said he had to go, but he said he had a message for you."

"Really? What was that?" I asked.

"It didn't make any sense. You know what dreams are like. He said to tell you that if you think you've lost something, it's because you left it in the ceiling. Isn't that silly?"

To me, it didn't sound silly at all. It sounded like my father, still keeping an eye on us.

Religion and beliefs are highly personal things. For most of us, they are a combination of ideals we are taught and truths we discover for ourselves.

I would never try to convince anyone that my beliefs are right, especially where ghosts are concerned, because it is not a something that can be proved. The only thing that will truly convince anyone about ghosts is personal experience.

I consider myself very lucky to have shared a home with Fred and the White Lady. I don't pretend to know who, or what, they were, but they had a profound effect on me and changed my view of absolutely everything.

When I was a child, I didn't believe in ghosts, but now I do. For me, that is enough.

Let's keep in touch

One of the best things about being a writer is being able to build a relationship with my readers.

Every month I send out a newsletter or two with details of my next book release, special offers and insights into my other writing projects.

And, to welcome you to my mailing list, I will send you a link to download my latest novella, Gin on the Rock, which tells the story of an unexpected adventure Bob and I had soon after we got married. We thought we were going on a two-week working holiday in Spain but things turned out very differently indeed!

To sign up to my newsletter, please visit my website www.dianatownsend.co.uk

Did you enjoy reading How It All Ended?

If so, I would like to ask you something.

As a new writer, my success depends largely on being able to draw attention to my work.

Much as I would love to take out full-page ads in the newspapers, or put posters on the underground, those options are simply not available to independent authors without the backing of a large publishing house.

However, reviews from readers can have a huge impact on the amount of exposure a title is given on online.

If you have enjoyed reading this book, I would be very grateful if you could spend just a few minutes leaving a review (it can be as short as you like) on the book's Amazon page.

Thank you very much,

Diana

About the Author

After growing up in Exeter, Diana trained as a silk-screen printer then joined with other members of her family to buy a derelict school and turn it into a popular tourist attraction.

Later, she helped form a company specializing in designing and installing Christmas displays for shopping centres and local authorities.

After writing several plays which were staged by schools and community groups, Diana began writing and producing short films.

Two of her feature film scripts, Deadly Intent and Scareycrows, have been produced and distributed by Inspired Toad Productions.

Diana lives in Devon with her husband Robert.

You can connect with me on:

- http://dianatownsend.co.uk
- https://twitter.com/Diana_Townsend
- https://www.facebook.com/dianatownsendwriter
- https://www.instagram.com/diana_townsend13

Subscribe to my newsletter:

- https://www.subscribepage.com/l4t3x4

Also by Diana Townsend

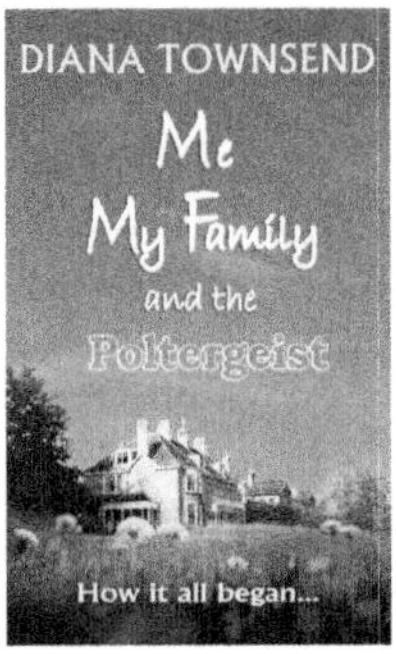

Me, My Family and the Poltergeist
A true story about living with a deranged grandmother, building a model circus, transforming a derelict school into a tourist attraction, and coping with a poltergeist.

Summer Days
After helping her family transform a derelict school into a tourist attraction, Diana Townsend expects to spend her days catering for happy holiday makers.

Instead, she finds herself contending with accident-prone staff, feuding craftspeople, grumpy clowns and an unpredictable ghost called Fred.

Printed in Great Britain
by Amazon

57902267R00149